50 HIKES IN NEW MEXICO

By

HARRY EVANS

$9.95

GEM GUIDES BOOK COMPANY
3677 San Gabriel Parkway
Pico Rivera, California 90660

CONTENTS

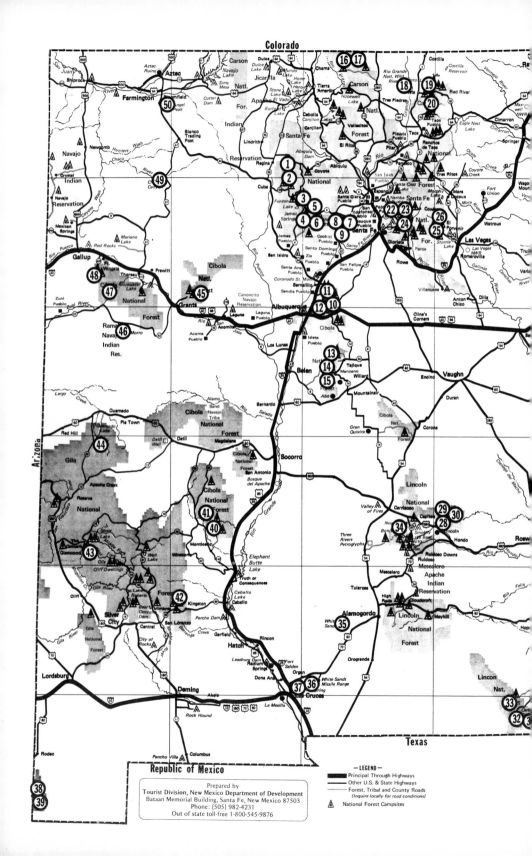

Hikes

ACKNOWLEDGEMENTS

I wish to thank the many people who have provided me with information or assistance. Representatives of each of the National Forests, Bureau of Land Management, National Parks, and National Monuments were supportive of my endeavor and provided me with information, and encouraged me to complete the book.

My special thanks go to Harry Steed, Ron Kerbow, Lee Singer, Rex Smart, Jeff Adams, and the numerous other federal employees who helped.

I'm grateful to my friends, too numerous to mention here, and to my grandson Kenyon Stewart, who accompanied me on some of my hikes. I am also grateful to my son Dale Evans and my daughters Teresa Stewart, Janet Evans, and Becky Johnson, along with Jane Kittleman and Janet Ketter for reading and commenting on my writings.

Special thanks to John Colburn of El Paso and Joe Repa of Santa Fe for sharing some of their favorite hikes with us, and to Joe for assisting me with photographing the hikes near Santa Fe. I want to remember my close friend Jim Middlebrook, who loved to hike the Gila Wilderness trails and who enlightened me with needed details of the Gila when my field notes omitted something.

Of course, I want to express my appreciation to my wife Mary Lou for her patience, waiting at some of the trailheads while I was hiking and at home when I was writing and drawing maps, and for her encouragement to work on the book when I would have much preferred to have been running, hiking, climbing, kayaking, bicycling, scuba diving, or indulging in some other outdoor activity.

COVER PICTURES:

(top left)   Looking southwest from near the trailhead on Brazos Ridge—Hike 17.

(bottom left)   Remains of the Butterfield Stage Station in Mills Canyon—Hike 27.

(top right)   Looking north along Black Range Crest Trail—Hike 42.

(bottom right)   An early morning hike alongside the Jemez River—Hike 4.

INTRODUCTION

"Land of Enchantment — New Mexico." The state's automobile license plates proudly bear this slogan, and the more you see of her varied beauty, the more appropriate it becomes.

Many things set this state apart from all the others. The sparsity of man and his works is evident in the broad vistas to distant blue-shaded mountains. Mountain peaks, which entice the energetic, are snowcapped much of the year and their slopes are blanketed by green forests. Beneath the peaks, mountains and hills are often dissected by captivating green valleys threaded by sparkling streams. In contrast, dry deserts are thinly covered with well-adapted and sharply defensive vegetation, which bursts into bloom in late spring. Rugged beauty is characteristic of the eroded and colorful mesa country. There are areas with impressive evidence of past volcanic activity, in the form of eroded plugs, cones, and lava flows. Vast expanses of grassy prairies, barren, sculptured sand dunes, and mystical prehistoric ruins are all part of this charmed land.

This spectacular scenery is embellished by skies clear and blue by day, but changing to wildly multi-hued at sunset, and black, punctuated by multitudes of brilliant stars by night.

The enchantment is not limited to land and sky. To a great extent, it is in the spirit of her people and their works. Spanish and Indian heritage is evident in the distinctive architecture and plan of village and city. This same heritage is apparent in the faces of more than half of the state's residents.

Each characteristic of land and people contributes to the uniqueness of the state. New Mexico, "me encanta."

PUBLIC LANDS IN NEW MEXICO

All of these hikes are on public land, primarily in national forests, with a few in national monuments, national parks, national grasslands, and lands administered by the Bureau of Land Management. There are nearly nine million acres of national forest land in New Mexico and about 13 million acres administered by BLM. Approximately 700,000 acres of this land has been designated as wilderness, and will remain in its unspoiled, natural state so long as this designation remains. The majority of the land is not designated as wilderness though, and is often exploited by mining, lumbering and ranching interests.

Recently, public land in New Mexico was studied for its suitability for designation as wilderness and much of it was found to meet the requirements. Unfortunately, not nearly enough was so designated and will not have the protection to keep it wild and scenic. Wilderness is an important resource that cannot be replaced once it is gone.

We are indeed fortunate to have access to this unspoiled land. I urge you to get out and see it for yourself. The hikes in this book will facilitate your sampling of what New Mexico has to offer to one who loves the outdoors. After you become acquainted with the land, I hope you will be stimulated to join with other conservation-minded individuals or groups to see that these resources remain unspoiled.

HOW TO USE THIS BOOK

50 Hikes in New Mexico will introduce you to many of the interesting places for hiking in the state, with one or more hikes in each area. These few hikes, long or short, will give you a sample of what that particular piece of public land has to offer. This book makes no pretense of being a complete guide to all of the trails in the state. Its purpose is to acquaint you with an area and if you are sufficiently interested after your visit, you will pursue further explorations. Most hikes include alternate routes and most all contain information on side trips that can be made from that particular area. I'm sure the information given in this book will yield much more than 50 hikes throughout the national forests and all areas covered in the state. I feel that those who hike will want to come back to see more of this beautiful, wild, and rugged region.

Included in the book are hikes of different lengths and difficulty to provide something of interest for and within the physical capabilities of just about everyone (many of these hikes could even be undertaken by the physically handicapped). The hike descriptions and accompanying maps should be adequate to enable an intelligent and physically capable person to follow the routes without losing the way. If a route is difficult to follow and requires an accomplished route finder, this is noted in the summary information at the beginning of the hike description. If you lose the trail or are uncertain of the route, turn around and go back to the trailhead or to an alternate route you can follow. Don't get lost! Photographs accompanying each write-up show you what to expect in the way of scenery and may influence your choice of the area you want to explore.

A map of the route accompanies each of the hike descriptions. Access routes to trailheads are sometimes shown on the maps, but not always. A paragraph in the hike description tells how to get to the trail. All of the hike routes are drawn on USGS topographic maps and appear as a heavy black and white broken line. Alternate routes and side hikes appear as black and white dashed lines. The trailhead is marked with "0" for zero miles. Distances along the hike are shown in miles, with significant features such as trail junctions measured to the nearest tenth, or sometimes hundredths, of a mile. A letter "T" followed by a number alongside a trail marked on the map is the trail number which appears on Forest Service maps and on trail signs.

A distance scale is included on each map to aid you in estimating distances on the map. True north is indicated on each map by an arrow with an "N" on it. Magnetic north, where your compass should point, is shown by a light arrow to the right (east) of true north. A tiny black square on a small map of New Mexico appears on each hike map to indicate where the hike is located in the state.

Roads on the map are marked with initials preceding the road number. F.R. prefix stands for Forest Road, N.M. for New Mexico highway, and U.S. for U.S. highway.

Hike summaries give the names of the topographic maps which cover the hike area, and it is suggested that you get the topographic maps and carry them on the hike, too, because they will show the surrounding country which doesn't appear on the map in the book.

In the introductory section of this book you will find information that can assist you in selecting the equipment needed for hiking and backpacking. These pages also tell you a few things about planning and organizing a hike, though there is more complete information on this subject in some of the books listed in the Suggested Reading section. The list of agencies and organizations in New Mexico will aid you in getting information and obtaining permits prior to making a hike. The large map of New Mexico has hike numbers in their approximate positions in the state,

facilitating your finding hikes for any specific area in which you might be interested.

Road distances stated in the "how to get to" paragraph of each hike description were determined from a car odometer and may vary some from your odometer reading. Consider the distances to be only approximate. I determined trail distances with an odometer wheel that measured distances in feet, with the exceptions noted in the hike descriptions.

At the beginning of each hike description is some commonly needed "quick look" information (summary), such as hiking time and distance, that will help you in selecting and planning your hike. The following discussions should aid you in interpreting the information as it was intended.

DISTANCE: The one-way or round-trip distance for each hike is given. Distances for side hikes or optional routes are not included in the hike distance. The distances for most hikes were measured with an odometer wheel, though the distances for Hikes 1, 2, 9, 10 and 11 were taken, in part, from those given on Forest Service and Park Service trail maps. The distances I measured were not significantly different from those that appeared on those maps. A few other hike distances were, as noted in the write-ups, determined in part from measuring topographic maps.

TIME: It is difficult to arrive at an average time for a hike because of the difference in speeds between individuals and the variations in loads which they might carry. On a relatively level, good trail a lightly loaded, strong hiker can average in excess of three miles per hour. On an uphill route a heavily laden hiker might average much less than one mile per hour. If you will record your starting time and arrival times at known points along the way you can determine your speed and can then anticipate how much time it will take you to get to your day's destination. After a few hikes you may be able to know what your approximate speed will be. There may be times when an individual's speed indicates that it would be wise for him or her to turn around and return to the trailhead and possibly try an easier hike. I tried to use actual hiking times when I hiked with companions I considered to be average hikers. When it was necessary to estimate hiking time, I used a speed of two miles per hour for level trails, a little faster for downhill, and one mile per hour for uphill. Times include hourly rest stops and intermittent stops to take pictures and to enjoy the scenery.

RATING: The assumption was made that all hikers will be in reasonably good physical condition and will not be overloaded. Longer, overnight backpack trips were usually rated as moderate or strenuous because of the loads that you have to carry and the distances that you must travel. Rough trails with lots of uphill and downhill, routes that are difficult to follow, or hikes of three days or more in duration were classified as being strenuous or very strenuous. Easy to moderate, or moderate to strenuous classification means that the difficulty is somewhere in between. You must realize that to a great extent the degree of difficulty of any hike depends on you, your abilities, and your attitude.

Temperature and other weather factors can also contribute considerably to the ease or difficulty of a hike. Extreme heat or cold, high winds, wet clothing and equipment, and muddy trails can consume energy rapidly, and postholing through deep snow can make the easiest route exhausting. When rating the difficulty of a hike, I assumed nearly ideal weather conditions. Bad weather (hot, cold, or wet) that you encounter will increase the hike's difficulty.

Some trails are easy walking, but in many instances following the route is so difficult that only experienced hikers, proficient with map and compass, should attempt them. This is noted in the "rating" statement.

ELEVATION RANGE: This tells you the highest and lowest elevations attained on the hike. Usually, the lowest elevation is at the trailhead, but not always. The range does not tell you about the ups and downs along the way. If you are prone to altitude sickness, "elevation range" will help you select hikes that remain at lower elevations, though I doubt that many hikers will have serious problems in the comparatively low (by world standards) mountains of New Mexico.

Not everyone experiences altitude sickness, and physical conditioning does not appear to affect one's susceptibility. When you go from a low altitude to a significantly higher one, chances are that you will experience some temporary discomfort, and it is certain that you will be short of breath and tire easily until you become acclimatized. The higher you go, the greater the chances are that you will experience altitude sickness, and the more severe the symptoms will be. Symptoms include headache (which medication will not relieve); impaired coordination; swelling (edema) of face, hands, ankles, eyes, etc., shortness of breath and tight chest; irregular breathing; nausea; vomiting; and a tired, unmotivated feeling. Mild symptoms should not cause you to change your hiking plans, but if you, or a member of your party, becomes ill, curtail your physical activities and don't go to a higher altitude until the symptoms improve, usually in two or three days. If after a couple of days the symptoms persist, or have worsened, go to a lower altitude. The only sure treatment for altitude sickness is to go to a lower altitude — a thousand feet lower is often sufficient to clear up the problem.

In New Mexico the mountains are not high enough to cause most people to have the more serious forms of altitude sickness which are a possibility at higher altitudes. But you should be aware that these potentially serious forms of edema have, very infrequently, been experienced at elevations as low as 10,000 feet. These problems are: high altitude pulmonary edema (HAPE), which is fluid accumulation in the lungs; high altitude cerebral edema (HACE), which is fluid causing the brain to swell. Don't expect anyone in your group to experience either of these problems, but you should be aware that they have happened to a few other hikers.

If you are interested in learning more about altitude sickness, you should read Dr. Peter Hackett's "Mountain Sickness," which is listed in "Recommended Reading." The June-July 1978 issue of *Backpacker* magazine (No. 27) has an interesting account of High Altitude Sickness happening at about 10,000 feet.

WATER: Water availability is often seasonal, related to snow melt and runoff or to rain. I suggest that you always inquire about its availability, particularly the places along the hike that are mentioned in the hike description. Always carry some spare water just in case a source is dry or you can't find it. I've spent a few thirsty days and nights myself and know that it takes some of the fun out of the hike for a while.

SEASONS: It would be impossible to predict when autumn's first snow will cover a trail, or when the snow will melt sufficiently to open the route in the spring. The months shown for hiking a trail are based on when the trail usually opens and closes, but each year is different. You should contact the agency that administers the area if you are planning a fall or spring hike to see if the trail is open, and when they expect conditions to change. I have started hiking in good weather and had the path obliterated by an overnight snow fall. At times like this you will need to know how to use a map and compass. The blazes on trees are very helpful, too.

If you like to cross-country ski, or snowshoe, you could use many of the trails year-round.

You may want to find out when hunting season is open. Deer and elk hunting is permitted in the National Forests and some of the Bureau of Land Management land, which may dampen your enthusiasm for hiking in these areas when the season is open. When I hike during hunting season, I wear bright colors and whistle a lot as I walk. So far, I have had no frightening experiences and all of the hunters I have encountered appeared to be quite knowledgeable or were with guides who were. But, it only takes one idiot with a gun to shoot you, so keep this in mind when you make the decision to hike during hunting season.

TOPOGRAPHIC MAPS of New Mexico are available from the USGS offices in Denver, Colorado and Dallas, Texas. See the list of "agencies" for USGS addresses. Most backpacking specialty stores sell topo maps of the more popular hiking areas. National Park and Monument headquarters sometimes sell topo maps of the areas they administer. Map and blueprint stores in the larger cities such as Las Cruces, Albuquerque, and Santa Fe may also sell some topo maps, and they usually sell maps of all of the National Forests in New Mexico, too.

A topographic map portrays the terrain with contour lines of equal elevation spaced at regular intervals, usually 40 feet. From the contour lines you can determine the locations, elevations, sizes, and shapes of mountains and valleys. Streams and rivers are shown, as are trails, roads, and other significant natural and man-made features.

Four or five of the hikes in this book are plotted on the smaller scale 15 minute topo maps because the larger, more detailed 7.5-minute topos are not available for those areas yet. The other hikes were plotted on 7.5 minute topographic maps, on which one inch on the map represents 2,000 feet on the ground. This size map covers 7.5 minutes of longitude (wide) and 7.5 minutes of latitude (high). Because all 7.5-minute maps are of the same scale, a number of adjacent maps can be spliced together to make a larger map, when desired. For some of these hikes it was necessary to join four or more topos together in order to plot the route on one continuous map.

An index map of New Mexico which shows and names all of the topographic maps covering the state is available from the USGS branch offices in Denver and Dallas. A brochure explaining topo maps is also available on request.

SPECIAL MAPS are available for most of these hikes. General Recreational Maps are available for each National Forest, backcountry maps or small maps and brochures for National Parks and National Monuments, and Visitor's Guides (maps) to the National Forest Wilderness Areas. Each Forest Service General Recreational Map is available from the offices for that particular forest, with three separate maps for the widely scattered units of Cibola National Forest and two for Lincoln National Forest. When you request a map from a National Forest Office be sure that you specify the ranger district that you want it for. The Bureau of Land Management has some maps available, but they don't usually show hiking trails.

PERMITS are required for making a number of these hikes. They are required for all of the backcountry hikes in the National Monuments and National Parks and for those into the parts of National Parks designated as Wilderness Areas. A permit is required for a lone hiker or for a group hiking together.

Proper management of these delicate areas necessitate the permit system. Permit records enable the Forest Service and Park Service to maintain usage data for the areas they administer, which enables them to manage the areas for maximum usage and enjoyment with minimum visitor impact on the wilderness resource. In some areas it is necessary to limit the number of visitors they receive.

Entry fees are charged by some of the National Parks and National Monuments, but the backcountry permits are free. National Forest Wilderness Permits are also free. Permits are available from District Forest Ranger Offices and from the National Park or National Monument Headquarters. Permits may be obtained by mail, by telephone, or in person. When you get your permit be sure to get the General Recreational Map or Visitor's Guide for the area.

THE LAND

The great topographic relief of New Mexico (from 2,840 to 13,150 feet) is largely responsible for the climatic extremes that can be experienced within the state.

New Mexico also has diverse physical geography, with three of the eight major physiographic divisions of the United States occurring here, and there are eight subdivisions of these three in the state. Those who are familiar with the region will not be too surprised to find that seven of these eight are found within 50 miles of Santa Fe.

Hikes 1 through 9 and 16 through 20 are in the region that is classified as the Southern Rocky Mountains. This area is made up of complex mountains of various types and is the highest, most forested part of the state, with very striking scenery. Outstanding features include the Sangree de Cristo, Jemez, and Nacimiento Mountains and Rio Grande Canyon.

Hike 27 is in Mills Canyon on the Canadian River, which cuts through the prairies of the northeast corner of the state, a portion of the Great Plains. This region is characterized by lava-capped plateaus, mesas, buttes, and volcanic cones standing above the grassy plains, and deep, picturesque canyons cut by the meandering rivers and intermittent streams. Far south of Mills Canyon is the long trough occupied by the Pecos River. The high plains of the eastern part of this region include the *Llano Estacado,* staked plains, as flat as any land found in nature.

Twenty-three hikes are in the Basin and Range province, which embraces the southwest quarter and central portion of the state.

This roadside marker relates a possible origin of the name Staked Plains (LLano Estacado) by which this extremely level terrain is known. The Spaniards called them Llano Estacado probably because of the yucca stems which dotted the vast expanses. Note the flatness of the land in the background.

Features of this area include narrow, isolated ranges of mountains separated by silt deposited desert plains, with occasional dry lake beds and sand dunes. Hikes in these mountains provide spectacular vistas to either side across the plains. Here faulting formed the great escarpments of the Sandia, Manzano, San Andreas, Caballos, Sacramento, and other mountain ranges. Mountain ranges in this part of the state that were not formed by faulting are the Magdelena, San Mateo, Black, and Mogollon.

The Sacramento section of the Basin and Range Province has mountains of greatly tilted-strata. These include Sierra Blanca, Sacramento, and Guadalupe mountains.

Hikes 45 through 50 are in the Intermontane Plateaus section, in the northwest quarter of the state. Much of the terrain here consists of plateaus, rock terraces, escarpments, mesas, shallow canyons, and dry washes. Exposed multi-hued strata make much of this area quite colorful, though it is extremely rough and rugged, and usually quite arid.

In the Datil section there are extensive lava flows, volcanoes, and volcanic necks (the material filling the central conduit of the volcano which remains after the cone is eroded away), such as the Zuni Mountains (Hike 47), Mt. Taylor (Hike 45), Cabezon Park, and others. This region is considered to have the finest display of volcanic necks in the world.

Additional volcanic features in the state include Capulin Mountain National Monument, Bandelier National Monument (Hikes 7 through 9), the great Valle Grande Caldera, Rio Puerco Field, Angel Peak (Hike 50), Shiprock, Zuni Salt Crater near Quemado, the very fresh lava of the Carrizozo and San Jose flows, and the ice caves near Grants. Volcanism continued until fairly recent times and some basaltic lavas are possibly less than 1000 years old.

Erosion and weathering produced some very striking features in New Mexico. These include Chaco Canyon (Hike 49), El Morro, which is better known as Inscription Rock (Hike 46), Enchanted Mesa, the volcanic necks (Hikes 45 and 50), Rio Grande Canyon (Hike 18), Osha Canyon (Hike 16), Mills Canyon (Hike 27), the Great Red Wall between Gallup and Thoreau (near Hike 48) and glacial phenomena of north central New Mexico (Hikes 20 through 24). The work of the winds can be seen at White Sands National Monument (Hike 35) one of the largest areas of gypsum sand dunes anywhere in the world.

New Mexico is indeed a beautiful and enchanted state and all Americans are fortunate that there is a place in our nation that remains largely unspoiled and unexploited.

We must be ever alert to preserve this enchanting land and take action to protect it. Get involved with conservation!

PREPARING FOR YOUR HIKE

PHYSICAL PREPARATION

A few of the shorter hikes described in this book don't really require any preparation other than just getting to your destination. As hikes get longer and more strenuous they will be more demanding of the hiker's physical and mental abilities. To prepare for physical demands you should initiate some sort of physical conditioning program. This may involve walking, hiking with a loaded pack, jogging, swimming, bicycling, rope jumping, or any other exercise that expands the lungs, exercises the cardiovascular system, toughens the feet and legs, and increases your stamina. Conditioning should be done on a regular schedule, daily if possible, with increasing activities as your condition improves. One of the conditioning books listed in "Suggested Reading" (such as Dr. Cooper's *The New Aerobics*) can be a big help in establishing a physical conditioning program.

MENTAL PREPARATION

Mental conditioning comes from knowing yourself and your capabilities, knowing your equipment and how to use it, and knowing that you can meet any problem calmly and handle it wisely. Fear is your worst enemy.

You can learn a lot about planning, equipment, using map and compass, coping with weather-related problems, first aid and such, from books, but the only way to try out what you have learned is by doing these things. There is no substitute for actual experience.

If you have friends who hike and camp, try to go with them on some outings. Consider enrolling in a backpacking class at the local community college or make some hikes with an outdoor organization such as the Sierra Club or the New Mexico Mountain Club. The store where you buy or rent equipment may have classes or should be able to put you in touch with individuals or groups with whom you can hike. When you hike with friendly, experienced people you can learn a lot from observing and listening.

COMPANIONS

You should not hike alone. When you plan a trip, choose your companions wisely. Consider their outdoor experience, physical strength and condition, mental attitude, and how they will affect the enjoyment of the trip by you and the other members.

Four is a good number of people to have in a group. If someone is injured or becomes seriously ill one person can remain with him while the other two go for help.

Someone has to be the leader and there must be an understanding before you start that after reasonable discussion if there is any disagreement, all will abide with his/her decisions.

THE ROUTE

In planning a trip you should become familiar with the potential problems along the route. Study the map, estimate the distances and amount of uphill and downhill and their gradients, and try to establish a leisurely schedule. From this you can plan campsites, water, food, and your overall time. Don't overestimate the abilities of members of your group.

If you are not familiar with the route you expect to take, try to get route, water, campsite and other pertinent information from acquaintances who have made the hike recently, or contact the Forest Service, Park Service, or whoever manages the area.

WEATHER

Consider the weather, current and the worst that could be expected during your outing. If it appears that it might turn bad, reschedule your trip or prepare for the worst the weather could bring. Weather is the major factor in most survival emergencies and it has a great effect on the morale of the group.

Be prepared for rain, wind, and an extreme change in temperature, especially in the mountains where conditions can deteriorate very quickly.

When you are wet and cold you get careless, your morale drops, and you are also a potential victim of hypothermia. Wet or dry, the wind increases the chill factor, quickening the rate at which your body loses its heat.

Cold, dry air can cause dehydration, which is a factor in altitude sickness. You may have to force yourself and your companion to drink enough liquids in order to stay healthy in below freezing temperatures.

At the other extreme, hot weather can cause heat exhaustion. When you exert yourself in hot weather much of your blood accumulates in the skin where cooling takes place. Heat exhaustion occurs when the accumulation of blood near the surface of the skin keeps the vital organs and muscles from receiving enough to function properly. In heat exhaustion the skin remains moist and cool, you may feel weak and have muscle cramps, and your skin will be pale. If you or a companion experience these symptoms, the victim should recline in a cool, shady place, drink plenty of water, and eat or drink something salty. After recovery be sure to consume plenty of water and salt, and limit physical exertion and heat stress that produced the problem. Though heat exhaustion is generally not considered to be serious, it can be, and the victim should be taken to a doctor as soon as possible.

A more serious and potentially fatal consequence of heat stress and physical activity is heat stroke (sun stroke). The victim's temperature control system breaks down and his/her temperature goes dangerously high. Symptoms include a reddish and dry skin that feels very hot when you touch it. Unconsciousness may result quickly. First aid must be initiated immediately. Shade must be provided and a conscious person should be given plenty of liquids and salt. Bathe the victim's skin (conscious or unconscious) with cool, wet cloth and fan him/her to enhance cooling. The temperature must come down! Get medical help as soon as possible!

If there is a possibility that the weather will be hot enough to cause problems, be alert to the onset of heat stroke or heat exhaustion in yourself and the others in your group. Carry something to provide shade, schedule a slower pace, carry plenty of water, plan frequent rest stops, and dress to keep cool and to give protection from the sun's rays. Good physical condition is essential in coping with high temperatures and physical exertion.

YOUR PACK

Keep your pack weight as light as possible; it will always weigh more than you want it to. The amount of load a person can carry varies quite a bit among individuals, but the heaviest load you should plan to carry is about one-third of a man's weight and one-quarter of a woman's. The only way to get accustomed to carrying heavy loads is to carry them. As you gain experience in hiking and camping, you will begin to leave behind many things because you learn you can get along without them.

Have your gear packed and ready to start hiking when you leave home. Nobody likes to stand around at the trailhead and wait for you to get packed. When you pack in a hurry you are more likely to forget something important, such as stove or sleeping bag. Food should be prepacked in plastic bags, by the meal or by the day, or whatever you consider to be the best way for you to organize it. Divide tent, stove, fuel, etc. among those who will be sharing in their use.

LET PEOPLE KNOW WHERE YOU ARE GOING

Write a note telling where you are going, your route, your companions' names, your anticipated schedule, your car description and license number and whom to notify if you don't return on schedule. Give a copy of the note to a responsible adult family member or close friend who will alert the proper authorities per your instructions.

At the hike area, sign out with the authorities and give them a copy of your note or write the same information on your permit, including home address and phone number. Check out with them or drop off your permit when you complete your hike, so they won't go looking for you.

WALKING TECHNIQUES

Walking for a long distance on a mountain trail with a pack of some sort on your back is quite different from a stroll around the shopping center. The heavy, stiff shoes you wear don't make walking seem any easier either. You will need to develop new walking techniques to conserve your energy and enable you to maintain a good average speed over long distances.

The stiff boots will make you walk flat-footed instead of springing from the toes as many short distance walkers do. Covering a number of miles in a day will require that you maintain a good steady pace, with infrequent rest stops. There will, of course, be times when you will want to stop and look at flora or fauna, or take pictures. If you can't take time to stop and smell the daisies, why bother to hike? But when you are moving, you need to

establish a steady pace that you can comfortably maintain for hours. Avoid the rush-ahead and stop-and-rest manner of the inexperienced. Since you will usually be hiking single file with a group, you must take up the pace of the others, which may be too fast or too slow for you. If you have trouble keeping up, ask the leader to let you set the pace for a while, then go at a speed that is comfortable for you.

Slow down when you go uphill. On very steep trails use the rest step. This requires establishing a slow rhythm. To do the rest step, you straighten and lock the knee on the downhill leg as you move the other foot forward. Pause momentarily, resting your legs, with the uphill knee bent and the weight all supported by the downhill leg. Next shift your weight over the uphill foot, step up on it, straighten the knee and lock it, and advance the other foot, which becomes the uphill foot. Repeat the procedure of straightening and locking the downhill knee and resting the uphill leg. The length of pause between steps depends on factors such as your physical condition, your load, trail steepness, and the altitude. Climbers at very high altitudes may take two or more breaths during each pause between steps.

Some hikers complain that going downhill is more difficult than going uphill, but I remain unconvinced. Going down, take fairly small steps, plant the downhill foot firmly, and shift your weight over it while both feet are solidly on the ground, before taking the next step. Some surfaces are rocky and unstable, and balance is very important. Maintain a comfortable pace downhill and don't let gravity get you started running, as it is difficult to slow down and creates a potentially dangerous situation.

Attitude is important. A person's ability to do something difficult or strenuous is largely psychological. Always try to think positively because if you are convinced that you can do something, such as carrying a heavy load up a steep hill, you probably will succeed.

Because hiking and backpacking are strenuous activities which require quite a bit of energy, you should plan to replenish your energy as you use it. I usually carry a plastic bag of mixed dried fruits, candy, and nuts (hikers call this Gorp), which I munch as I walk. You will probably enjoy experimenting with these ingredients to come up with a Gorp mixture that suits you.

You should make a short water and rest stop

every hour or so, and more often in hot weather, to prevent dehydration and regain some energy.

When hiking in cold weather you will have to stop and peel off some clothes as soon as you get really warmed up, so you won't sweat and get your underclothes wet. This is why you should dress in layers. Remove just the right amount of clothing to be comfortable. When you make a rest stop, you should immediately put plenty of clothing back on to prevent becoming chilled. When the weather is cold, be sure that you don't remove too much clothing, because you will have to use more energy just to keep warm, and may exhaust your energy supply. If this happens you will not be able to keep warm when you stop, and hypothermia can set in quickly.

Be sure to drink plenty of water when hiking, in either hot or cold weather, to prevent dehydration. The higher the altitude the more rapidly you lose water, and dehydration makes you more susceptible to altitude sickness and other altitude related problems.

CAMPING MANNERS

A goal for all of us who use and enjoy our existing wilderness should be to keep it wild and unspoiled for future generations. We must minimize our impact, with the objective of leaving no signs of our visit. "Leave only footprints and take only pictures!" Those of us who go into the backcountry must help by taking the necessary precautions, setting good examples, and educating those who are ignorant of appropriate conduct.

Many of the following rules were taken from the Sierra Club's "Camping Manners for Wilderness," copies of which I have often provided to students and novice hikers prior to backpacking trips. These include conservation measures and camping conduct necessary for keeping our wild country clean and unscarred, and for making the trip enjoyable for all. There is a deep sense of satisfaction and personal achievement in the knowledge that you have camped in and traveled through an area without leaving visible traces of your passing.

CAMP LOCATION AND CONSTRUCTION

Set up camp where foot traffic does the least damage to the fragile vegetation. Never camp in meadows; try to find sandy or rocky areas. Minimize building, whether for a kitchen or place to sleep. Don't modify the natural setting with rock walls for fireplaces or windbreaks. Don't cut limbs or small trees for tent poles or tarp supports; tie lines between two trees if you need a support, and don't put nails into trees. Don't disturb the soil with trenches, even though you may have been taught to always ditch your tent. Instead, locate your shelter or tent so water will drain away naturally. When you break camp, remove all evidence that you were there.

In many places you will find established campsites in the wilderness. Try to use one of these existing sites instead of making another.

CAMPFIRES

Some areas such as Carlsbad Caverns National Park do not permit campfires, and during extremely dry periods fires may not be permitted in national forests, so always be sure to inquire about campfires when you get a camping permit. Use existing fire sites whenever possible. If you camp where no one else has camped before, build a minimum fireplace. In a safe place, clear a circle to bare soil about 10 feet across, being sure to remove all burnable materials. Don't let decayed vegetation fool you into thinking it is soil. Never build a fire near trees, or in meadows, brush, rotten logs, stumps, dry grass, or litter. Don't build your fire against a log or a big rock. Keep your fire small, in a small pit or circle of rocks.

Never leave any fire unattended at any time. To do so violates state and federal laws.

When breaking camp put your fire out completely before you leave. Let the fire burn down, separate the embers, mix and stir the coals with dirt and water. Make certain the fire is out by feeling it with your hands. Bury the ashes and charcoal. Cover all traces, and, except in well established camps, return fireplace rocks to their natural positions with black areas on them hidden.

Smoke only in camp and at rest stops, never while traveling. Field strip all cigarettes and carry out all of your filter tips because they seem to be indestructible.

WOOD

Keep fires small. Conserve wood, particularly where it is scarce. Use small down wood only. Do not cut standing trees, living or dead, nor break off their branches. The dead trees and limbs are picturesque, a part of the forest setting. I never carry an axe because chopping on logs and stumps mars the wilderness appearance (and because axes are heavy).

STOVES

Stoves will be needed above timberline, in areas where firewood is scarce, and in places where fires are not permitted. They are clean and easy to use and do not scar a fragile campsite.

BED SITES

Avoid digging or leveling. Try to find a flat, sheltered, and well-drained spot that won't require any reworking. When you leave remove all signs of your having been there.

SANITATION

Dig latrines whenever a large party plans an overnight camp or when a small group plans a longer stay. Use them when available. They should be inconspicuous and placed well away from water. If there is no latrine, go far from camp, trail, and water, dig a small trench in the "live" top few inches of organic soil so that waste will decompose rapidly, and bury it. Burn toilet paper so it will not be strewn about. Placing a rock over the site is not satisfactory.

WASHING AND BATHING

Swim, bathe, and wash dishes downstream from where you get water for camp. Do all bathing, dishwashing, and laundry well back from the shores of lakes and streams. Prevent pollution by keeping soap and detergent out of the waters. Opinions differ as to the merits of using soap versus biogradeable detergent. For laundry and dishes use a wash basin. For bathing find a secluded spot where you can lather and rinse ashore before taking a dip in the lake or stream. One reason I carry a gallon or half-gallon plastic jug for camp and drinking water is that I use it to pour rinse water over myself when bathing.

CLEAN-UP AND GARBAGE

Burying garbage is not acceptable. Park and Forest Services prohibit digging pits and burying trash. In many areas soil is too shallow; animals, wind, and water expose the garbage, and disturbing the soil may initiate erosion. Put food wrappers, foil, orange peels, etc. in your pocket, pack, zip-lock bag, or trash sack for later disposal. Where fires are permitted you can burn everything that will burn. Pack out everything that won't burn: cans, bottles, foil, egg shells, big pieces of plastic, etc. Foil does not burn, and some paper wrappers for food are laminated with foil. Attempts to burn foil produces so many little sparkling bits that it is impossible to pick all of them out of the ashes. Cans can be carried out more easily if they have been smashed flat with a rock, or both ends have been cut out and the cans washed or burned and then flattened. Edibles may be scattered thinly, out of sight, and well away from camp and trail. Double check for litter-bits of paper, plastic, clothing, etc. Leave your campsite cleaner than it was when you found it. Make every trip a clean-up trip for campsite and trail.

STOCK ON THE TRAIL

Mules and horses are sometimes unpredictable and difficult to manage, so on the trail they have the right of way. When you see horses or mules coming, get off the trail to a place where the animals can see you plainly, preferably on the uphill side. Stand and talk quietly until they have passed because any unexpected movement or noise may spook them.

TRAILS

Stay on the trail. Cutting corners and cutting across switchbacks are the quickest ways to break down trail edges and start erosion and gullying. Dislodged rocks may fall on others below you.

CROSS-COUNTRY

Restrain your impulses to blaze trees or build rock cairns (ducks) to mark the route. Let the next hiker find his way as you did.

FISH

Catch only as many fish as you can eat. After cleaning them, bury the heads, scales, and entrails ashore; never throw them back into the water.

COURTESY

Be a considerate neighbor. Don't crowd other camps or sleeping areas. Noise is not in harmony with the wilderness, nor should radios be taken on hiking trips.

GRAFFITI

Do not carve on or paint rocks or trees. Pictures will probably remain until the tree dies. I have seen names and peace symbols carved and painted on trees, rocks, historic structures, and beautiful irreplaceable Indian pictographs.

FIREARMS

Guns are appropriate for hunting trips, but not for hiking and backpacking outings.

*Graffiti by an anonymous artist. The "artwork" is
on a dead tree which will fall soon and the felt pen
ink should fade before that event occurs.*

PETS

Pets (dogs) should not be taken into the wilderness. They are specifically prohibited in national parks and should be in wilderness areas too. Most hikers go into the wilderness to see the wildlife and to get away from annoyances. It is not enjoyable to have the peace and quiet shattered by an outburst of barking by another camper's dog, or have to fight it off while you are trying to prepare or eat a meal. There will be little opportunity of seeing deer or smaller animals when a dog is running ahead of you.

At Easter time there is still plenty of snow in the mountains.

SUGGESTED EQUIPMENT

Before we get into discussion of the major items of equipment it would be prudent to mention some relatively small items that may be vitally important in your surviving an unexpected emergency. Some of these items such as map, compass, and knife, are things you might use on any hike you make, while some are for use in emergencies only. I suggest that each person carry the following articles on any hike where one can't depend on help being nearby in case of an emergency.

A good knife
A good compass
Maps of the area (and know how to use them)
Matches (waterproof) and a lighter
First aid kit
Flashlight (with spare batteries and bulb)
Candle
Extra pair of socks (they can be used as gloves too)
Extra clothing (windbreaker, wool cap, etc.)
Three or more large plastic garbage bags
Canteen or durable water container, with water in it
Lightweight tarp or poncho, with grommets
Extra food (high energy)
Police-type whistle
Sunglasses
Insect repellent
Sewing kit
50 feet of parachute shroud line or heavy nylon twine

You may have something to add to the list or may want to omit an item or two, such as sunglasses or insect repellent. Every item on the list is important, and I will discuss each briefly.

KNIFE

I carry two, with one as a spare in case I lose the other. The knife I use most is a Swiss Army Knife, or Camper Spartan model. These knives are available at most specialty shops, with many different models offering a variety of blades. The Camper model is thin enough to fit comfortably in a pants pocket. I have a loop of red shoestring attached to my knife, which I secure to a belt loop when I'm hiking. The shoestring also helps me keep track of the knife in grass and leaves. My spare is usually a Gerber folding knife, which holds a very sharp edge.

COMPASS

I carry two compasses (plus a small one, used by scuba divers, on my watchband). I want a spare in case I lose one, but these two also have special uses. One (a Sunto) hangs on a string around my neck so it is handy for taking bearings or checking my heading. It is my favorite for taking bearings and can be read accurately to 0.1 degree. In the pocket of my pack I carry one of my assortment of Silva compasses because I find it best for plotting and measuring bearings on a map.

MAP

I carry the topographic maps and any special maps of my hiking area folded and encased in a watertight zip-lock plastic bag in the back pocket of my pack, or in my hand. The plastic bag protects them from precipitation and from sweaty hands.

MATCHES

Waterproof matches are available, but I usually carry regular ones in a watertight pill bottle. I also have book matches in zip-lock bags and carry a matchbook in the zip-lock bag with my toilet paper (paper towels) so I can burn it. Also, I carry two butane lighters, which are small, lightweight, and dependable. You should be aware that butane lighters can, and have exploded in pants pockets from hard blows or when they leak and a spark ignites them. It would be best to carry this type of lighter in your pack rather than in your pocket.

FIRST AID KIT

Everyone has his or her own idea about what should be in a first aid kit. Mine includes chlorox for water purification and for disinfecting; Neosporin antibiotic ointment; a dozen regular size bandaids; a small roll of ¾-inch adhesive tape; six 3x3 sterile pads; a bottle of Visine (for eye irritation); and a small tube of opthalmic ointment; Presun or Uval sunscreen; a stick of Cutter's insect repellent; small scissors; a scalpel blade and a pointed Exacto knife blade; tweezers; magnifying glass, sewing kit; 10 butterfly laceration dressings; a dozen aspirin; vitamin C tablets; antihistimine tablets; a dozen or more 3x4 inch pieces of thin type of moleskin; two three-inch wide Ace bandages; a small cake of soap; assorted safety pins; salt tablets; a large bandana; some Lomotil tablets for diarrhea; and a copy of "Mountaineering Medicine."

SNAKEBITE KIT

There are a number of varieties of rattlesnakes in New Mexico, but chances are remote that you will ever be bitten by one.

Coral snakes, the other poisonous type, are so rare that you will probably never see one. Though it is unlikely, snakebite is a possibility you should prepare for. You should know what to do if someone is bitten and should always carry a couple of rubber bands or Ace bandages to use in restricting dispersal of the venom.

If a snakebiting accident occurred on a hike, I would make the victim comfortable, lower the limb with the bite slightly, install restrictive bands, apply cool wet compresses if possible, and send a companion (two companions if available) for help. Help might be a horse to carry the victim out or it could be a helicopter with paramedics aboard. The objective is to get him/her to a medical facility as soon as possible so that antivenom can be administered.

I try to watch where to step when I hike, but snakes blend with their surroundings so well that they are sometimes impossible to see.

FLASHLIGHT

I prefer a flashlight that uses two "C" cells. This size is lighter than the more popular size that uses two "D" cells. An advantage of the C-cell flashlight is that it is small enough for you to hold in your mouth when you need to use both hands. You can also do this with a light that uses penlight cells, or a small throwaway light, but the very small batteries wear out rather quickly. I carry a small Tekna Lite as a backup. Also, I recommend that you carry spare batteries and bulb for your light. Battery life decreases as the temperature decreases. In very cold weather, battery life may be only 25 percent of normal.

CANDLE

I carry a six-inch candle (in a plastic bag) primarily for use in starting a fire when wood and tinder are wet. Use one match to light the candle and it will outlast hundreds of matches for fire starting. The candle can also be used as an emergency light. I sometimes bring along a compact, lightweight candle lantern, which provides enough light for reading, and it also warms and cheers up a tent on a long evening in bad weather.

EXTRA CLOTHING

This would depend on the time of the year and where you are hiking. I always try to take along a rainproof parka on backpack trips, and also on day hikes if rain is a possibility. If there is a chance of the weather turning colder, longjohn tops and bottoms are light and compact and really help keep you warm. A down vest with nylon shell stuffs into a small space and adds very little weight to your pack. A wool balaclava or the hood for a down jacket can save a lot of heat loss and doesn't weigh much, however, the down hood would be useless if it got wet. Plastic rain gear tears easily.

LARGE PLASTIC GARBAGE BAGS

These are useful for lots of things. I put one inside my sleeping bag stuff sack in rainy weather to keep the bag dry, and line the clothing and camera compartments of my pack with one each for the same purpose. If you don't have a rain cover for your pack you can use a plastic bag, with holes for the straps, to keep it dry. In camp I slip a plastic bag over my pack at night to protect it from dew or surprise showers. I have used a large plastic bag with a face hole in one edge near the bottom corner, as a rain or wind parka quite a few times when I didn't anticipate any bad weather. I have used the plastic bag parka and a plastic bag around feet and legs combined as an emergency sleeping bag when I didn't get back to camp from a long day hike. Large plastic bags have kept my pack and cameras dry as I swam and floated them across the Rio Grande. A bag can be rigged on sticks to provide shelter from rain and wind for your cook stove. One is also handy for carrying your garbage and other trash which you pick up along the trail. When ground, logs, rocks or whatever you want to sit on are wet, spread out a plastic bag and sit. I'm sure you can find other uses for them, too.

FOOTWEAR

No matter how warm you sleep or how comfortable your pack, you can't enjoy a hike if your feet hurt. I consider boots to be the most important articles of backpacking equipment. Boots or shoes must fit properly; they must support your feet and ankles adequately and protect them from rocks and cactus underfoot and on the sides. They must be comfortable and as lightweight as possible and still do their job well.

You may want the high quality, expensive footwear sold in the specialty stores or you may start with a high-top work shoe, a gum-soled hunter's boot, or with surplus G.I. boots. Whatever footwear you get should fit you properly and give your feet the support and protection they need. Backpack and sporting goods store personnel will be able to advise you.

BOOTS — LIGHTWEIGHT

I would not recommend the lightweights for rough trails and/or heavy loads. They do not provide sufficient protection from rocks and thorns and I don't believe that they would support arches and ankles adequately under these demanding conditions. The boots may not survive the punishment of rough, rocky trails too long.

JOGGING SHOES

When hiking with a light day pack on a trail that is not too rocky I often wear a pair of good jogging shoes. These have a good arch support and plenty of cushion underfoot for such hiking conditions, and are lightweight and comfortable. Though they are very comfortable, on long hikes my ankles and feet get tired and ache due to lack of support, and even with moleskin I often get heel blisters at the tops of the shoes. I believe that the new lightweight boots would be a good alternative to wearing jogging shoes.

GAITERS

A pair of short, lightweight gaiters with hiking boots, cover the tops of the boots and keep rocks and gravel out. Gaiters can also help keep your feet dry in wet grass or when you accidentally step in water that comes above the boot tops.

MOLESKIN

Before you make your first hike, regardless of what shoes you have, go to your local drug or discount store and buy at least one package of Dr. Scholl's Moleskin (not the thick Molefoam). The package of precut three by four inch rectangles is easiest to use because it saves cutting. It is quite a bit cheaper to buy by the roll and cut into the three by four inch rectangles. Before putting on your socks and boots, apply a full three by four inch piece of moleskin across each heel — don't cut it, use a whole piece on each heel. On later hikes you may try leaving it off, but it is good insurance against blisters. It is best to apply moleskin prior to hiking because by the time you feel a hot spot you usually already have a blister.

PACKS

Another important item of equipment that you will need is your backpack. You should have a light day-pack in addition to the frame type backpack. There are so many manufacturers and styles of packs that reaching a decision on which to buy may be difficult.

The day-pack is not so critical. I like a fairly large one to carry all of the camera gear, survival equipment, spare clothing, water and food for a day's outing. For this one I prefer moderately wide and padded shoulder straps, and the bottom of the bag should be reinforced. I usually carry a lightweight (no padded straps or reinforced bottom) day-pack in my backpack, for making side trips.

Your backpack should have a good sturdy frame, either external or internal. Do not get a plastic frame or one with plastic fittings. I prefer external frame for most trips because this type rides away from my back and allows air to circulate and keep me cooler. An internal frame pack might be better in cool weather. The external frame pack generally permits carrying a bigger load because more things can be piled on top, hung underneath, and tied on the outside.

The backpack *must* have a padded hip belt (or waist belt) to carry most of the load on your hips, rather than hanging it from your shoulders. Some packs have hip-suspension arrangements to suspend the load from the sides of the belt rather than from the back.

Be sure the frame is not too long (or short) for you, and can be adjusted to fit you. With the hip belt cinched up snugly, the point where the top ends of the shoulder straps attach to the frame should be level with or slightly lower than your shoulders, so you can carry some of the load on your shoulders.

External frame packs with lots of external pockets and provisions for attaching numerous items are popular. Some backpackers prefer cavernous internal frame packs with no external pockets or things that might get snagged during a technical climb. Most pocketless packs now have provisions for add-on pockets. The backpack frame should be well made, preferably of welded aluminum tubing. Before you take it on a hike, load it very heavily and bounce it around a lot to see where it is likely to fail. When the high stress points have been determined put in some additional stitching and further reinforce it to preclude failure. Carry plenty of heavy nylon thread, pack cloth, some large needles, a thimble, and a small pair of pliers when you hike so you can make repairs.

Quality should be a prime consideration when you buy equipment. External frames should be welded, heat-treated aluminum tubing. Machined aluminum fittings are good too, but plastic fittings or small screws are not. Internal frames are not usually as rigid as external ones and may consist of aluminum strips joined with pins. Pack bags should be made of tough, heavy-duty nylon or comparable material, and coated to make them as waterproof as possible. Seams should be straight, with about 12 stitches per inch. High stress areas should be double stitched and places where loads are concentrated should be reinforced. Zippers should be good quality and a flap should cover them to keep out rain. Shoulder straps and hip belts should be padded with a fairly firm closed cell foam that does not compress and roll up when the strap is loaded. Hip belts should be wide, padded, and encircle you completely, not just across the front. The belt buckle should be easy to fasten and unfasten under load and you should be able to tighten it while fastened and loaded. A sternum strap, to keep shoulder straps from slipping off, is a nice feature, but should not be a major consideration when choosing a pack.

Lightweight, fitted rain covers are available for Kelty packs and can be used on other packs as well. A rain cover is recommended because even the best, coated pack fabric leaks some in a downpour.

WATER CONTAINERS & PURIFIERS

I carry my trail water in a plastic bottle that fits in a side pocket of my pack. Extra water is carried in one-half gallon plastic jugs inside my pack and, if needed, in gallon plastic jugs on the outside of my pack. I'd rather have too much water than not enough. When I know there will be plenty of water along the hike I carry a plastic container for use in bathing and for holding cooking and camp water. A good rule to follow in hiking is to have at least a gallon of water per person per day. Remember, cold, dry air dehydrates too.

All stream and lake water (and that found in storage tanks at Forest Service cabins), regardless of how clear and pure it appears, should be purified before you drink it or use it in food preparation. Exceptions may be made for water taken from a spring as it flows out of the ground or a pipe.

Water purification is not difficult, but does require time and the proper materials. There are four ways in which a hiker can purify water. These include: boiling, mechanical filtration, chlorination, and iodination. Each of these methods has advantages and disadvantages, and some don't give complete "kills" of organisms which can transmit infections through water to humans. There are three basic categories of human enteric pathogens which are normally of consequence in the water you will find: bacteria, viruses, and amoebic cysts.

Water can be disinfected by boiling it vigorously for 20 minutes (longer at higher altitudes) to assure that all organisms are inactivated. This is the most effective method of purification, but the time and fuel required are major deterrents to doing it this way.

Mechanical filtration units are available from most backpacking specialty stores. These units utilize activated charcoal or resin beds or other substances that can give filter pore sizes of 0.5 to 1.0 microns. These filters are effective in removing cysts and bacteria but the pores are too large to catch viruses. This means that viruses such as hepatitis, poliomyelitis type I, cholera, and of course esch. coli (which is the culprit which causes the "touristas," the nausea and dysentery most frequently associated with impure water) can pass through the filter. For this reason it is suggested that one of these filter units be used prior to, and in conjunction with, chemical treatment. Some purification materials now available purportedly filter out or chemically kill all organisms, including viruses, which may indeed do. A quick and thorough treatment process would certainly be convenient to use.

Chlorination kills bacteria and most viruses by the reaction of chlorine products, primarily hypochlorous acid, with the enzymes that are essential to the metabolic processes of bacterial and virus cells. The rate and extent of disinfection is dependent on contact time, concentration of the chemical agent, and water temperature. The disinfection time decreases by approximately one-half with each 10°C (18°F) increase in water temperature, so allow more time when purifying colder water.

Sources of chlorine for disinfection of water include Halozone tablets and bleach, such as Chlorox. Each of these produce the hypochlorous acid essential in disinfection, when they are fresh, and when the water isn't too badly polluted with organic material and is within the proper ph range. Halozone has a very short shelf life (five months at 90°F) so it is essential that Halozone tablets be fresh. Bleach has a much longer shelf life. I usually replace my bleach a couple of times a year just in case it loses its strength. This is no problem because there is always plenty in the laundry and the cost is negligible.

I use bleach, which I carry in a discarded synthetic sweetener bottle. Dosage depends on turbidity of the water, because sufficient chlorine is needed to satisfy both the chemical oxygen demand and the biological oxygen demand in order to do its job. Proper filtering to remove the organic and other suspended materials, will make the water taste better and will require less bleach. Use four drops of bleach to a quart of clear water in a container that can be tightly closed. Shake the container to mix, loosen the cap and shake again to disinfect the cap and threads. The minimum time for disinfecting lukewarm water is 10 minutes, so allow a half-hour to be safe and an hour for water colder than 41°F. Chlorine (and iodine) must be used in the shade because sunlight breaks down the disinfecting chemicals. After 12 hours remove the cap from the water container and smell the contents. If it has a slight chlorine odor, similar to a swimming pool, there is residual chlorine indicating that the dosage was adequate and the water is safe to drink. If there is no chlorine odor, add another four drops of bleach and repeat the procedure.

I have used bleach for treating water in many countries in Africa, Central and South America, Asia, etc., and have never been sick from drinking the water. I also use it to treat the water in my hotel room in most foreign cities, including some parts of Europe. Bleach and Halozone produce the same chlorine compounds that "purify" your hometown water.

Iodine is a more effective chemical for disinfecting water than chlorine. A few people I have hiked with used iodine crystals, others used tincture of iodine (10 drops per quart), and others used a solution of iodine dissolved in water. I don't recommend any of these because you can't control the dosage adequately. Too much iodine, possibly 15 grams, can be fatal. Insufficient chemical won't disinfect the water.

If you prefer to use iodine, I recommend hyperiodide tablets. Use two tablets per quart of water and allow one-half hour after tablets have dissolved. I have a number of small bottles of these that the military uses (from Army Surplus). They are sealed with wax to keep out moisture and apparently can be stored indefinitely if kept sealed and dry. Hyperiodide tablets are available commercially as Globaline, Potable Aqua, and as Coughlans. The procedures for using iodine are similar to those for using chlorine compounds, except that you must taste it to test for residual rather than smelling it. Some people find the taste of iodine unpleasant and prefer Halozone or bleach treatment.

In summary, water can be adequately disinfected if you first filter it mechanically with one of the kits available at backpacking shops, then follow up with Halozone, Chlorox, Potable Aqua, or Coughlans.

EXTRA FOOD

Always carry enough food for at least one day more than you plan to be on the trail. This can consist of granola bars, soup mix, chocolate, a Mountain House dinner (for two), cheese, gorp, and maybe some kind of canned or dried meat. This could be stretched for two or three days or more if necessary. You can live about 10 times as long without food as you can without water.

WHISTLE

If you are lost or injured, a whistle signal can be heard a lot farther than your voice can. I carry a small plastic police whistle in my first aid kit, and a brass one on a string in my pocket. Whistles are also good for locating companions in forest or fog. All children should wear whistles at all times where they could wander off and get lost.

SUNGLASSES

These are necessary on snow and in the desert, particularly White Sands.

INSECT REPELLENT

Insects are not usually a problem in New Mexico, but when you do encounter them, you'll enjoy the outing if you have some repellent along.

SEWING KIT

A sewing kit could include heavy nylon thread and a couple of large needles for pack harness repairs, along with a thimble and small pliers to get the needle through thick material. A couple of small needles, dacron thread, some patch material, plus a button or two are useful in clothing repairs. To keep it all compact, wrap the thread around a finger-sized piece of open-cell foam rubber and stick the needles into the foam, inside the thread. Some duct tape wrapped around a short piece of pencil is handy for making quick repairs to equipment, clothing, or water jug.

SHROUD LINE

Fifty feet of this can come in handy for everyday use, as well as for emergencies. I've replaced the ropes that came on my tents with shroud line, and spare line is handy in case a tent tie is lost. There are numerous other uses for shroud line.

TENTS

You need a tent to protect you from the weather and insects, and sometimes to give

An inexpensive three or four person tent. A two person version is also available. A rain fly can be added for extra protection.

Hikers using a gasoline stove for cooking.

you some privacy. Your tent should be able to withstand strong wind and remain dry inside in a hard rain. It should also breathe and let the moisture that you produce escape, rather than condense on the inside. There are numerous tent manufacturers and a wide variety of tent shapes and support techniques. With so many to choose from, the tent you buy will depend on your personal preference, and possibly on the advice of the salesperson.

Tent weight should be a prime consideration in your selection, along with ease and speed of setting it up. It should have adequate space for occupants and some equipment, with sufficient headroom for sitting, dressing, stuffing sleeping bag, etc. If possible, you should borrow or rent a few different types of tents to see which you like best before you buy.

Regardless of what tent you have, always have a plastic ground sheet to put under it. The plastic provides an extra moisture barrier on wet ground or snow, and gives the waterproof tent floor some protection from sharp rocks, etc. This ground sheet should not extend beyond the sides of the tent because you don't want water to run down the side of the tent onto the plastic and under the tent.

Whether you buy a tent, rent one, borrow one, or a friend has just borrowed and returned yours, always put it up before you take it on an outing. Be sure all of the parts are there and you know how to put it up. If possible, practice putting it up in the dark, as you may have to do this on a hike sometime.

SLEEPING BAGS

There are plenty of different sleeping bags available to choose from. You will first have to consider what type of camping you expect to be doing, the anticipated minimum nighttime temperatures, humidity, shelter, sleeping pad, and your metabolism. If a bag is too warm for the weather, there is no way to make it cooler except by opening the zipper, which should be full length two-way for best ventilation. On the other hand, if your bag is not quite warm enough for the weather you can add longjohns and even more clothes to get comfortable.

I recommend that you consider only the "mummy" style bag, with the full length separating two-way zipper. You will have to decide what type of fill is best for you. The more expensive bags have goose down fill, which is warmer and lighter than synthetic fiber fills, and stuffs into a much smaller volume for carrying in, or on, your pack. Both down and synthetic fills have their advantages and disadvantages. There is plenty of information about sleeping bags in the equipment catalogs and backpacking books, so I suggest that you read some of these.

The ground pad you use will make a difference in the warmth of your sleeping bag, particularly on very cold or moist ground or on snow. Air mattresses take time to inflate and have a habit of going flat in the middle of the night. They also are not good insulators because the air in their chambers is free to circulate and carries heat from the warm body in the sleeping bag to the cold ground, or snow. A closed cell foam pad made of ensolite, volara foam or ethafoam, does not soak up water and does not compress much because air is trapped in each of the closed cells. Open-cell foam may be softer and cushion better because it does compress, but it does not insulate as well as a much thinner closed cell pad. It takes three to four times as much thickness of open cell foam to give insulation equivalent to closed cell.

You should carry your sleeping bag in a waterproof stuff sack to protect it from precipitation.

STOVES

On a backpacking trip the quickest and most convenient way to cook is with a stove. Traditionally, a camping trip doesn't seem like a camping trip unless you have a nice campfire for cooking and sitting around until bedtime. But backpack cooking is different from cooking while car-camping, or canoeing, or at a base camp. Going light is the name of the game and you don't want to carry the types of foods that require a big fire or hot coals for cooking. Especially if you have been carrying a heavy load all day and are tired and hungry, or it is raining and you and the firewood are wet, you will be glad that you don't have to go to the trouble of starting a fire, and waiting to get a bed of coals to cook on. Campfires are not permitted in many National Parks and Monuments, including Carlsbad, and in dry periods they may be prohibited in national forests as well. You will need a lightweight backpacking stove.

The least expensive device would be a can of sterno and a small folding fire shield/ cookpot support, but I would not recommend it. Sterno does not produce enough heat to do much more than heat a cup of soup, and it takes a long time doing this.

The less expensive stoves use butane or

propane containerized fuel. This type of stove is easiest for the beginner to use, is easy to start (in moderate weather), and is clean and quiet. The disadvantages with this type of stove include high cost of fuel, and the difficulty in finding the fuel cartridges in any place but a specialty stove. In addition, fuel containers may leak and leave you without fuel when you think you have plenty. In cold weather butane and propane do not vaporize readily, necessitating warming your fuel by carrying it around inside your jacket or by some other equally inconvenient manner.

Most experienced hikers use stoves that burn white gasoline. There are many makes and models to choose from. The SVEA 123R has been a standby for years and is widely used by backpackers. Optimus is also a popular brand of stove and has at least three models that burn gasoline (white gas) and two models that burn kerosene. Coleman, which has long been the leader in large gasoline camping stoves now has a small one-burner backpack stove. It is heavier than the other lightweight stoves and burns quite a bit of gasoline, but it puts out lots of heat.

The MSR Model G/K will burn quite a range of fuels including auto or aviation gas, kerosene, diesel fuel and stove oil. It is a very lightweight stove as it doesn't have any fuel tank. It screws into a Siggs aluminum fuel bottle, which becomes its fuel tank.

These are some of the many reliable stoves which should give trouble-free operation through a wide range of altitudes.

FLORA

Six of the seven life zones present in North America are found in New Mexico, each with its distinctive assemblage of plants and creatures. A simplified picture of the life zones would have them stacked one on top of the other, with clearly defined elevation (above sea level) limits for each. This would be an oversimplification because even though temperature, rainfall, and soil are the primary factors that determine life zones, they are in turn affected by many factors. The north slope of a hill or mountain doesn't receive as much direct sunlight as the south, particularly in winter, and therefore is much colder. Life zone limits will occur at a lower elevation on the north slope than on the south. West facing slopes receive direct sunlight during the warmer afternoon and are consequently warmer than the east slopes. You should take these factors into account when trying to avoid snow during spring and fall hikes, or when hiking in the summertime.

As an air mass moves uphill, it cools. If the temperature is lowered to the dew point clouds form and precipitation may be "squeezed" out. The precipitation usually falls on the upwind slope, leaving the downwind side of the mountain dry. In New Mexico most of the weather comes from the west or north. This difference in precipitation influences life zone limits. Plants that grow on the wet side of a mountain are often different from those that grow on the dry side. The latitude (distance from the equator) difference between the southern part of the state and the northern part affects the life zone elevations significantly, but is not as great a factor as elevation.

Life zones in New Mexico and their approximate limits are: Lower Sonoran or Desert Zone (up to 4,500 feet), Upper Sonoran or Plains Zone (4,000 to 7,500 feet), Transition or Foothills Zone (7,000 to 9,000 feet), Canadian or Montane Zone (8,500 to 11,500 feet), Hudsonian or Subalpine Zone (10,000 to 12,500 feet), and Arctic or Alpine Zone (above 12,000 feet). The zone limits reflect variations between northeast and southwest facing slopes, but as you hike you will find a much wider variation in them.

The life zone for an individual species of plant is different from that of any other species. The upper limit of a plant's life zone is where it is too cold for the plant to survive.

The lower limit is where it is too dry or hot for it to live.

More than 5,000 species of plants have been identified in the Rocky Mountains and possibly half this number live in New Mexico. A number of these are unique to this state. Many extraordinary plants, particularly cacti, peculiar to the southwest deserts are found here.

In the following paragraphs I will list some of the many plants found in each of the life zones in New Mexico. When I started compiling the list and trying to tell something about each, I found that to do the job adequately would require a separate volume which I'm not qualified to prepare. Instead, I recommend that you go to your local library or bookstore and evaluate the many excellent tree and flower books that are available. Purchase one or two that you think would be most helpful in identification, to carry in your pack. Book weight and compactness are important and should be considered in making your selections. The suggested reading list in this book includes some excellent plant books.

LOWER SONORAN PLANTS

Lower Sonoran life zone vegetation is typically that of the hot, dry desert. A definite indicator of this zone is the Coville Creosote bush, which is generally recognized as the most adaptable of all desert plants. Several species of grama grasses and root grasses such as Curly Mesquite are found here, and there are many varieties of cacti.

PLANT LIFE

Agave
Barrels
Chollas
Desert Broom
Fishhooks
Jojoba
Lechugilla
Mormon Tea
Ocotillo
Prickly Pear
Rabbitbush
Sotol
Sagebrush
Saltbush
Tesajo
Hedgehogs

TREES

Big Sagebrush
Fremont Cottonwood

Net Leaf Chokecherry
Valley Cottonwood
Velvet Ash
Honey Mesquite
Catclaw Acacia
Desert Willow
Hairy Mountain Mahogany
Western Soapberry
One Seed Juniper
Screwbean Acacia

FLOWERS

Buffalo Gourd
Broom Bacchrais
Desert Buileva (Desert Marigold)
White Stem Paperflower
New Mexico Thistle
Evening Primrose
Coulter Lupine (Bluebonnet)
Desert Zinnia
Malacothryx (Desert Dandelion)
Senna
Coast Erysimum
Bladderpod
Big Sagebrush
Gilias
Millein
Prickly Poppies
Windmills
Wild Verbenias
Nama
Goats Beard
Desert Parsley
Blazing Star
Phacelia
Starflower
Desert Willow
Tackstem

Woody plants such as Big Sagebrush, Freemont Cottonwood and Velvet Ash are found along streams and in moist places. One Seed Juniper is found scattered throughout the Lower Zone; Honey Mesquite is abundant in the grasslands and along streams and dry washes in southern parts of the state. Catclaw Acacia is also found in grasslands and along washes. Desert Willow grows along dry washes in central and southern New Mexico, and Velvet Ash along creeks and washes in the south. Hairy Mountain Mahogany is found in the southern half of the state as is Western Soapberry.

Numerous flowering plants are found in the Lower Sonoran Zone. A number of them are restricted to this zone, but the majority of them grow also in the Upper Sonoran and some in the Transition Zone and higher.

Ponderosa pine. Battleship Rock is at the extreme right.

UPPER SONORAN PLANTS

The Upper Sonoran is the most economically important in the state. Its lands have valuable grasses (grammas, galleta, buffalo rye, bunch grass, foxtail, etc.) and are well suited for ranching. When you drive through the state and see cattle grazing on ample grass out on the plains country, you can be reasonably certain that you are in this life zone. Extensive forests of Ponderosa Pine in the Upper Sonoran produce much of the state's valuable crop of timber. Some of the hikes I have described as passing through Ponderosa forests may someday pass through clear cut areas instead. On a warm afternoon a Ponderosa forest is filled with an aroma similar to that of vanilla extract. If you can't recognize this tree by sight you can do so by smelling the bark. Ponderosa are widely distributed in the state. Gambrel Oak are found in or near Ponderosa forests, on mountain slopes.

Woody plants and trees grow well here because of the moderate climate and adequate rainfall. There is quite a bit of overlapping of plants between life zones, with Lower Sonoran plants generally found in the lower levels and Transition Zone plants in the upper levels of the Upper Sonoran.

PLANT LIFE AND TREES

Grasses
Lower Sonoran Plants
Lower Sonoran Trees
Redbud
Chokecherry
Arizona Walnut
Arizona Sycamore
Arizona Cypress
Chihauhau Pine
Apache Pine
Arizona Pinon
Canyon Live Oak
Silver Leaf Oak (small)
Arizona White Oak

FLOWERS

Stone Crop
Service Berry;
Long Plumed Avens
Bitterbrush
Fireweed
Desert Parsley
Umbrella Plant
Bluebonnets
Scarlet Falsemallow
Manzanita

Collomia
Cromwell
Black Nightshade
Indian Paintbrush
Bluebell
Rocky Mountain Bee Plant
Yarrow
False Dandelion
Thistles
Spotted Knapweed
Morning Brides
Golden Aster
Rabbitbrush
Hawksbeard
Gumweed
Sunflowers
Gayfeather
Lush Pink
Coneflower
Horsebrush
Yellow Columbine

Alligator Juniper is associated with the Upper Sonoran in the south-central and southwest portions of the state. Another widely distributed tree associated with this zone is the Piñon pine, which produced the "Piñon Nut" seeds that are coveted by birds, animals, and man.

The majority of the flowering plants grow in the Transition Zone also, and a few grow at even higher levels. In moist places on cliffs or canyon walls near seeps, springs, or waterfalls you may find the beautiful Yellow Columbine.

TRANSITION (FOOTHILLS) ZONE

The transition zone has a cool, but moderate climate and receives more precipitation than the Sonoran. It is the habitat for a variety of vegetation, including many plants from the Sonoran and some from the Canadian life zone. Ponderosa grows in the lower levels and Englemann Spruce grows here, in the higher levels, and on up to timberline. Both are valuable for their timber and some of these hikes will take you through areas where they have been logged.

Trees found throughout the Transition Zone in mountain forests statewide include Limber Pine, New Mexico Locust (see Hike 42), Blue Spruce, Douglas Fir, and Quaking Aspen. Ponderosa, Narrow Leaf Cottonwood, Gambrel Oak, Wavy Leaf Oak, Rocky Mountain Juniper, and Gray Oak are widespread throughout the state, but grow at lower levels in this zone; while Rocky Mountain Maple and Sub Alpine Fir occur only in the upper levels and

Bark of the Alligator Juniper.

into the Canadian Life Zone. Those trees that are associated with wet places (streams, bogs, ponds, etc.) over the state include Inland Boxelder, Big Tooth Maple, Choke Cherry, and Narrowleaf Hoptree. Some trees are only found in the southwest corner of the state, including Emory Oak, Silverleaf Oak, Arizona Alder, Arizona Cypress, Arizona Pine, Chihauhau Pine, and Arizona Sycamore. Those found only in the northern part of the state include Water Birch, Black Hawthorn, and Curlleaf Mountain Mahogany.

Bushes found in this zone include Buckthorn, Currant Gooseberry, Thorn Apple, Barberry, Wild Rose, and Snowberry.

Many of the Transition Zone flowers prefer moist or wet soil along stream banks, around ponds and lakes, or in bogs. Some prefer shade and grow in moist woods while others grow in moist or wet meadows. In the summer you find flowers just about anywhere you go in the New Mexico Mountains.

Wild flowers and flowering shrubs that are found in the lower levels of this zone and down into the Upper Sonoran include the water plants: Bull Rushes, Cattails, Arrowhead, Water Ladies Thumb, Water Hemlock, Pond Weed, and Bunchberry. At this same elevation, those that grow in wet or moist areas near water include Blueeyed Grass (open areas), Mountain Spray, and Silverweed or Cinquefoil.

At higher levels of the Transition Zone and into the Canadian Zone and above, there are many flowering plants, most of which prefer moist or wet soil. The following grow along wet creek banks or in bogs, usually in the shade: Mountain Ash, Twinflower, Elk Thistle, Chokecherry, Sedges (more than 100 species are found in the Rocky Mountains and quite a few of these can be found in New Mexico), Dogtooth Violets, White Bog-orchid, Mountain Sorrell, Baneberry, and Shrubby Cinquefoil.

Giant Hyssop or Horsemint (a nettle-like plant that stings bare skin that rubs against it, as noted in Hike 34) grows on open hillsides and in shady places where the trail crosses streams and bogs. Blue Columbine (Colorado state flower) grows in moist or wet areas, in rock slides, open rocky areas, and sometimes in aspen groves, where you might also find Mountain Lover and Yampa, Arnica, and Little Sunflower.

Transition and Canadian Zone flowers that grow primarily in open, wet meadows include Milk Thistle, Coulter's Daisy, Red-osier Dogwood, Rocky Mountain Iris, and Monkshood. Those that prefer dry soil, primarily in open areas, include Fairybells, Yellow Fritilary and Bitterbrush (both are associated with Sagebrush), Wallflower, Sweetclover, American Vetch, and Goldeneye. Yampa, Green Gentian, Blue-eyed Mary, and Pussytoes prefer semi-dry or moist soil.

CANADIAN (MONTANE) ZONE

The Canadian Life Zone lies generally above 8,500 feet in New Mexico and is important for the water it stores for the lower elevations. The variety of trees decreases with increases in elevation because minimum temperatures that limit the growth range of plants get lower as elevation increases. In this zone you will find primarily Quaking Aspen, Inland Boxelder, White Fir, New Mexico Locust, Douglas Fir, Blue Spruce, Limber Pine, Rocky Mountain Maple, Thinleaf Alder, Sub Alpine Fir, Engelmann Spruce, Cork Bark Fir, and Bristlecone Pine.

Engelmann Spruce and Subalpine Fir, along with occasional Bristlecone Pine and Cork Bark Fir, grow all the way up to timberline. The life zone of the Blue Spruce coincides almost completely with the Canadian Zone, where it usually grows near streams. Aspen, Inland Boxelder, and White Fir are widely distributed over the state, grow only in the lower portion of the Canadian Zone, and at lower elevations. New Mexico Locust, Douglas Fir, and Limber Pine seldom grow at elevations higher than the lower half of this zone; while Rocky Mountain Maple and Thinleaf Alder (which grows on only a few small areas in the north and the southwest portions of the state) may be found alongside streams throughout the Canadian Zone.

Many of the Canadian Zone flowering plants were listed with Transition Zone plants because they are found in both. The following plants are found in this zone and on up into the Hudsonian Zone. Plants that are found in wet, boggy areas or beside streams include Marsh Marigold, Milk Vetch, Parry Primrose, Red Lily (from the plains up), Lily of the Valley (lower elevations), and Strawberry. Rocky Mountain Iris, Fireweed, Western Fringed Gentian, and Elephanthead prefer wet meadows. Those which grow in dry to moist soil include Kinnikinnick, Scarlet Gilia, White Phlox, Silky Phacelia, Big Sagebrush, and Sego Lily (which ranges from the desert up to here).

HUDSONIAN (SUBALPINE) ZONE

Vegetation in the Hudsonian Zone is similar

*The rare Texas madrone tree may be found on
Hikes 31, 32 and 33.*

to that which grows far to the north near Hudson Bay. This is a harsh environment and trees which are exposed to the wind and wind-driven snow are often stunted and deformed. Trees of this zone are Engelmann Spruce, Sub Alpine Fir, Cork Bark Fir, and occasional Bristlecone Pines. Aspen and White Fir sometimes grow in the lower levels of this zone, but cannot survive in exposed places or the cold temperatures of higher elevations. Near timberline, the upper limit of this zone, Engelmann Spruce and Subalpine Fir are the only trees that can survive except for a few Bristlecone Pines in the north-central portion of the state.

Nearly all of the flowering plants that grow in the Hudsonian Zone are also found in either the Canadian or Alpine Zones, or in both.

ALPINE ZONE

The Alpine Life Zone experiences extreme cold, strong winds, and wind-driven ice and snow particles. In many places deep accumulations of snow persist much of the year. The plants that can survive in this hostile environment must be very hardy and well-adapted. No trees can endure the harsh conditions, so this region is often referred to as being "above timberline." The plants that do grow here are the low, compact tundra, which can hide behind small rocks or withstand exposure to the elements. These plants are able to survive snow cover and immediately burst into bloom as soon as they are exposed to sunlight, in their rush to complete their reproduction cycle in the brief summer.

Alpine vegetation is characterized by dwarf flowers which include Forget-me-nots, Saxifrages, Sedges, Rushes, Dwarf Gentians, and Alpine Larkspur. From the following list of flowering plants, which is quite incomplete, you can get an idea of how colorful it can be above timberline on a pleasant summer day.

Alpine flowering plants include American Bistort, Springbeauty (Groundnut), Sandwort, Moss Campion, Anemone (Windflower), Rosecrown, Parry Primrose, Western Fringed Gentian, Silky Phacelia, Alpine Forget-me-not, Elephanthead, Yarrow, False Dandelion, Alpine Sunflower, Milk Vetch, Indian Paintbrush (many colors), Kinnikinnick, Sedges and grasses. Also, you might find the occasional beautiful Blue Columbine, Scarlet Gilia, White Phlox, Mountain Bluebell, Strawberry, Fireweed, Yellow Monkeyflower, and Pearly Everlasting.

In addition to flowering plants, rocks may be patterned with a variety of colorful lichens, which are very durable in the harsh climate, but grow extremely slowly.

Rocky Mountain Iris.

33

FAUNA

Wildlife is abundant in New Mexico, but you will probably see more in your car headlights at night than you will see on your hikes. Though the environment seems very inhospitable and dry, there is a greater number of animals and reptiles in the desert regions than in forested mountainous areas. The majority of animals, particularly in the desert, are nocturnal.

The most numerous creatures you will see on your hikes, aside from insects, are birds. More than 300 species have been identified in the state. In fact, more than 300 bird species regularly occur in the region encompassed by the southwest corner of New Mexico and southeastern Arizona (Hikes 38 and 39), and about two dozen of these are not ordinarily found anywhere else in the USA.

Rodents are the most abundant animals in the state, ranging in size from the smallest mouse to the good-sized beaver. They occupy all regions, from the hottest, driest desert areas to the cold alpine climate above timberline.

Small rodents found in the state include three species of Pocket Mice, six species of Grasshopper Mice, House Mice, Norway Mice, three species of Voles (found in isolated areas in the north and the east part of the state), three species of Kangaroo Rats, three species of Wood Rats, and Muskrats.

Rabbits are common on many of these hikes, particularly in the desert. The most frequently seen is the Blacktailed Jackrabbit. It is possible that there are Antelope Jackrabbit in the extreme southwest corner of the state. The Desert Cottontail is widely distributed at lower elevations, while the Eastern Cottontail's range is limited to the southeastern region.

Watch for Pikas (Conies) in rocky areas in the higher mountains near the Colorado Border. You may first hear their shrill whistling call. They are out and active during the day, eating or gathering grass. Higher mountains in the northern part of the state are also home to the Yellow-bellied Marmot, relative of the Woodchuck. You may hear it whistling near its den in rockslides and rocky areas below and above timberline. Marmots will sometimes allow you to approach close enough to get a good photograph with a telephoto lens.

There are many squirrels, chipmunks, and prairie dogs in New Mexico. They are found in all areas, from the low desert to near timberline. The Antelope Ground Squirrel is a desert-dweller, while the Thirteen-lined Ground Squirrel occupies the prairies and plains country. The Spotted Ground Squirrel is found in sandy, rocky areas at lower elevations. Largest of New Mexico ground squirrels, the Gray Rock Ground Squirrel is quite common from desert to timberline. It is often seen sitting on large rocks that afford good views of its surroundings.

Golden Mantled Ground Squirrels are fairly common in pine forests, as are Cliff Chipmunks (at lower elevations), and these are most likely to be the ones you see scampering around forest campgrounds looking for food scraps or handouts. The small Least Chipmunk prefers the open country.

There are three species of tree squirrels in New Mexico. The Albert (Tuft Eared), a very attractive species, is found only in Ponderosa forests. Not so numerous, the Red Squirrel may be seen in coniferous forests in the southwestern region, while the Western Gray Squirrel occurs in a small area in the northwest.

Blacktailed Prairie Dogs used to be fairly common in the plains and prairies, but eradication programs have drastically reduced their numbers. They are found only in relatively flat, overgrazed grasslands, where they build extensive "towns." The less numerous Whitetailed Prairie Dog's range seldom overlaps that of the Blacktailed. The Whitetailed is found at somewhat higher elevations on mesas and grassy mountain slopes.

Three species of pocket gophers occur in New Mexico. You are not likely to see any of them, as they spend their lives underground, but the mounds of dirt they push up as they build tunnels give evidence they are underfoot. The Western Pocket Gopher is widely distributed over the state, while the Plateau species is found in the eastern plains region. Plains Pocket Gophers have a very limited range in the southeastern realm.

Porcupines may be encountered in most parts of the state in a variety of habitats. They feed primarily on the inner bark of certain species of trees. They are forest dwellers, but apparently can live wherever there is an adequate food supply and favorable climate. Porcupines are nocturnal, so you won't see many of them in the daytime. They apparently crave salt and have been known to chew items

*One of the beaver dams that enhance the fishing in
Rio Cebolla.*

that have salty sweat deposits, including pack shoulder straps, boots, walking sticks, etc.

You will see beaver dams and ponds on some of these hikes. The dams are interesting structures, and they and the ponds they create enhance the valley scenery. Beaver are New Mexico's largest rodents and are relatively numerous as you can tell by the gnawed stumps of willow and other trees that border streams and ponds. You will be lucky if you see this interesting mammal because they are nocturnal and if any happen to be out in the daytime they are ever alert and will dive and disappear as soon as they see you. Along larger streams and river beaver do not build dams and lodges, but instead burrow back in muddy banks, with underwater entrances. The telltale stumps indicate their presence.

Carnivores have been the victims of extensive eradication programs for years. It seems that man, the ultimate predator, is prone to exterminate any creature that competes with him or which he thinks harms any of his possessions.

Black Bears are the largest carnivores in New Mexico. Evidence of the Black Bear is visible in the tooth-scarred trail signs that mark many of these hikes through forested mountains, its preferred habitat. In our northwestern states it is often necessary to hoist food up between trees at night to keep it out of reach of bears, but this practice is not necessary in New Mexico.

There are still some Mountain Lions (also known as Puma or Cougar) in the state, but you will be very lucky if you ever see one. Mountain Lions prefer rough, desert country and may travel many miles on a night's hunt.

Bobcats prefer the forests and Upper Sonoran life zone, but are not limited to this habitat. Their population is not large, and they are seldom seen by hikers.

Some ranchers believe that wolves kill their livestock, but the Red Wolf, if not extinct, is extremely rare and could not be responsible for all the villany for which it is blamed. If you were to see one, it would not be in a desert environment.

Coyotes are not on the endangered species list yet. In fact, their numbers have increased in some areas in the past few years, probably due to the increase in rodents, their primary food supply, which resulted from the elimination of other predators. The coyote is mainly a plains and desert dweller, but in New Mexico they may be found in all habitats, from low desert to high mountains. It is a real thrill to me to hear the barking/howling of a coyote in the night or early morning hours. One animal can sound like a whole pack.

Gray Foxes may occur just about all over the state, but their preferred habitat is open brushy country at lower elevations. At a glance you might think a Gray Fox is a small coyote, but a closer look should note the short legs and big bushy tail of the fox.

Red Foxes may be present in the extreme northern part of the state, though they are not common. If you see a reddish fox in New Mexico it will probably be a Gray Fox with this form of coloration.

The Kit, or Desert Fox, is smaller than the Gray Fox and its ears are much larger, proportionally. These animals are found primarily in the desert country, though some may still survive in the plains.

The raccoon and its relatives, Ringtails and Coatis, are present in New Mexico. Raccoons are found near permanent water. It inhabits desert canyons and valleys and is found throughout the state, except at high elevations. It frequents campgrounds and will raid your food supplies if you leave them out.

Ringtails inhabit much of the state, primarily in the desert and foothills habitats. The Coati is a recent arrival from Mexico. It prefers the Upper Sonoran life zone and its range is limited primarily to the southern half of the state.

The weasel family, which includes skunks and badgers, is well represented in New Mexico. American badgers are quite easily distinguished from other mammals because of their short legs and broad, heavy body, and their black and white face patterns. They prefer the plains country, but are found in the desert habitat also.

There are three species of skunks in New Mexico. The most commonly seen is the Striped Skunk, which is found all over North America. The little Spotted Skunk, also known as the Civet Cat, ranges throughout the state, but is not seen as frequently as the Striped species. The Hog-nosed Skunk is a migrant from Mexico, and the relatively few that have crossed the border are found only in the southern region.

Of the weasel-like animals, the Longtailed Weasel is by far the most common. I observed a family of these near the Colorado border, on Hike 16. Shorttailed Weasel (Ermine), Mink, and Blackfooted Ferret are infrequently seen, and then, only in colder realms in the northern part of the state. A large relative of the weasel, the Marten, possibly occurs in this same habitat. The River Otter is also a member of the weasel family, and there may be a few of them along streams in the northern region. A tell-tale sign of otters is the "slide" they make down muddy stream banks.

The largest wild animals you will likely see on your hikes are the hoofed ones. These include elk, deer, antelope and sheep.

It is exciting to unexpectedly encounter a small herd of elk, or an individual one, on a hike. Unfortunately, this doesn't happen frequently. I have seen more elk in Gila National Forest than in any other part of the state. This is probably because I have hiked more there than in most of the other areas, and at times when the elk were driven out of the high country by deep snows. The extensive Gila Wilderness is a refuge free of hunters, permitting increased populations of both "game" animals and predators.

Pronghorns may be seen grazing in herds on the vast open prairies, primarily in the eastern half of the state.

Elk may be seen in meadows or above timberline in the high mountainous country from Gila National

Forest and the Capitan Mountains in the south, northward into Colorado.

A small herd of elk has been reintroduced into the Guadalupe Mountains, near Carlsbad, and I have seen elk there, but the real elk country is in the high mountains of the northern region.

The most frequently seen of the large hoofed animals is the Mule Deer. It is found from the lowest, hottest deserts to the highest mountains, and places in between.

Whitetailed Deer are found more in the southern and eastern portions of the state. They are not as big as Mule Deer, but are spectacular to see, with the big white tail telling you goodbye as they make a quick and graceful retreat.

Small herds of Pronghorn are often seen grazing with cattle in the plains and prairie country. They are plains animals and are not found in the desert, forest, or mountains.

The Bighorn Sheep was hunted to extinction in New Mexico years ago. A few have been reintroduced in a small number of scattered, isolated areas. Though their habitat extended up the mountains of the west from Mexico to Canada, the few that have been reintroduced are in desert mountains, such as the Guadalupe.

Herds of 10 to 20 Collared Peccaries may be encountered in the extreme southern part of the state. Also called Javelina, they resemble pigs.

We don't always think of bats as being mammals, but they are. About 15 species of bats are found at Carlsbad, and the most common, the Mexican Freetail, is found in all of the desert country.

Reptiles are frequently thought of as being primarily desert dwellers, but this isn't necessarily so. Most of the species of lizards and many of the non-poisonous snakes are found in all areas of the state where it is possible for them to survive the winters. Three major groups of reptiles are found in New Mexico. These are: turtles, lizards, and snakes. Reptiles are cold-blooded, with a body temperature about the same as the surrounding ambient ground and air. This is why few reptiles are found in the colder climate zones. You have probably seen turtles, snakes, and lizards sunning themselves on logs or rocks, or on a sunny patch of ground. Warm sunlight, warm air, or a warm surface is the only source of heat for these creatures. Many snakes are killed by vehicles at night when they crawl out on the warm pavement to gain some heat. Reptiles must be careful about getting too hot,

so they remain in the hot sun for only a short time.

Do not kill snakes just because you've been taught that this is always the thing to do. They belong in the wild areas and are interesting creatures. Leave them alone so others can have the pleasure of seeing them too. Reptiles feed primarily on insects and rodents, and in this way help us with pest control.

Next to birds, lizards are the most frequently seen form of wildlife, at lower elevations. These include Earless Sand, Banded Gecko, Collared, Leopard, Horned, Whiptail or Racerunner, Spiny Swift, Ground and Climbing Uta, Alligator, Skink, and the poisonous Gila Monster species.

The Collared Lizard grows to be more than a foot in length and is very colorful. Its body is often bright turquoise, mottled with brown and yellow. Two black bands around the back of its neck give it the name. It can run very fast, sometimes on its hind legs, balancing with its upturned tail. The Leopard Lizard is similar to the Collared Lizard in size and conformation, but its coloration is quite different.

Horned Lizards (Horned Toads) are unusual creatures. Their skins are spiny, but enlarged spines on their heads give them their name. They live in dry, sandy soil and eat ants and other small insects.

There are many other interesting lizards in New Mexico. The Sand Dune Lizard is a small, white lizard that is endemic to the White Sands (Hike 35). Its color, or lack of color, makes it almost invisible when it rests quietly in the white sand.

If you see a fairly large brown lizard climbing around on the smaller limbs of trees it is probably the Alligator Lizard. It has a prehensile tail that helps it hold onto twigs and branches.

It is interesting that there are no males of the sand-dwelling New Mexico Whiptail Lizards (Racerunners). Litters are parthenogenic — the females, without needing the service of a male, lay eggs that all hatch into females.

The Gila Monster is the only poisonous lizard occurring in the USA. It is quite rare and is found only in the Gila River area of this state. It is found in damp, sandy places in washes and stream beds.

Poisonous snakes are probably uppermost in the minds of novice hikers. There are quite a few different species of rattlesnakes in New Mexico, but no Copperheads or Cottonmouth

Moccasins; and Coral snakes are very rare. Although there are quite a few rattlesnake species in the state, they are seldom seen. If you want to see one, they are said to be relatively numerous in the area around Sitting Bull Falls (Hike 33).

In the mountains in the southern part of the state, and around Carlsbad and Sitting bull Falls, the Mottled Rock Rattlesnake is the common species. The Blacktailed Rattlesnake is also common in the southern region. The Banded Rock species is more commonly found in the southwestern part of the state. Chihauhaun Ridge-nosed Rattlesnake from Mexico occur in the Peloncillo Mountains (Hikes 38 and 39). The Western Diamondback is widespread throughout the state, at elevation below 5,000 or 6,000 feet. The Blacktailed Rattlesnake is interesting in that its coloration varies with the area in which it occurs. In the southern part of its range it is silver-gray with a black pattern, while north of Albuquerque this same snake is golden yellow with black markings. Prairie Rattlers are found in the plains in the northeastern part of the state. Massasaugas are smaller than the other rattlers and, accordingly, are less dangerous than the big ones. The dark blotches on their backs seem to stand out in more contrast with the background than on other rattlesnakes. Massasaugas usually have a silver-gray background.

Though hikers are most concerned about poisonous snakes, there are two or three times as many species of nonpoisonous ones. These include Bull, Glossy, Gopher, Western Hognosed, Patch-nosed, Leaf-nosed, Long-nosed, Ring-necked, Black Headed Blind, Garter, Ground, Ribbon, King, Milk (Red King), Blue Racer, Whip, Coachwhip, Rat, Corn, Fangless Night, and two species of Lyre snakes. Smooth Green Snakes are found in the Sangre de Cristo Mountains.

The Lyre Snake probably should not be included here with the nonpoisonous ones. They have back fangs and cannot bite like other poisonous snakes, but if you play with one and your finger gets in its mouth it could poison you. Children have died from Lyre Snake bites.

There is great diversity among the nonpoisonous snakes. Sizes range from the seven-foot maximum length of Bull, Rat, and Coachwhip snakes to the eight to 12-inch adult Blind, Ring-necked, Hook-nosed, Ground, Flat-headed, and Leaf-nosed snakes. Some are very specialized, such as the Hog-nosed which dines almost exclusively on toads, or the Blind Snake which lives underground, can't see, and eats only worms and insect larve. Some are nocturnal while others are active in the daylight hours.

If you are fortunate enough to encounter a snake on one of these hikes (or any place else) please do not harm it. Observe it and photograph it, but leave it alone. While the human population has more than doubled in the past 50 years, snake and other wild populations have diminished at a frightening rate.

*View of distant forest enroute to San Pedro Peaks
and San Pedro Parks.*

1 RED ROCK TRAIL TO SAN PEDRO PARKS
SANTA FE NATIONAL FOREST

Distance: 14.8 miles round-trip (this is a circle route)
Time: 7 hours minimum, better as a two or three day trip
Elevation Range: 8,300 to 10,560 feet
Rating: Moderate to strenuous, route finding is a problem at times
Water: Reliable at places
Seasons: Usually May through October depending on snow
Topographic Maps: Regina, Gallina, Nacimiento
Special Maps: Santa Fe National Forest, Grid B4, B5; San Pedro Parks Wilderness Guide

This hike is in San Pedro Parks Wilderness, where a permit is required for remaining overnight. Permits can be obtained from the Ranger Stations in Cuba and Coyote, in person or by mail (except for staying at San Gregorio Reservoir, for which you must apply in person). Be sure to get the San Pedro Parks Wilderness Guide and Map, and the Santa Fe National Forest Map, when you get your permit. They are necessary in order to follow the trails. They give trail names and numbers, distances, and topographic information. Permits are free.

At the trailhead, alongside Rio Gallina, there is a nice camping area. This is convenient if you want to stay here overnight before or after the hike, or if there are non-hikers who will need to camp while you are hiking. The area is small and primitive, but delightful.

There are quite a few optional routes for this hike, because of trails which join or cross the route described. The hike can be done as a day hike or as an overnight; it can be a loop or an up and back; it can be modified shorter or longer by taking other routes; or, if a car shuttle or key-exchange is planned there are other possibilities. Beginners may want to go only as far as the junction with Trail No. 36 where there is excellent camping with plenty of water. Others may go to San Pedro Peaks and camp along the way, near Capulin Creek, or in the open forest on top of the ridge (no water).

It is recommended that hikers on this route be well versed in the use of map and compass and be experienced trail finders. Most of the route is on excellent, well-prepared and maintained trails that are easy to follow. But there are places where the trail disappears or gets mixed up with well-worn cow trails. In such places you must either turn back or be able to navigate until you can pick up the route again.

Trail No. 30 starts at the end of Forest Road 14. A sign marks the route which goes up the east side of the canyon. The trail is easy to follow and easy walking. It is well maintained to the junction with Trail 36 (1.2 mile). If you plan to go on to San Pedro Peaks, continue on Trail No. 30, turn left at the junction and continue straight for about 200 feet. A blazed fir tree and a blazed aspen mark the way. The route then turns northeast, crosses a stream bed and rises fairly steeply uphill. Look to your left (NE) through the trees for the wide, well-worn path going uphill. It is well marked and is nearly as good walking as the first part.

If you have other plans, you may wish to travel uphill on Trail No. 36 from this junction. It is easy to find and follow. Either route takes you away from the water in Rio Gallina, which was parallel to this junction.

At 0.1 mile past this junction (1.3 miles) on Trail No. 30 is a fork. Take the sharp switchback to the left, even though there are old blazes on the trees along the abandoned route to the right. At 2.9 miles, hikers go left, cows go right. The trail crosses Capulin Creek at 3.1 miles. There is water in the creek and good campsites nearby, but flies may be bad. Trail No. 30 ends at its junction with Trail No. 31, at 3.4 miles. Go right (south) on Trail No. 31.

Capulin Creek is the last water for a while, as the ridge along San Pedro Peaks is quite dry. The trail is being rerouted around washed-out sections, so some new sections will depart from the old, blazed route. There is a sign, "San Pedro Parks Trail No. 31," at 3.8 miles.

A good picture of Tom Mix is carved in an aspen tree 20 feet beyond the sign. This was apparently done by a WPA worker who worked on the trail in the 1930s. Please do not carve on trees — graffiti remains until the tree dies.

You are near the highest portion of the San Pedro Peaks ridge at 5.4 miles. The forest is small, widely spaced coniferous trees, with many good campsites all along the top of the ridge.

The farther you proceed along the ridge, the less distinct the trail becomes. Watch for blazes on trees, rock piles (cairns), posts, posts standing in piles of rocks, etc. marking the way. You start losing elevation at 6.2 miles and cross many cow trails, marshy meadows, and patches of forest. Farther along is a sign (away from any indication of a trail) proclaiming "San Pedro Peaks."

From here on trail finding is a problem. When you lose the trail you might try going to the east and to the west to see if you can cross it, but remember where you started from. But if you just use your compass and continue a bit west of "south" you should hit Trail No. 32 at about 7.2 miles (3.8 miles along Trail 31).

If your trail following and navigation have been good, you should come to three posts with signs at the junction of Trails Nos. 31 and 32. It seems that Trail No. 32 runs more southwest than the map shows, but follow it (alongside a small stream part way) to the broad marshy meadow (park) and the major trail junction with Trail No. 51. Vacas Trail No. 51 is a major route (see Hike No. 2), well defined and maintained, joined at 7.8 miles. The junction with San Jose Trail No. 33 is reached at 8.7 miles after a very scenic walk through some of the San Pedro Parks. The beautiful scenery continues along No. 33 on the northwest also. There is plenty of water at intervals upon arriving on Trail No. 32, with numerous good campsites.

Gallinas Trail No. 36 junction is well-marked, and there is a good view to the northeast at this point (10.7 miles). Trail No. 36 is going to be difficult to follow for the first half-mile or so. At 0.1 mile from the junction a rock cairn will show where to enter the forest. From 0.2 to 0.3 mile on this leg continue to follow rock cairns and blazes on trees and whatever path you can find. At .3 mile (11.0 miles total) there is a spring, which has been dug out to make a small pool. Rock cairns and blazes are still helping to mark the route. Shortly, the trail enters the forest and the old route is very obvious. The trail in the forest has been recently rerouted. Many switchbacks have been added, avoiding much of the old, steeper and eroded route.

The sign at the junction of T-33/T-36 reads, "Red Rock Trail 1¾ miles." The additional switchbacks now have increased this distance to 2.9 miles, but the good walking surface and easy grade more than compensate for the increased distance. From here to the car there should be no trail-finding problems. You rejoin Trail No. 30 at 13.6 miles, and it is an easy 1.2 mile walk downhill on the very good trail to the car. Total walking distance has been about 14.8 miles, with a variety of beautiful scenery.

This is a fairly hard day-hike for an experienced trail-finder and strong hiker. It would be much more enjoyable as a two or three-day backpack trip. The scenery is excellent, with quite a bit of variety. Water is available on much of the route, though you should always treat it with your preferred chemicals.

To reach the trailhead, get on N.M. 96 and go to Forest Road 76, which goes south from N.M. 96 a mile or so west of the rather ill-defined place shown on the map as Gallinas. The turnoff is 4.4 miles east of the N.M. 96/112 junction, or 2.4 miles west of the F.R. 8 French Mesa Road, which is well-marked. A brown and white Forest Service sign marks the F.R. 76 turnoff, pointing to Gallina Trail and San Pedro Parks.

There is a good, new cattle guard as you go onto the gravel road. To help be certain you have turned onto F.R. 76, it turns left quickly after the cattle guard and for a short distance runs east almost parallel to N.M. 96. Shortly, there is a F.R. 76 sign. F.R. 76 is a very good all-weather gravel road, with signs identifying side roads, including F.R. 14. It is 4.3 miles from N.M. 96 to F.R. 14, which is dirt surface, and rough. In dry weather a pickup or small car can make the 1.6 miles to the trailhead without much trouble, but if the road is muddy don't attempt it — and don't get rained in. Look it over for yourself.

Looking north into San Pedro Park from the "trail," which is indistinct, momentarily, along here. The *Forest Service cabin is in a small branch of the park, on the left.*

Primitive camping area at the trailhead. The small stream in the foreground is Rio Gallina.

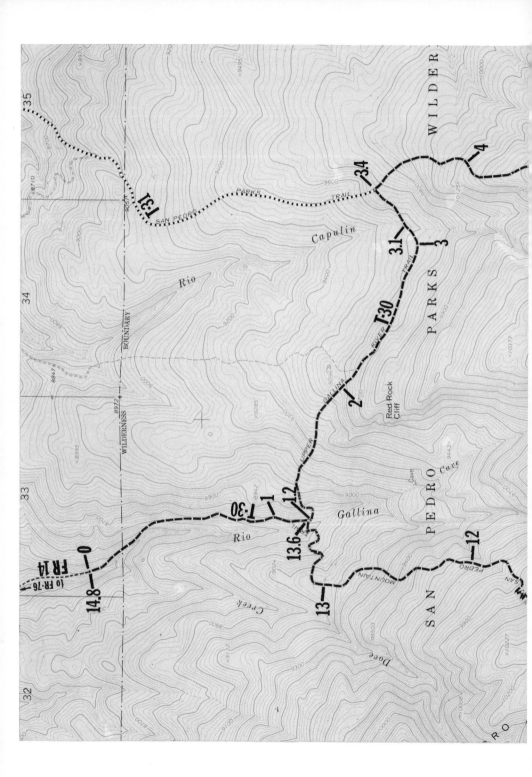

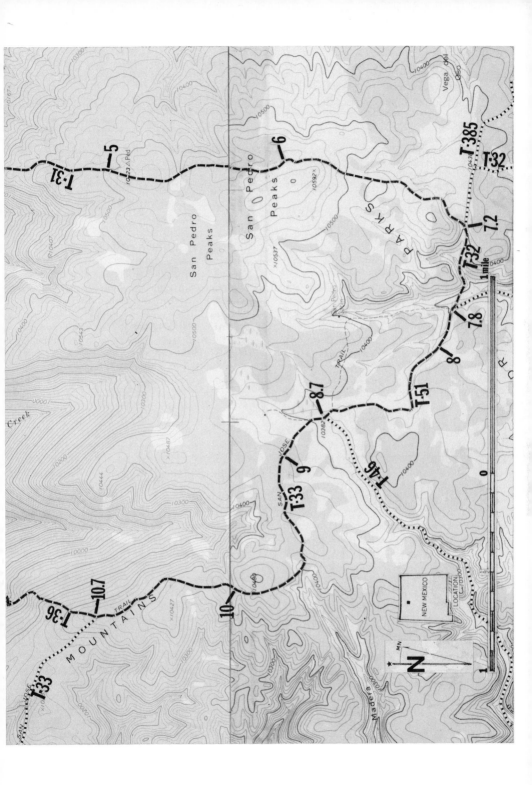

2 VACAS TRAIL TO SAN PEDRO PARKS
SANTA FE NATIONAL FOREST

Distance: 17.9 miles round-trip
Time: 9 to 15 hours round-trip, but plan to camp awhile
Elevation Range: 9,200 to 10,400 feet
Rating: Easy
Water: Available much of the way, but must be properly treated
Seasons: Usually May through October, but depends on snow
Topographic Map: Nacimiento Peak
**Special Maps: Santa Fe National Forest, Grid B5; Visitors Guide (map) to San Pedro Parks
    Wilderness**
Permit: Required for overnight camping

This is a hike that should please everyone. And, from the number of cars there when you arrive at the parking lot, you'll think everyone is out hiking it. But don't be dismayed by the apparent crowd, because the majority of the people parking there will be fishing at San Gregorio Reservoir, a mile or so up the trail. Weekends are crowded, and probably only 10 percent of the cars are from out-of-state, indicating that it is mainly local people who know about and use this beautiful area.

This trail has a number of advantages over others in this area. An excellent all-weather road runs all the way to the trailhead. You start hiking at 9,200 feet and climb only to 10,400 feet in San Pedro Parks, so there isn't much uphill. The trail is broad and easy to follow, with no steep grades.

The scenery is outstanding, with open green forest, open valleys and parks, wooded hills, open marshes, and clear streams along the way. There is water frequently until you get in the parks area. When you get ready to camp you never have to go far to find an excellent site. Though there may be a number of other hikers in the area, you seldom see many of them because they are so widely scattered in a place this large.

Before you hike in this area be sure to get the special map of San Pedro Parks Wilderness. Without it, the trail signs sometimes don't tell you enough. The map gives distances in addition to trail names and numbers, and topographic information.

This trail starts at the parking lot near the end of Forest Road 264. From there to San Gregorio Reservoir the path is quite wide and heavily used, passing through a forest of large trees. Keep the reservoir to your right and follow the path which skirts the east shore. At 0.9 mile the trail forks at two posts (no signs). The left branch continues around the lake.

The right branch is Vacas Trail. At about 1.2 miles, a side trail joins from the left. A post in the marsh marks the route. There are a number of side trails along the way, which are not marked and are not shown on the wilderness map. There is no problem in following the main trail. The major trail junctions are well-marked, such as the one with Palomas Trail No. 50 at 5.2 miles and with Anastacio Trail No. 435 at 5.5 miles.

Along a portion of the route, between 3.5 and 4 miles swarms of aggressive mosquitos were encountered. It was a relief to find that they were troublesome in only a small, forested area.

There are other major, marked trail junctions at 7.9 miles and 8.8 miles. Vacas Trail ends near the source of Rio de las Vacas near a large, open, marshy area in San Pedro Parks, at about 9.1 miles. You may want to camp in this area, or you may want to continue farther on one of the other trails.

You can return on a loop route by taking Rito de los Pinos Trail No. 46 southwest to Anastacio Trail No. 435. Take Trail No. 435 back to Vacas Trail. This way you will see more of this beautiful area.

Please note that even the major trails may become obscure in the dense marsh grass, so look for posts marking the route. Also, cow trails in the San Pedro Parks area are sometimes more heavily used than the hiking trail. If you have trouble finding the trail, take careful note of the route you have been following, so that you can return the way you came.

To get to this hike, go east out of Cuba on N.M. 126 for about 10 miles to Forest Road 264. Turn left (north) on F.R. 264 and follow it about three miles up to the trailhead. The N.M. 126/F.R. 264 junction is 0.7 mile east of the end of the pavement on N.M. 126.

Trail junctions are usually well marked, but you need the Visitors Guide to the San Pedro Parks Wilderness map in order to know which route to follow.

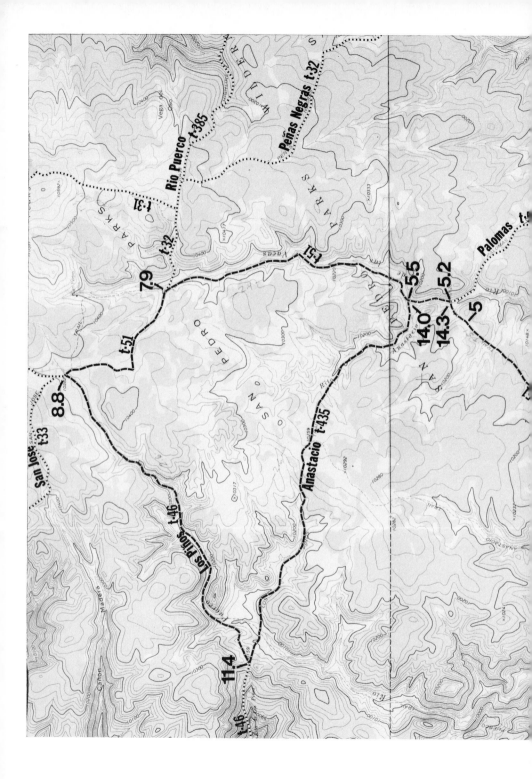

48

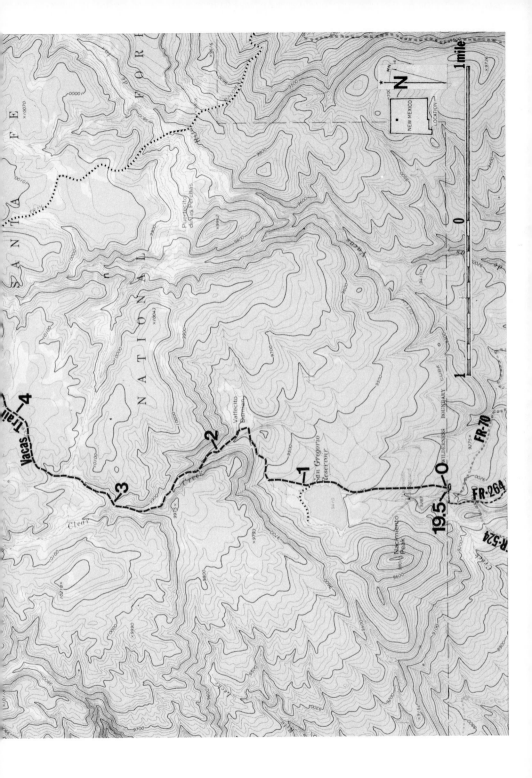

SANTA FE

FOR

NATIONAL

Vacas Trail

Puertecito de las Perchas

Vallecito Damian

San Gregorio Reservoir

Nacimiento Peak

4

3

2

1

0

19.5

WILDERNESS BOUNDARY

FR-70

FR-264

Clear

N

NEW MEXICO

LOCATION

0   1   1 mile

3 RIO CEBOLLA TRAIL NO. 68
SANTA FE NATIONAL FOREST

Distance: 8 miles round-trip
Time: 4 to 8 hours
Elevation Range: 8,060 to 8,550 feet
Rating: Easy
Water: Dependable in Rio Cebolla, which the route follows
Seasons: All. Hiking April through December. Cross-country skiing January through March.
  Varies, depending on snow
Topographic Map: Seven Springs
Special Map: Santa Fe National Forest, Grid C6

This hike starts one mile upstream from Seven Springs Campground at the end of the road. Steep creek crossings restrict vehicular travel beyond road's end to four-wheel drive vehicles and pickups. A jeep trail continues much of the way along the route. The hike takes you through a moderately wide, open, grassy valley bordered by forested hills. Rio Cebolla, fringed by small willows, meanders through the valley, its flow halted briefly by occasional small beaver dams. It is a delightful little stream and you often encounter fishermen. If the fish are not biting, just being in this lovely valley is reward enough.

At 0.7 mile a trailhead on the left is marked by a small sign, "Calaveras Canyon 2½ miles." This trail, T-66, has recently been rebuilt and is a scenic and interesting trip. You could explore it instead of continuing up the valley, or you could hike it another day. An old route follows blazes up the slope directly up the hillside from the sign and will intersect the new route. The new trail starts a bit to the left, going uphill, and is marked by blazes on a number of aspen growing close together. After you get on this trail it is easy to follow. The route has a good gradient and switches back a few times as it works up the slope. Before it reaches the ridge crest the trail goes rather steeply up a small, narrow drainage. At one-quarter mile up from T-68 the terrain levels and you pass by some large boulders. This area is excellent for camping (no water). Nearby, rocks projecting above the trees at the top of a small cliff provide an exciting view of the valley below and the mountains beyond. This trail continues for more than two miles, crossing Calaveras Canyon along the way. It is a very nice hike, but there is no reliable water, so carry what you will need.

The terrain in Rio Cebolla Canyon near the head of T-66 gives little indication of having been disturbed in the past, but this was once the site of a large corral and adjacent to it, downstream, was a dance hall. Across the valley had been a large lodge, dining hall, swimming pool, and cabins for 150 people. In the 1960s the Forest Service acquired the private land, saving this beautiful valley from further development. In 1967 they removed all traces of the Lazy Ray Ranch.

Continue up Trail No. 68, and fish along the way if you wish. At 1.5 miles the route forks, with the right branch, F.R. 381, crossing the stream. The sign indicates this is Road Canyon. T-68 continues for another 2.5 miles along the river. This is recommended more as a day-hike, with camping at Seven Springs Campground or at the suggested area on T-66.

In the winter this route is ideal for cross-country skiing. It is open, with moderate grades, and is quite scenic. The road may not be cleared of snow beyond the fish hatchery, which would give an additional mile to ski.

To get to this hike, go north out of Jemez Springs for about 20 miles on N.M. 126, or west out of Los Alamos on N.M. 4 to N.M. 126 which you take to F.R. 381. From Cuba go east for 30 miles on N.M. 126. The turnoff, northeast, to Seven Springs Campground is onto F.R. 314, but no sign gives this road number. There is a sign pointing to the State Fish Hatchery and another which reads, "Seven Springs Campground, 1½ miles," and these should be adequate marking for the turn. Go past Seven Springs Campground one mile to the end of the road. The hike starts there.

Rio Cebolla Valley from the Calaveras Canyon trail.

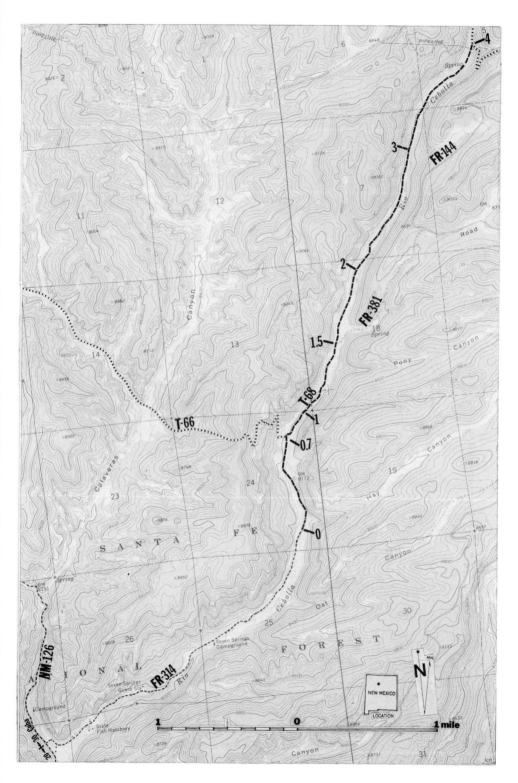

Much of this hike is in the valley alongside Rio Cebolla.

Sign points to side trail to Calaveras Canyon.

4A BATTLESHIP ROCK TO HOT SPRINGS
SANTA FE NATIONAL FOREST

Distance: 3.2 miles, round-trip
Time: 2 to 3 hours, with day-pack
Elevation Range: 6,775 to 7,330 feet
Rating: Easy
Water: Warm water at spring
Seasons: March to December usually, but depends on snow
Topographic Maps: Redondo Peak, Jemez Springs
Special Map: Santa Fe National Forest, Grids 7C, 7D
Permit: None required for hiking or camping at spring. Note: Vehicle will be towed away from Battleship Rock Picnic Area if left after 10:30 p.m. If you want to camp, go to Jemez Falls (Banco Bonito) campground end of trail, hike 4-B.

This is a super hike for family, small groups, or individuals. The path is easy-walking and the route is blazed on trees along the way. The trail follows alongside the Jemez River for the first 150 yards, until it gets past the base of the 200 foot vertical "prow" of Battleship Rock. It then turns abruptly left and climbs somewhat steeply, with switchbacks, up the side of the canyon. Don't miss the left turn, as the streamside trail continues for another mile or so. The steep portion of the route is brief and should not be a deterrent to anyone in reasonably good physical condition. The gradient soon eases and the majority of the route is nearly level. A mixed forest of hardwood and conifer surround the path at the lower elevations, but large ponderosa are dominant near the spring. Openings through the trees along the steeper portion of the route afford brief views of Battleship Rock and the forested sides of the canyon to the west and south.

The hot spring is situated nearly midway between Battleship Rock Picnic Area and Jemez Falls (Banco Bonito) Campground. Water flows from a small patch of gravel and rocks immediately above the triangular pool, which measures about 25 feet on each side. Its dam appears to be man-made, and the pool is probably no deeper than three feet. Warm water (about 80°F) flowing from the spring makes for good soaking in all kinds of weather.

To get to Battleship Rock Picnic Area get on N.M. 4 or N.M. 126. From the N.M. 4/126 junction, just southeast of La Cueva, go 3.4 miles south on N.M. 4. The picnic area is well-marked, on the east side of the road. The trail starts beside a circular picnic shelter.

These bathers are enjoying the warm water on a cool October day.

4B JEMEZ FALLS CAMPGROUND TO HOT SPRINGS
SANTA FE NATIONAL FOREST

Distance: 3.4 miles round-trip
Time: 2 to 3 hours, with day-pack
Elevation Range: 7,925 to 7,330 feet
Rating: Easy; 1.1 mile uphill grade on return, but not bad
Water: Warm water available from spring
Seasons: March to December usually, but depends on snow
Topographic Maps: Redondo Peak, Jemez Springs
Special Map: Santa Fe National Forest, Grid 7C, 7D

The hike to the hot spring from this campground is not as popular as from Battleship Rock, probably because the picnic area is more heavily used. Jemez Falls Campground is shown as Banco Bonito on the forest map and on the topographic map. It is a large, spread-out area, and there are a few picnic tables and outhouses near the end of the road. The forest here, primarily widely scattered large ponderosa, is quite open with very little underbrush. It is a short walk downhill to the Jemez River from the picnic tables, and Jemez Falls are not far downstream from here.

The trail to the hot spring is in excellent condition and is easy to follow. It starts behind the outhouse near road's end in the campground. There are two signs down in the low area behind the outhouses, each pointing along a trail. One sign says "McCauley Hot Springs 2 miles." The other points to "Jemez Falls ¼ mile."

Jemez Falls Trail is a new one which takes you to an overlook immediately above the falls. The falls are beautiful and this short hike is very easy. I highly recommend this side trip for everyone, hikers and non-hikers alike. If you have children along, hold onto them when you get to the overlook because even though the overlook itself is fenced — the remainder of the cliff top and the top of the falls are not.

To get to the hot springs from the trailhead just follow the path. It goes down across a broad depression where the signs are, and then follows along a ridge for one-half mile before dropping rather steeply for the next 1.1 miles to the stream which flows from the spring. The path to the spring and pool goes uphill along the east side of the stream.

To get to Jemez Falls Campground go east on N.M. 4 for 5.5 miles from its junction with N.M. 126, near La Cueva. The turnoff onto Forest Road 133 (not marked as such) is sharp back to the west. The sign at the turnoff says "Jemez Falls." The turnoff is near milepost 32 on N.M. 4 and is just west of where it drops down and crosses the east fork of the Jemez River. It is 1.4 miles from N.M. 4 to the end of F.R. 133 in the campground.

Jemez Falls are a short side trip from the Hot Springs hike.

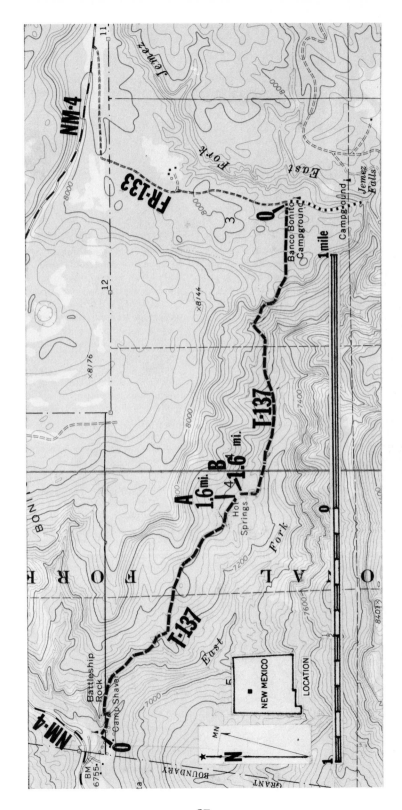

57

5 EAST FORK OF THE JEMEZ RIVER
SANTA FE NATIONAL FOREST

Distance: 4 miles, one-way (you should have transportation back)
Time: 2½ to 4 hours, one-way
Elevation Range: 8,400-7,950 feet
Rating: Easy for first 1.6 miles, moderate in places after that
Water: Available in Jemez River (treat it before drinking)
Seasons: April through November usually, but depends on snow
Topographic Map: Redondo Peak
Special Map: Santa Fe National Forest, Grid 7D

This trail is currently a fisherman's path alongside the east fork of the Jemez River. It is so popular that the Forest Service is considering making a good forest trail which will follow the present route much of the way. This is a beautiful, scenic hike beside the river through forest and open bottom land framed by steep, forested hillsides. You will find numerous outstanding places to camp adjacent to the stream in the first 1.8 miles. There are places to camp along the remainder of the hike, but the streamside ones are better and they are on public land. There are a number of river crossings, with stepping stones when the water flow is low. When the water is up, plan to get your feet wet.

The hike starts on the north side of N.M. 4 just east of mile post 36, where the river crosses from the south to the north under the highway.

Las Conchas Campground is one-half mile east. You can park your car either at the trailhead or one-half mile away at the campground. Or, better yet, if you can arrange it, shuttle the car four miles west to near mile post 32 where the river again crosses under the highway in Cajete Canyon, at a picnic area. For an easy overnight camping trip, it is suggested that you hike in for a mile or more, camp, and return to your car at the trailhead.

Start walking the path that runs along the west side of the river. At one-quarter mile you come to a fence and gate. Near the gate was (in 1982) a plaque on a tree that said, "This area is in memory of Eric Hamlin." Such a beautiful memorial!

Your path crossed the stream about 0.3 mile along, and shortly after crossing you come to an excellent campsite. After you cross the river three more times there is a deluxe campsite on the west side at 1.3 miles. You cross over and back again, and at 1.6 miles you come to an east-west fence. Here the river turns sharply west, into a small sheer-walled canyon, pouring over a small waterfall in the canyon. Cables across the stream in line with the fence indicate that in the past there must have been a hanging fence across it.

This is about the mid-point of the hike and you will have to make a decision about what to do next. You may want to camp in one of the excellent areas mentioned previously, return to the starting point, or continue the hike. There are a couple of ways to continue; you can go north up the side canyon that joins the stream at its sharp turn to the west, or you can take the trail that goes west along the north side of the fence on the west side of the stream. If you go north up the side canyon for about one-quarter mile you will come to a power line. Go west on the truck tracks that roughly parallel it all the way to hike's end.

If you take the route that goes west along the fence, you will encounter some confusing trails on the hillside. Possibly one continues west on the slope for some distance and bypasses the sheer canyons downstream, but I don't believe so. I have always dropped down the steep hillside and crossed the river and gone north up the next side canyon downstream. This route bypasses the first small waterfall and takes you to the top of a larger one immediately downstream of the side canyon you follow to the north. It appears very difficult to wade the stream because of waterfalls and deep pools for quite a distance downstream.

Go about one-quarter mile north up the side canyon to the power line and follow the tracks west. This part of the hike is not streamside, but it is quite scenic too. The power line is on private property so conduct yourself accordingly. It is less than two miles to the picnic area on Highway 4 where you should have transportation waiting.

To get to this hike, get on N.M. 4 between La Cueva to the west and Bandelier National Monument to the east. The trailhead is between mile posts 36 and 37. There is a small parking area north of the road on the west side of the stream. If you prefer, you may leave a car at Las Conchas Campground a half-mile to the east. There is a large area for parking at trail's end, beside the river near mile post 32, where you should have transportation waiting.

AVOID HIKE # 5
UNTIL FURTHER CLARIFICATION
OF PUBLIC & PRIVATE
PROPERTY BOUNDARIES

Here, near the trailhead, the path is on the left side of the Jemez River.

A hiker enjoying the good trail and beautiful valley.

Waterfalls and deep pools such as these, make it difficult to wade through the canyons.

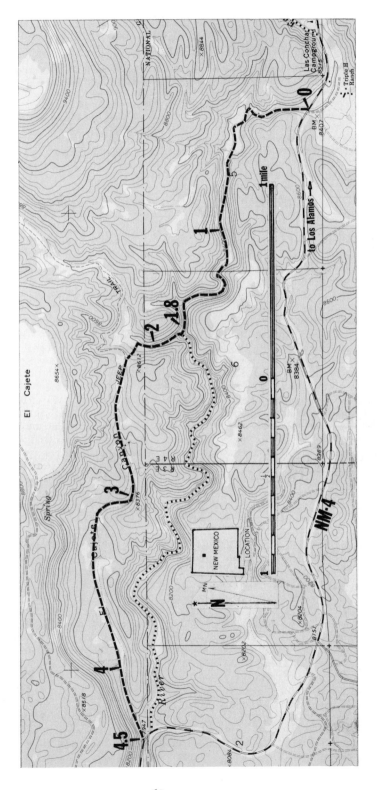

6 PERALTA CANYON TRAIL NO. 140
SANTA FE NATIONAL FOREST

Distance: 12.6 miles round-trip to forest boundary (additional hikes available)
Time: 9 to 12 hours round-trip (you can adjust hike length to fit time schedule; best to make an overnight trip)
Elevation Range: 8,440 to 6,660 feet from mile zero to forest boundary
Rating: Depends on distance hiked. The walking is easy, but 12.6 miles is moderate to strenuous, particularly with the return nearly all uphill
Water: Trail follows a reliable stream much of the way
Seasons: May through December usually, but depends on snow
Topographic Maps: Bland, Redondo Peak, Canada, Bear Springs Peak
Special Map: Santa Fe National Forest, Grid D7, E7

This is a place for those who like seclusion; for those who enjoy hiking through a beautiful mixed forest alongside a small, crystal-clear stream and probably not see another person (except on weekends). Go downstream from the starting point and follow the well-used trail. Though they are not needed, blazes on trees mark the route alongside the stream.

Trail No. 126 joins from the west at mile 3.12. This would be a good side trip, if you have the time. At mile 4.26 the trail begins to climb the left (east) side of the canyon, and in a quarter of a mile the path is well above the stream with some good views.

The trail divides at 4.72 miles. There is no sign here, but take the path to the right. The left fork may be T-109 that is shown on the forest map. There is a ridge to the right of the trail at 5.05 miles. If you walk out to the rocky tip of this ridge you get excellent views both up and downstream of the canyon below and the surrounding mountains. From along here the trail begins to drop and is back at the stream at 5.61 miles.

There are many good areas to camp all along the hike, but the best is in an open, flat area next to an old log cabin at 5.71 miles. A short distance farther along there is a mine entrance on the east side of the path and a partially filled well on the west.

A trail which follows an abandoned roadway comes down on the left (east) at 6.00 miles. There are two sign posts here, but no signs. This should be Trail 132, as it is in the proper place and goes in the proper direction.

Santa Fe National Forest boundary is reached at 6.30 miles. Surroundings here are drier and less green. The valley is opening up and you no longer have the shut-in feeling that you had at the start of this hike. You should have permission from the Jemez Pueblo prior to continuing the hike onto Tribal Land.

On one hike here, when I returned to the starting point, I remained in the streambed all the way, instead of taking the path up on the hillside. Brush was thick much of the way and there was no path in many places. The canyon walls steepened and narrowed so that I had to do some wading. At one point I waded into a small box canyon which had a 15 foot waterfall at the head of it flowing into a big, clear pool. This is a beautiful spot. To get around this obstacle I had to do some rock climbing to the west (left) of the stream, over the formation that caused the waterfall. While on top of this formation I went over and looked down into the canyon and found some other nice waterfalls which can only be seen from that vantage point.

Hiking back along the stream is much more strenuous than hiking up the short section of trail on the hillside and I don't recommend it for any but the strongest hiker who is not carrying a large pack.

When you begin this hike it is a short walk down to the stream-side path from the trailhead at the effective end of the forest road. There are excellent campsites in the deep shade near where this path joins T-140. A small sign by the road says "Peralta Canyon" but there are no signs, except at the T-126 junction, that identify the route as T-140. T-140 goes upstream as well as downstream from the access point. The upstream trail can be explored in less than a day and the longer downstream route can be done in a long, moderately strenuous day.

To get to this hike, get on N.M. 4 west of Bandelier National Monument and east of the village of La Cueva. Turn south on Forest Road 280 just west of mile post 39 on N.M. 4. There is a good sign on the highway marking this turn. Go through the gate (be sure to close it) and go uphill past the sign that says, "Not suited for passenger cars." The sign is wrong, as this is a better than average forest road.

About two miles in, the road forks. Go right, toward Elmer Canyon. A bit more than six miles from N.M. 4 the road widens briefly to provide a place to turn around. Beyond this point the road becomes virtually impassable. A sign beside the road here says "Elmer Canyon." Another small sign to the south (downhill) side of the turnaround says, "Peralta Canyon ¼." This sign is right beside the trail to Peralta Canyon, and it is only 300 yards from the sign to Trail No. 140, alongside the stream.

This clearing alongside the log cabin is a fine spot to camp for a couple of days.

Bears apparently like the taste of trail signs.

One of the waterfalls and a deep pool in the narrow canyon that the trail bypasses.

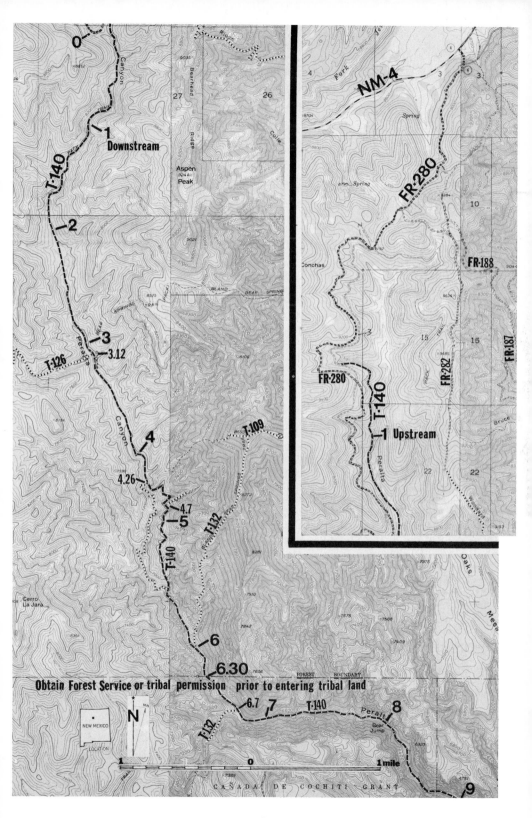

Obtain Forest Service or tribal permission prior to entering tribal land

N

NEW MEXICO
LOCATION

0   1 mile

7 FRIJOLES RUINS AND CEREMONIAL CAVE
BANDELIER NATIONAL MONUMENT

Distance: 2 miles round-trip
Time: 2 hours
Elevation Range: 6,100 to 6,340 feet
Rating: Easy
Water: Available at Visitor Center (a canteen is advisable in hot weather)
Seasons: All
Topographic Map: Frijoles
Special Map: Guide booklet and map available at Visitor Center

Bandelier National Monument is 46 square miles of rugged juniper and piñon forested, arid mesas, cut by deep canyons. Some of the canyons are floored with forests and meadows of grass and flowers, watered by small, clear streams. Most of the backcountry remains undisturbed and is designated as wilderness. It is a fragile environment, so treat it gently and leave no marks or debris that would tell others of your brief presence. If you build a fire, keep it small. Carry out all of your trash. Do not pollute the water. Take proper sanitation measures. Pets are not allowed on trails.

The La Mesa forest fire in 1977 destroyed many of the trees on mesas in the northern half of the monument, but the area still retains its scenic attraction. The region near this hike was not involved in the fire.

The primary attraction of Bandelier to many visitors is not its rugged beauty but its prehistoric Indian Ruins that are so extensive. The monument is named for Adolph Bandelier, who studied these ruins in the 1880s. His book *The Delight Makers,* available from the Visitor Center, is recommended reading prior to your visit to the monument. The Frijoles Ruins Trail starts at the Visitor Center and goes west along the foot of the cliffs on the north side of Frijoles Canyon. This trail takes you to a group of ruins that are in various stages of excavation and restoration. Read the guide book to learn details about the ruins and about local history and geology. Along the route, side trails permit return to the Visitor Center. See all of the ruins on this hike and get the most out of it by climbing the ladders into caves, kivas, etc. After Long House, petroglyphs and pictographs, continue up the canyon one-half mile or so to Ceremonial Cave. Everyone who is physically and psychologically able, kids and adults alike, will enjoy the 150-foot climb, by a series of four ladders, to the ledge on which a few dwellings and a kiva were built. The ledge provides an excellent viewpoint, too.

This short hike should be made before you go into the backcountry, as it will help you to understand more about who the Indians were, when they lived there, and give you a look at some excavated or restored structures similar to some undisturbed ruins you may see on your longer hikes. No permit is required for this hike.

To get to Bandelier National Monument go north of Santa Fe on U.S. 285 to Pojoaque, then 12 miles west on N.M. 4 to a fork; go left (south) through the town of White Rock and follow the signs to Bandelier. There is an excellent, spacious campground soon after entry into the monument with restrooms, water and designated campsites. A permit is required for backcountry hikes, so if you plan to get an early start, before headquarters opens, arrange to get one ahead of time.

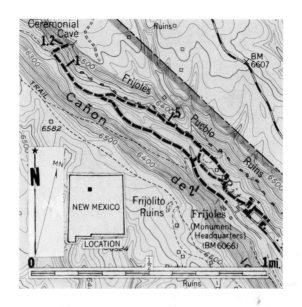

A ladder provides access to Cave Room, which was dug into the soft volcanic rock of the canyon wall. This type of rock is called "tuff."

8 STONE LIONS AND PAINTED CAVE
BANDELIER NATIONAL MONUMENT

Distance: 28.0 mile loop
Time: 3 days or more. Strong hikers can hike in 2 days
Elevation Range: 6,060 to 7,430 feet
Rating: Strenuous, due to distance and steep gradients coming up out of canyons (excellent trails most of the way)
Water: Dependable in Frijoles, Upper Alamo, and Capulin Canyons, but to be safe, confirm stream flows when you get your permit
Seasons: All. Snow is possible November through March
Topographic Maps: Frijoles, Cochiti Dam
Special Map: Trail Guide and Back Country Trail Maps available at Visitor Center
Permit: Required to enter Wilderness Area. Obtain at Visitor Center, or call (505) 672-3861, or write: The Superintendent, Bandelier National Monument, Los Alamos, NM 87544

This is an excellent, interesting hike. You might say that it is a two-level route; you are either up on dry, forested mesas or down in green forested and watered canyons. The trails in Bandelier are among the best prepared and maintained that you will find anywhere. The new portion of trail from Capulin Canyon and the Rio Grande to the rim of Frijoles Canyon is rougher and rockier than most of the other backcountry trails, but it is still not bad, considering the rough, rocky country that it traverses.

There are camping rules that you must observe and take into consideration when you plan your hike. Study the backcountry map, available at no cost from the Visitor Center, when you get your permit. It is a topographic map with all of the trails marked on it and indicates no camping and restricted camping zones. You must camp at least 75 feet from the spring and 50 feet from stream. Camping is not allowed in Frijoles Canyon from the Rio Grande to two miles above Ceremonial Cave nor within one-half mile of Upper Frijoles Crossing. Camping is not permitted within one-quarter mile of Painted Cave nor within one-quarter mile of the Stone Lions. Camping is also restricted in Alama and Capulin Canyons near the trail, so check these restrictions when you get your permit.

This hike starts at the Visitor Center and goes up forested and shady Frijoles Canyon to Upper Frijoles Crossing, six miles distant. It takes three to four hours to get to the crossing. If you get a late start you may wish to make your first camp along Frijoles Creek before you get to the no camping zone at the crossing.

After crossing the stream at Upper Crossing the climb out of the canyon begins. This climb, up the south side of Frijoles Canyon, takes you

to a high ridge (7430 feet), 1¼ miles from the crossing. You may see Alamo Springs Trail going to the right (west) up the ridge. Continue southeast and at 7.7 miles the trail forks. Keep right, going southeast, and at mile 7.9 a trail crosses the one you are on. Turn right on this trail and go southwest. In a half-mile or so, you will start dropping into Alamo Canyon.

The mesa this trail crosses was burned in the June 1977 La Mesa fire and most of the trees were killed. The grass and flowers have come back in abundance and it is a beautiful place even with the stark skeletons of the dead trees about.

As the trail descends into Alamo Canyon you get some good views of the canyon and the surrounding countryside. Alamo Creek is a fairly reliable source of water at upper crossing only, but to be certain it is flowing check when you get your permit. You can take enough water from here to get you to Capulin Canyon, via the Stone Lions. There are some very nice places to camp in this canyon, if your schedule permits. Alamo Canyon gives you the feeling of being boxed-in, because it is narrow, with high, sheer walls. The canyon floor is green with fairly dense patches of forest. It is a nice place to be in.

Climbing out of Alamo Canyon is a bit strenuous as the trail is rather steep, but the good quality of the trail minimizes the effort. It is about 1.6 miles from Alamo Creek to the next trail junction on the mesa. The mesa in this area has also been burnt, but is still pretty. It is rolling terrain with no big ups and downs. Time for hiking this 1.6 miles is more or less 1½ hours, to the trail junction. At this junction you may want to leave your pack and day-hike the 0.2 mile to the life-sized mountain lions which were carved from the soft volcanic rock. You should really take time to see these remarkable rock carvings because they are unlike anything else done by Indians of the southwest.

From the trail junction near the Stone Lions it is a mile to the streamside trail in Capulin Canyon. You come to the canyon rim rather abruptly and the view of the area below and the country beyond is excellent. You lose altitude slowly at first, then drop steeply to the canyon floor. There is a three-sided shelter near the trail junction here similar to the one near Upper Crossing. You should not plan to camp in it as it will probably be filthy because of inconsiderate campers who preceded you. The stream here, larger than the one in Alamo Canyon, is a reliable source of drinking water. As always, take care not to pollute it, and always treat the water from these streams with Halozone or other appropriate chemicals.

There are good campsites at frequent intervals along in the canyon; just observe the restrictions established for this area. This is such a delightful place with its rushing, clear stream, flat grassy areas shaded by large trees, and framed by the high sheer walls, you may want to relax here for a few days. Painted cave can be visited from camp, or you can stop there when you pass nearby on the next leg of the hike. When you visit this interesting archaeological site, take care not to damage or deface the pictographs, and see that no one else does either.

To continue the hike proceed two miles downstream from Painted Cave to the trail junction. At this junction a path continues downstream, but you want to take the route that goes to the left. This junction is well marked, so you should not have any trouble seeing the turnoff.

The trail to the east climbs out of Capulin Canyon over a little ridge and drops down into a small, but deep canyon. You cross this canyon, climb over a ridge and drop into Alamo Canyon. This is a fairly new route that keeps you above the Rio Grande River Trail, which is often flooded when the lake level is allowed to rise. You will note that the new portion is steep and rocky in places, not too representative of other Bandelier trails.

In the mouth of Alamo Canyon you cross mud flats which could be a sticky problem when the river backs up, or when softened by rain. The lake level was raised for a while, killing all of the juniper and many of the pine that stood in the water. The dead trees detract from the beauty of the river valley immensely. While crossing the mud flats be alert for the trail going to the left. If you end up hiking along the river you have missed this turn and gone too far. The river trail seems to follow the same path across Alamo Canyon and the mud flats, so be alert for the turnoff.

The trail turns north and climbs up a steep slope to a mesa top where there is a fenced plant study enclosure. At this enclosure a trail that forks off to the right goes to the river trail. Keep left and continue basically north for a while. At 21.1 miles you are back in the bottom of Lummis Canyon. Follow it upstream a short distance before climbing to the right, east, to the mesa top again. This mesa was not burnt in the 1977 fire, so you walk through an open juniper forest. The trail across the mesa is very easy walking and passes a number of small ruins. The route approaches the rim of Frijoles Canyon at about 25 miles and turns left toward NNW to parallel it. The route passes Frijolito Ruins at about 26.1 miles but they are hard to spot unless you are an expert.

At the trail junction at 26.8 miles you turn right and start down the side of Frijoles Canyon, toward the Visitor Center, which is 1.2 miles and a half-hour distant. It is a good day's hike from Capulin Canyon back to the Visitor Center, which is reached at 28 miles.

I believe that you will agree that this has been an excellent hike; remote, scenic, and with significant historical features.

At the beginning I indicated that this trail could be hiked in all seasons. This statement should be qualified because in snow the trail, particularly on the mesas, is difficult, if not impossible, to see. For this reason, the winter hiker must be very familiar with the trails when they were free of snow, and must be proficient with map and compass. Winters are cold, but generally dry and sunny. January, the coldest month, averages 39°F for a high and 18°F for the low, but has dropped to a record low of - 18°F. As a precaution, carry extra food and fuel in the winter and be prepared to sit out a heavy snow instead of wandering around and getting lost or taking a chance with hypothermia.

Summers are cool and pleasant, with cool nights usually in the 50s, though it can freeze in June and September. Daytime temperatures rarely exceed 90°F.

See Hike #7 for instructions to get to this hike.

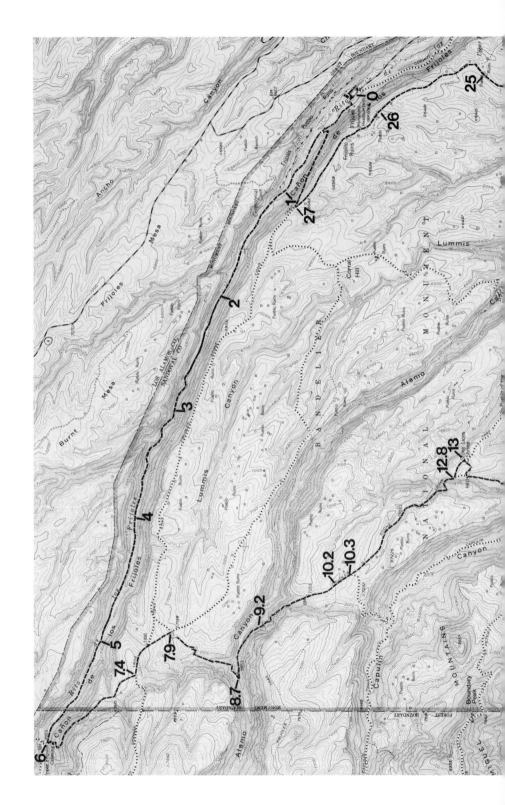

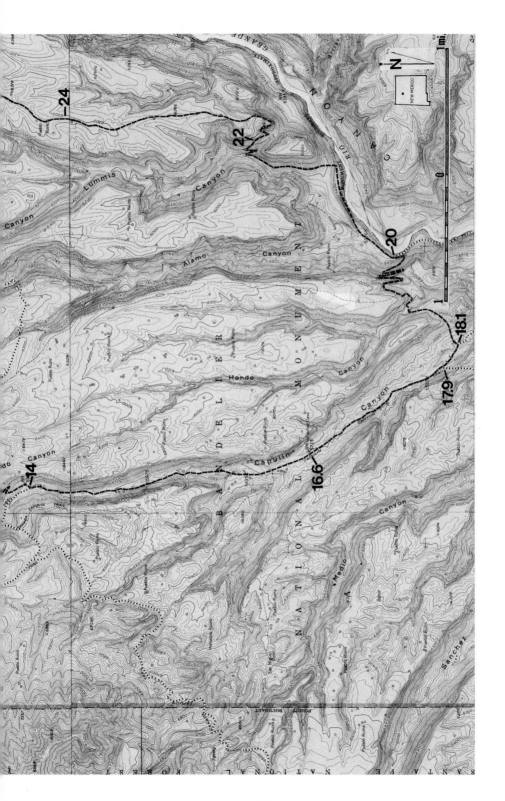

The Stone Lions were carved in place from the soft tuff. They are weathered and worn, so please treat them as the unique and fragile treasures they truly are. The Stone Lions were religious objects to the ancients and continue to be a shrine to inhabitants of nearby pueblos who still bring offerings to them.

The upper end of Lummis Canyon with its open forest of ponderosa, piñon, and juniper.

9 UPPER AND LOWER FALLS TRAIL
BANDELIER NATIONAL MONUMENT

Distance: 4.6 miles round-trip to Rio Grande
Time: 2½ to 5 hours
Elevation Range: 6,060 to 5,360 feet
Rating: Easy
**Water: Carry what you will need; plenty in Rito de los Frijoles, but it must be treated before
   drinking**
Seasons: All (it can be hot in summer [90° F] and cold in winter)
Topographic Map: Frijoles
Special Map: Trail Guide Map, Falls Trail Guide Booklet from Visitor Center
Permit: Not required for day hiking

The falls trail is a popular hike. It is easy walking, though slightly steep in places, and takes you to two beautiful waterfalls. From the Lower Falls you can continue an additional 0.8 mile to the Rio Grande, if you wish. It is recommended that you hike on down to the river and see the whole route. On the Falls Trail Hike the environment changes considerably from the forested, shady area near headquarters to the relatively dry juniper and pinon forest with cactus and open grassy areas along the Rio Grande.

The trail begins at the southwest corner of the headquarters parking lot and takes you along the west side of the stream much of the way to the lower falls. You cross the stream a few times along the way. Typical of those in Bandelier National Monument, the trail is clean and well-maintained. It is wide, easy to follow and has a good stable surface.

About 1.3 miles from the start is the section of trail that overlooks picturesque Upper Falls and the lovely valley at its foot. It is best photographed near midday, when sunlight reaches it in the narrow chasm. Along here the path gets fairly steep and rocky as switchbacks drop you to the canyon floor. The steep section is brief and 0.2 mile below Upper Falls is Lower Falls. The path crosses the stream on a wooden bridge just above Lower Falls in a green, shady area. This is an ideal place for resting and picnicking. A sign here tells you it is not safe to go upstream to the foot of Upper Falls. If you think you'd be tempted to walk up there anyhow, see if you can get permission at headquarters before you start your hike.

The top of Lower Falls is immediately downstream from the bridge and rest area. You can climb on the rocks on either side of

the stream and look down the falls, but be very careful if you do because it is a long fall to the rocks below. Better views can be had from the trail 100 yards or so down toward the river. You can scramble through the rocks and brush to the foot of the falls, but the clear, cool pool at the foot of the falls which was shielded from view by surrounding trees and bushes is no longer there. The pool and most of the trees were washed out by flood waters in 1977 or 1978. Flash floods are a potential hazard in the canyons of Bandelier, and you should always be alert for one when you are alongside a stream or in a dry wash.

It is 0.8 mile from Lower Falls to the Rio Grande. The trail is a bit steep and rocky in places, and the temperature gets warmer the lower you go, but it is still a pleasant hike to the river. The path crosses Rito de los Frijoles four or five times along the way and a quarter of a mile or so before you get to the Rio Grande the route leaves the Frijoles with its streamside trees and bushes and goes through juniper and pinon forest. Before you get to the river you enter a zone of dead juniper; scattered piñon and ponderosa appear to be the only surviving trees. This is because water in Cochiti Reservoir has been allowed to rise so high that it sometimes floods this area, and the juniper are unable to survive. There are some shady places by the river, or you may prefer to sunbathe on the sandy bank, but plan to spend a while here. You may also want to try your luck at fishing; the river is wide here and the fish may be big ones.

The trip back uphill is slower and warmer than coming down. If you get hot and tired on the way down, turn around and go back. On warm days carry adequate drinking water,

Trees provide welcome shade when the path is near the water of Frijoles Creek.

74

which will be about one-half gallon per person. Frijoles Creek water must be treated prior to drinking and this requires that you have Halozone, iodine, or chlorox, a suitable container, and time to wait one-half hour (in the shade) for the treatment to do its job. Carrying water on this short trip is much easier.

To get to this hike follow the directions for getting to Hike #7.

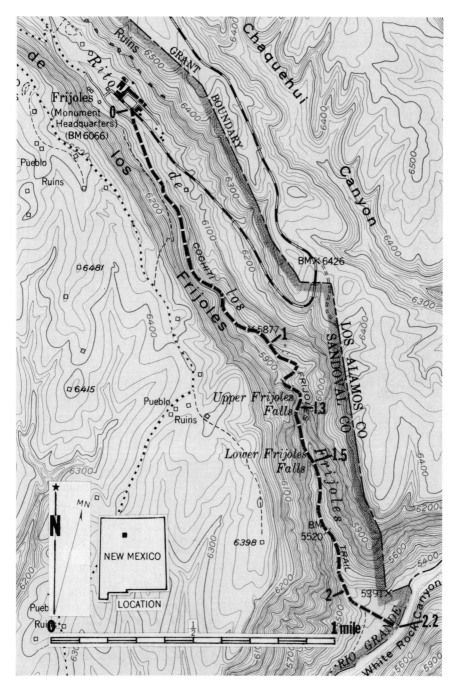

10 SANDIA CREST TRAIL NO. 130, SOUTH
CIBOLA NATIONAL FOREST, SANDIA DISTRICT

Distance: 15.8 miles one way
Time: 9 to 14 hours one way, overnight camp recommended
Elevation Range: 10,678 to 6,550 feet
Rating: Moderate going from north to south; strenuous from south to north
Water: Spring at 10.7 miles
Seasons: Usually April through October, depending on snow
Topographic Maps: Sandia Crest, Tijeras
Special Maps: Cibola National Forest, Sandia-Mountainair Ranger Districts, Grids C-2, Sandia Recreation Area Cibola National Forest

The Crest Trail has been written as two separate hikes, north and south, because the paved road to Sandia Crest provides good access to near its midpoint. The nearby tramway provides additional access from the west side of the mountain.

In order to hike only one way on this trail, a car shuttle must be made or a ride otherwise arranged. The shuttle distance to get a car to Canyon Estates at the south end of the trail is 20.4 miles. I have written both the north and south Sandia Crest Trail hikes starting from Sandia Crest because it is easier to descend 4,000 feet than it is to climb that distance.

If you plan to hike the full Crest Trail, combining hikes Nos. 10 and 11, it is recommended that the trip start at the south end. There is water available on the crest near the end of the steep climb up from the south end, and also, there is a large amount of spring water at the north end of the route at Tunnel Spring to refresh you when you arrive at the end of your long walk. The car shuttle from Canyon Estates to Tunnel Spring is 33.6 miles one-way.

This hike starts at the south end of the parking lot at Sandia Crest. Distances were measured from the foot of the stairs that go from the lower parking lot up to the observation point.

This hike is extremely scenic due to the many dramatic views to both east and west, as the route follows the crest. The vegetation changes from a high altitude forest of spruce, fir, pine, and aspen similar to the forest in the far north near Hudson Bay, to juniper and cactus and other semi-desert plants at lower elevations near the trail's end.

Along the crest, near the Visitor Center and tramway terminal, there are many side loops from the trail to the ridge crest and back.

Disregard these and remain on the main, most heavily used route. The tramway and chair lift are encountered at 1.5 miles. There is drinking water in the Visitor Center here. The trail doesn't go to the buildings but instead passes some distance down the slope, east, from them. There may be a slight problem in finding the path south of the chair lift, but keep walking and you'll find it.

There is a trail sign at a bend in the trail at 1.6 miles, which tells you this is Crest Trail No. 130, U.S. Hwy. 66 is 15 miles south and Sandia Crest is 1.5 miles north. You will find many good campsites along the crest, though you must carry all the water you'll need between the Crest and the spring at mile 10.7. T-130 signs usually indicate that a trail junction is near. Trail No. 147, Tree Spring Trail, joins the Crest Trail at 3.1 miles. T-130 from the north comes into this intersection from the south-west and turns to the southeast to continue toward the south. T-47 departs from the intersection in a northerly direction.

There is another trail junction at 4.9 miles, in a saddle with grand views to both east and west. Cienega Trail No. 143 goes southeast and the Crest Trail continues south (or north). Cienega Picnic Area is 2.25 miles down the side trail.

The trail is excellent for the first six miles, then it begins to get a bit rocky. There are a couple of signs at 6.2 miles marking a trail junction. It is six miles back to the Crest and 10 miles to Hwy. 66. The sign for a side trail to the east says; "Canoncito Trail No. 150, Canoncito Spring 2¼ miles, Forest Road 299 3 miles." There are rock cairns and a new side trail at 6.8 miles but no signs, so continue on the main trail.

Bear Shelter, a three-sided shelter is at 7.9 miles. Sometimes it is a mess inside, so you will probably not want to stay in it except in case of an emergency. If you do use it, please carry out all of your litter and some of that which others have left. A sign here tells you that it is Bear Shelter; Sandia Crest is eight miles to the north, and U.S. Hwy 66 is nine miles to the south.

Prior to arriving at 8.9 miles the trail has been going through dense oak brush with scattered open patches, and with low peaks to the west. There is a sign post at 8.9 miles with no sign on it. South Sandia Peak is directly west of this point, and it is a short climb to the top. A faint path to the summit is reached by going into the clearing west of the trail about 300 feet north of the post. Go to the extreme west end of this triangular clearing where a faint path leads into the forest. Take your time picking it out through the brush and fallen trees. It leads up onto the ridge north of the summit and continues up the ridge. If you lose the path, it is a tough fight through the oak brush. The view from the summit is excellent. From here you can see the concrete water tank which marks the beginning of Hike No. 12 and the route it follows up through the forest and valleys below. Albuquerque spreads out in the Rio Grande Valley beyond, to the west. To the south are the Manzano Mountains. The view is certainly worth the half-hour round trip.

Embudito Trail No. 192 meets the Crest Trail at 9.6 miles. Signs here tell you that Crest Trail No. 130 goes north and south, Bear Shelter is 1.75 miles and Sandia Crest 10 miles to the north, and U.S. Hwy. 66 is seven miles to the south. Embudito Trail No. 192 is the route to the west and Deer Pass is a quarter mile and Oso Pass 1.25 miles along the way. It is 5.25 miles to the end of Trail No. 192 at the edge of Albuquerque. (See Hike #12 for information on this route.)

The welcome sound of running water alerts you to the spring at 10.7 miles. A 1½ inch pipe is embedded in the trail, but dense oak brush prevents your seeing the water. A small side trail to the east goes a few feet to where water is pouring from the pipe into a metal water trough. A welcome surprise!

From about this point the trail begins to lose elevation more rapidly and becomes, at times, quite rocky. The route is not steep enough to be a problem, but the footing is rough at times. This condition continues much of the remaining five miles to trail's end.

There is a new trail to the left at 14.8 miles, but no sign. At 15.1 miles a stream appears along the left of the path and soon crosses it, with a small waterfall below and to the right of the trail. The route forks at 15.3 miles. The branch that continues straight ahead is abandoned, so take the fork which doubles back to the right. Shortly there is a sign indicating a side trail that leads to a travertine deposit (on the waterfall).

The hike ends at 15.8 miles at the end of Canyon Estates Road.

To get to this hike, get on N.M. 14 at Tijeras, 15 miles east of Albuquerque or seven miles southwest of Santa Fe. Turn west off N.M. 14 at San Antonito, about six miles north of I-40, onto N.M. 44. This road is paved and goes to Sandia Peak Ski Area. At about five or six miles along N.M. 44 the pavement turns left and becomes N.M. 536. Follow the pavement to Sandia Crest. If you missed the turn off N.M. 44, you will soon know it because the next six miles or so are all-weather gravel surface.

To get to the south end of the hike, at Canyon Estates get on N.M. 14 south of I-40, and go north under I-40 as if you were going to get on I-40 going west to Albuquerque, *but* turn right immediately after going under I-40 and go east on the paved road marked "dead end." Shortly it turns north and the Canyon Estates sign is visible. Go 0.7 mile north to the end of the road. The trail signs are quite obvious here. There is plenty of room to leave your car here and it should be safe, with a house nearby.

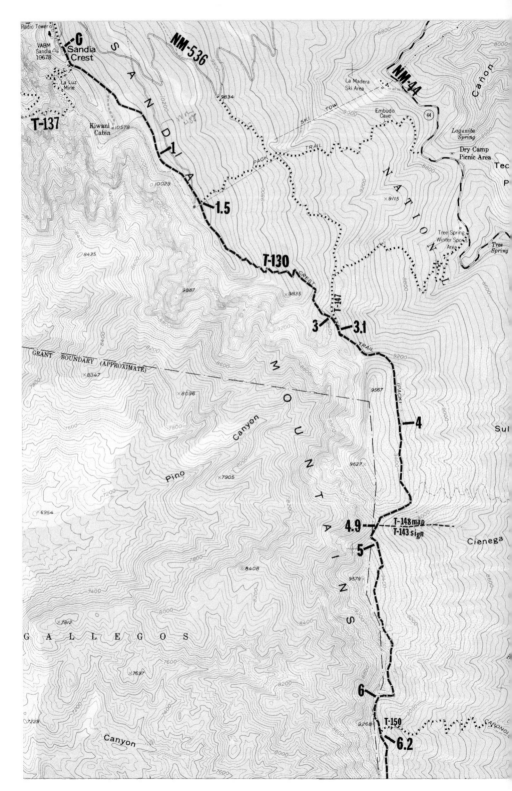

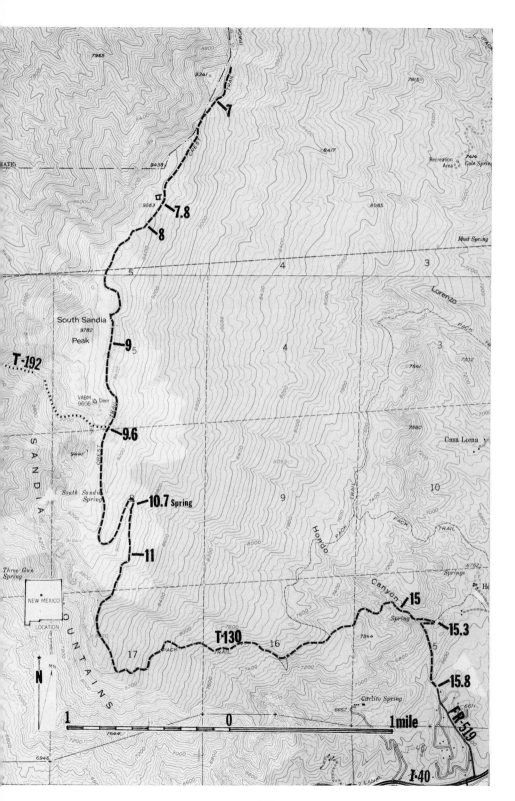

Looking north toward Sandia Crest.

11 SANDIA CREST TRAIL NO. 130, NORTH
CIBOLA NATIONAL FOREST, SANDIA DISTRICT

Distance: 10.6 miles one-way
Time: 4 to 7 hours down, 6 to 10 hours up (plan to camp overnight if possible)
Elevation Range: 10,678 to 6,400 feet
Rating: Easy to moderate if hiking north, strenuous if coming up from north end
Water: None along the way, only at each end
Seasons: Usually April through October, depending on snow
Topographic Maps: Sandia Crest, Placitas
Special Maps: Cibola National Forest, Sandia-Mountainair Districts, Grids C-1, Sandia Recreation Area Cibola National Forest

This hike is the north portion of the Sandia Crest Trail. (See Hike No. 10 for a description of the southern portion of the trail.) It is possible that you will want to combine the two hikes.

It will be necessary to shuttle a car or have someone pick you up at Tunnel Spring if you plan to hike only one way. It will be much easier to hike downhill than up. The shuttle from Sandia Crest is 19.2 miles. Tunnel Spring is 19.2 miles. The turnoff north onto N.M. 44 from N.M. 536, six miles from the crest, is not marked with a road number; only a couple of signs about maintenance of next eight miles in winter time. Go north on N.M. 44 through the town of Placitas. Just west of Placitas turn left on F.R. 231, which is marked with a brown and white sign. F.R. 231 is rough, but all-weather and passable by a passenger car to Tunnel Spring.

Trail distances were measured from the foot of the stairs that go from the lower parking lot to the observation point on Sandia Crest. The trail, which is well marked, starts from the north end of the parking lot. The first half of this hike is particularly scenic because it follows the high ridge crest, presenting many views of the Rio Grande Valley, Bernalillo, Coronado Ruins, and the desert beyond. The vistas on the lower half of the route aren't quite so grand, but are still very good.

A sign at the beginning of the hike tells you that Del Agua Overlook is three miles, Agua Sarca Overlook is six miles, Tunnel Spring is 11 miles, and also gives estimated hiking times. The first part of the route passes through a Hudsonian Forest of spruce, fir, and aspen, near the crest. The trail near the parking lot and radio/TV station is fairly heavily used and there are many side paths, so keep to the main trail and disregard the others

which usually go to the top of the crest.

At 0.6 mile the route forks; keep left. The crest, farther along, is heavily notched and the trail is at times right by the steep dropoff and at other times is some distance from it. There are some concrete and stone benches in an open area in the forest at a good overlook at 2.1 miles. There is a similar bench at another good viewpoint at 2.3 miles. This may be Del Agua Overlook, which the sign said was at three miles.

A transition in vegetation slowly takes place as trail elevation drops, and at 3.2 miles the Hudsonian forest has given way to an extensive thicket of oak brush. The trail surface is still good, but getting rockier. By the time you have gone 5.3 miles the vegetation is predominately juniper and is about the same for the remainder of the trip to Tunnel Spring.

The trail goes by the edge of a dropoff to the west, at 5.7 miles providing excellent views to the west and north. There is an overlook at 7.5 miles with a concrete and stone bench. One of these must be Agua Sarca Overlook, which the sign said was at six miles.

There is a one-third mile uphill grind, which is not steep but seems long, ending at the 10 mile point.

The hike ends at 10.6 miles at Tunnel Spring. The crystal clear, cool water gushing out of that six-inch pipe is a welcome sight on a warm day. And, it tastes and feels as good as it looks!

To get to the start of this hike, at Sandia Crest, get on N.M. 14 at Tijeras, 15 miles east of Albuquerque or seven miles southwest of Santa Fe. Turn west off N.M. 14 at San Antonito, about six miles north of I-40, onto N.M. 44. This road is paved and goes by Sandia Peak Ski Area. At about five or six miles along

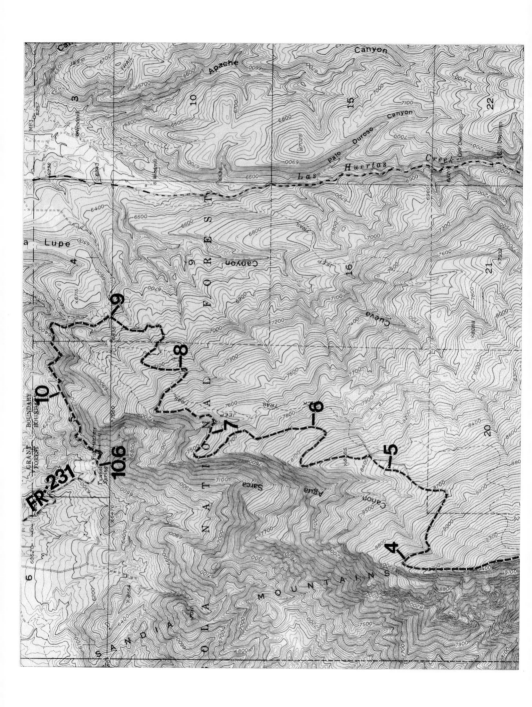

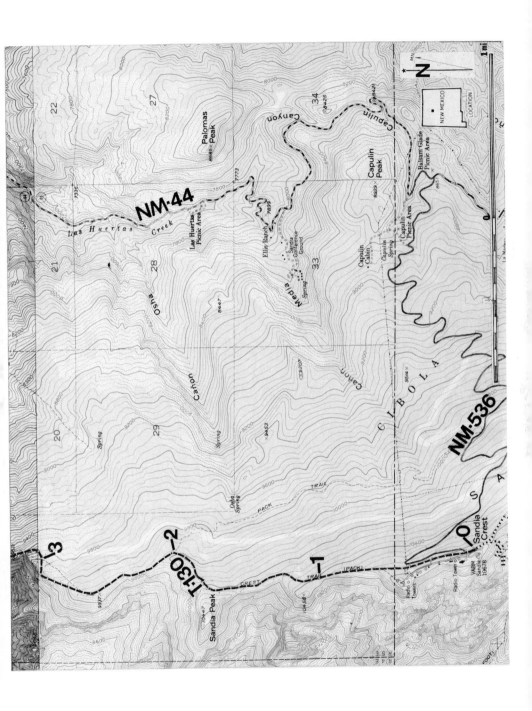

N.M. 44 the pavement turns left and becomes N.M. 536. N.M. 44 goes straight ahead and is gravel for the next eight miles. This is the route you take for the car shuttle. Continue on the pavement to Sandia crest and the trailhead.

There are no formal camping areas anywhere along N.M. 44 or N.M. 536 and camping is not permitted in the picnic areas. Camping is permitted in places where you can pull off the road on a couple of switchbacks and in a couple more places. This is inconvenient when you arrive at night to start hiking the next morning.

One of the almost continuous views provided by Hike 11, showing Albuquerque sprawling in the Rio Grande Valley toward the foot of the Sandia Mountains.

12 EMBUDITO TRAIL NO. 192
CIBOLA NATIONAL FOREST, SANDIA RANGER DISTRICT

Distance: 5¼ miles one-way (from Water Tank to Crest Trail No. 130)
Time: 5 to 7 hours up; 2½ to 5 hours down
Elevation Range: 6,240 to 9,600 feet
Rating: Moderate to strenuous (the grade average is 12 percent, so some of the trail is steep)
Water: 0.5 mile, 1.1 miles, 2.25 to 3.5 miles
Seasons: All. Snow may close upper portions December through April
Topographic Maps: Sandia Crest, Tijeras
Special Maps: Cibola National Forest, Sandia-Mountainair Ranger Districts, Grids C-2, and City of Albuquerque, Sandia Recreation Area Cibola National Forest

This trail starts at the edge of the city of Albuquerque and will take you up to the Crest Trail No. 130 via Deer Pass. Deer Pass is on the south shoulder of South Sandia Peak (9,782 feet).

A big advantage of this trail is its accessibility to hikers who may arrive in Albuquerque by public transportation and not have a car available for a drive to the mountains. To reach the trailhead by city bus, take buses #1, #2, or #3 from the center of Albuquerque to Gerard and Central. From this intersection take bus #5 (Carlisle-Montgomery) to Tramway and Montgomery. From the bus stop walk east about a half-mile on Montgomery to Glenwood Hills Drive. Go left, northeast, up Glenwood Hills Drive past Desert Hills Place and you should be in a position to see the big concrete water storage tank a few hundred yards to the northeast. There is so much construction in progress currently that I can't give an up-to-date description of how to get to the water tank from Glenwood Hills Drive but this should not present any problem.

The trailhead formerly was at a fence with a ladder over it, at the north end of Glenwood Hills Drive, but the fence has been removed and excavation indicates that the street is being extended and additional residences built along it. For this book, the trailhead is considered to be at the south side of the concrete water tank, and this is where the distances were measured from.

The route starts cross-country along the south side of a broad, gently sloping valley floor. Vegetation growing in this area includes tumbleweed, beargrass, various cacti, juniper, sunflowers, and many other desert-type bushes and flowers. Currently it is best to go around the southeast end of the earth dam behind the water tank and pick up the old trail.

The trail follows upstream along a small, dry drainage which narrows and gradually changes direction from east to southeast.

The trail goes into a larger drainage and follows it upstream (south) for a short distance before exiting on the east side to climb up the steep bank. If you miss the trail going to the east out of the dry stream bed and continue upstream, in 100 yards or so you will come to a limestone ledge with a small waterfall (which may dry up at times) trickling over it. This is a popular picnic spot. However, the water may be polluted; so don't drink it.

Look around for the good, wide trail which switchbacks up the steep stream bank. This area is heavily used and there are many steep, rocky paths worn into the hillside. After you find the trail, the route from here on (except for a couple of places) is very obvious for even a novice hiker. Since the route gains about 3,400 feet in the next five miles, the path leads persistently upward. Typical of most trails in Cibola National Forest the route is well planned and maintained. The surface on most of the route is packed, sandy soil with small rocks in it and doesn't get muddy when it is wet, and is stable to walk on when it is dry.

From the stream bed the trail climbs steeply then becomes virtually level along a hillside on the north side of a drainage, as the floor of the drainage rises to join it. The trail goes alongside the flowing (usually) stream for only 50 feet or so before departing abruptly up the north bank of the drainage behind a big box-elder bush. The trail sign marking this turn was reclining in the box-elder and the post standing signless. The level area beside the stream provides a small but good campsite and appears to be heavily used. The water in this stream may be safe to drink if you go upstream far enough to get it, but it would be

85

best to treat the water before drinking.

The trail stays away from drainages for a while and the vegetation gradually changes from desert-type plants to coniferous forest on the slopes as the altitude increases. When the path returns to stream-side, the vegetation is quite lush and green.

At about 1.9 miles, in a piñon and juniper forest, South Sandia Peak is quite visible to the east. Along here the good trail is being damaged by lazy, thoughtless hikers who cut the corners, causing it to wash where they walk. The path is in a moist stream bed at 2.2 miles, with mixed conifers and hardwood forest. A stream is pouring over a rocky bed, and provides refreshing drinking water at 2.25 miles along the way. This is a shady, cool place for a brief stop.

There is a fork in the trail at 3.0 miles. Trail No. 192 goes to the right slightly. The other path, which goes sharply to the left, crosses the crystal-clear little stream into a large, excellent camping area under big trees. A few scattered shingles and boards are all that remain of a cabin that was here many years past.

The junction with Three Gun Trail No. 194 in Oso Pass is at 3.8 miles. Keep left on No. 192. There are small signs on each of the paths about 100 feet from the intersection which give the number of the trail, so check that you are on the correct route. From near this junction, there is a good view, through the trees, of South Sandia Peak. Deer Pass is a bit over a mile uphill east from Oso Pass through primarily conifer and later conifer and aspen forest. The area is rather open from Deer Pass to Crest Trail No. 130. The junction with the Crest Trail is at 5.25 miles. If you need water here, 1.1 miles south, a good spring can be found flowing through a pipe which crosses under the Crest Trail and pours into a metal water trough. There is little elevation change enroute to this spring and is an easy 20-minute walk each way. There are many neat camping areas along the crest, if you'd like to spend a night or two up here.

If you wish to climb the South Peak, go less than three-quarter miles north from the Trail 192/130 junction to a low scrub-oak covered hill, west of Trail 130. Look closely as you approach it and you can see an indistinct animal path going up through the brush on the south end. This route is fairly easy and the view from the summit is well worth the effort. As a matter of information, there is a post beside Trail No. 130 at a point directly east of the summit. See Hike 10 for directions to a better path to the summit, starting from this post.

To return to Albuquerque, the route is the reverse of the one up, but is much easier and quicker. You could return by another route if you wish. One possibility is to hike the La Luz Trail, and another is to ride the cable car from the terminal 8.1 miles to the north, near Sandia Crest.

South Sandia Peak as seen from a vantage point.

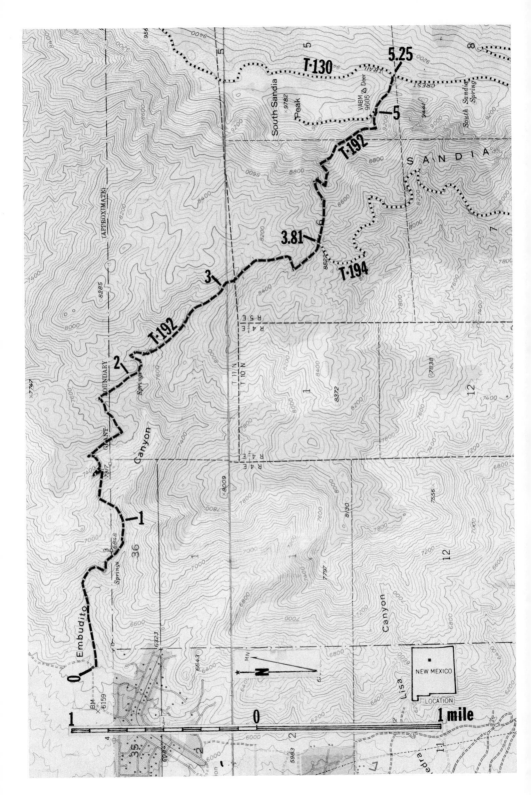

13 FOURTH OF JULY CAMPGROUND TO MANZANO CREST TRAIL
CIBOLA NATIONAL FOREST, MOUNTAINAIR DISTRICT

Distance: 5.3 miles
Time: 4 to 6 hours or overnight
Elevation Range: 7,600 to 8,850 feet
Rating: Moderate
Water: Near beginning and end only
Seasons: April through December usually, but depends on snow
Topographic Maps: Tajique, Bosque Peak
Special Map: Cibola National Forest, Mountainair Ranger District, Grid C5

This loop route provides a variety of environs and scenery, and can be made as a day hike or overnight. It will be necessary to carry all of the water you will need, as cows have messed up the springs in the high country.

The hike starts and ends near the Fourth of July Campground. To get there, take N.M. 14 to the town of Tajique. F.R. 55 joins N.M. 14 near the south edge of town and goes basically WNW from town to the campground, a distance of 6.5 miles. The campground is large and offers a variety of settings for campsites, with picnic tables. There is drinking water available from hand pumps.

The hike starts up Albuquerque Trail, which follows the two-track Forest Road 55C for the first mile. F.R. 55C leaves F.R. 55 about 0.4 mile northeast of the road which goes into the campground. This is easy walking, with springs along the first part of the route, and some nice campsites. It follows a drainage which has only a slight gradient.

At one-half mile there is a sign post with fragments of a T-78 sign, and at 0.6 mile is a spring that supplies most of the water you've been walking in at times, and just beyond the spring is another T-78 sign. The two-track ends at one mile and the trail joins an abandoned two-track at 1.7 miles. Go left (northwest) on this road. There is a sign post but no sign, so look for blazes on the trees, if in doubt. The gradient is still gentle and the walking surface still excellent. At 1.91 miles is a fence and gate, and a good campsite. A trail runs along the fence to the left, destination unknown. Beyond this fence the route steepens considerably. The slope remains very steep to a fence in the saddle at the ridge crest, 2.01 miles. This is the boundary between the national forest and the Isleta Indian Reservation. The abandoned road and Albuquerque

Trail continue downhill on the reservation, but don't go this way.

An abandoned road, or wide trail, runs steeply uphill to the left (west) generally alongside the fence, on the reservation side. To get to Crest Trail No. 170 go west up this route paralleling the fence. This must be one of the steepest roads ever made!! After one-half mile uphill the route turns north (right) away from the fence and after about 200 or 300 feet the trail leaves the old road and goes west again, up the hill. This trail departure is difficult to see because of a dead tree across it. Don't continue on the old road (it starts downhill shortly) north, but look for the not-too-obvious route west. The wide route again turns north at 2.62 miles and goes about 200 feet before switching back to the southwest and becomes a good one-track hiking trail. This is the beginning of Crest Trail No. 170. At 2.75 miles the trail switches to the north and at this point there is a grand vista to the east. The route switches back to southwest at 2.82 miles and at 2.93 miles turns due south and continues to a fence and gate, the national forest boundary, at 3.05 miles. Mosca Peak, 9,509 feet towers above to the west, and would be interesting to climb, but I found no route through the very dense oak brush. The trail is almost like a tunnel at times, through the dense oak thicket. Cattle have made side paths through the thicket, so take care to stay on the main trail, which at times, is almost blocked by branches. Keep a cool head when you think you have lost the route and look to either side until you have found it. There is a good view at 3.31 miles to the southwest, of mountains and valley. There continues to be so many cow trails that it is difficult to discern the Crest Trail. Farther along is a wet, boggy area in a clearing to the east of the trail, but the water is messed up by cows.

The trail, which has been very level through the oak brush for some distance, starts to drop off a plateau at 3.85 miles with a big view to the south. At 4.0 miles the trail is in a flat saddle just below the north end of a rocky peak. The route is still in the oak brush. There is a trail sign here pointing north and south to Crest Trail No. 170, north to forest boundary, one mile, and south to Fourth of July Trail No. 173, 140 feet. One hundred forty feet later is a sign pointing to Fourth of July Trail No. 173 and Campground. The sign is broken. At the first set of signs, one points to Ojito Trail branching to the west. Cerro Blanco Trail No. 79 branches to the southeast from Trail No. 173. A look at your forest map will show you where these trails go.

Trail No. 173 through the brush and grassy clearings is difficult to follow, so look for rock cairns marking the route. There is a big clearing with grass and flat rocks for a campsite at 4.1 miles but where is the trail? Keep to the northeast end of the big clearing to find the trail. At 4.1 miles a T-173 sign marks the route, but you are right on it before you can see it. The trail has been rerouted around some badly washed and worn sections on the steep hillside, but it is still rough in places. The trail continues to be popular, so this condition is no deterrent to hikers. The slope eases at 4.5 miles and is easy going for the remainder of the hike.

A small, clear stream comes in from the right at 4.61 miles and 150 feet down the trail from a pipe is flowing more clear water into a metal tank in the stream bed. This is good (and welcome) drinking water. About 400 feet farther there is a large metal water tank and through this area the trail is marshy, so step carefully to keep your feet dry. Farther along you zig-zag through a couple of fences. The trail is good, with gentle gradient through here. The hike ends at the loop road in Fourth of July Campground at 5.32 miles.

Hike No. 14 starts where this one ends and reverses the route up to the Crest Trail, which it follows to the south. If you like No. 13, try Hike No. 14 which is longer, easier to follow, and more scenic.

This is a view to the south of Manzano Mountains Crest, from near the junction of T-70 with T-171 and T-173.

89

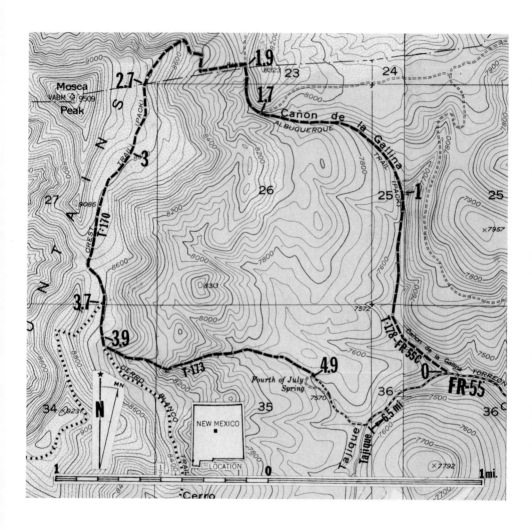

14 MANZANO MOUNTAINS CREST TRAIL
CIBOLA NATIONAL FOREST, MOUNTAINAIR DISTRICT

Distance: 10.2 miles to Capilla Peak Campground and 19.5 miles to Red Canyon
 Campground
Time: 2 or 3 days
Elevation Range: 7,400 to 9,600 feet
Rating: Moderate to strenuous
Water: Capilla Peak Campground
Seasons: April through December usually, but depends on snow
Topographic Maps: Bosque Peak, Capilla Peak, and Torreon
Special Maps: Cibola National Forest, Mountainair Ranger District, Grid C5
Permits: Contact U.S. Forest Service Office, Mountainair, New Mexico

This trail is only 50 miles southeast from Albuquerque by road. Though it is close to the city, the trail does not seem crowded after you get a couple of miles from the Fourth of July Campground, even on weekends. The campgrounds get crowded at times, but not the trail. This hike is written as a one-way trip, so unless you backtrack to your starting point, it will be necessary to arrange to have transportation waiting at the end of your hike. A road runs up to the campground on Capilla Peak. You can end your hike here if you wish, or could day-hike the trail and car camp here. There are many alternatives on this trip.

The hike starts on Trail 173 in Fourth of July Campground. After hiking the first 2.25 miles of the route you will understand why it is classed as moderate to strenuous. Trail No. 173, as described in Hike No. 13, has a steep section as it climbs from the drainage up to its junction with the Crest Trail. Other portions don't seem too steep, but must be, as the route gains 1,600 feet in this 2.25 miles, for an average grade of 13 percent. At one mile, Trail No. 79 joins from the left. Crest Trail No. 170 is joined at 1.25 miles.

Go south on the Crest Trail. After 2.3 miles you are on the ridge and from here to Capilla Peak subsequent elevation changes are insignificant, except at 5.8 to 6.8 miles (downhill) and 9.1 to 10.1 miles (uphill). North of Capilla Peak the vegetation is fairly open, with patches of ponderosa, piñon, and oak brush. The open places provide fine vistas to east and west. There are numerous excellent campsites along the route, but the only reliable and easy to find water is at Capilla Peak Campground. If you plan to camp prior to reaching the peak (about 10.2 miles for the day) take adequate water for drinking and cooking. The amount of water to take will vary with individuals and

temperature, but on a warm day take at least 1½ gallons per person. Night camps on the ridge are outstanding, with brilliant stars above and the lights of Albuquerque and other towns to east and west visible below.

At 4.2 miles Trail No. 174 from Canyon de Tajique comes in from the left (east) and Bosque Peak is one-half mile to the west. You should dump your pack and make the 30 to 45 minute side trip up the peak. Continuing south along the trail, it begins to lose elevation at 5.8 miles and at seven miles in a saddle, is a trail junction. Trail No. 176 joins from Canyon de la Verde, to the east, and Commanche Canyon Trail No. 182 comes up from the west.

The path crosses Canyon del Ojo del Indio at 9.2 miles and then begins its climb to Capilla Peak (9,368 feet), where it joins Forest Road 245, at 10.2 miles. Capilla Peak Campground is a short distance across the road, to the east, and the lookout tower is to the north. There are shelters, tables, and water in the campground. The University of New Mexico Astronomical Observatory is nearby, but is not open to the public. On leaving Capilla Peak the trail follows F.R. 245 for nearly a mile to where a sign marks its departure beside a microwave tower on the right. The trail follows the ridge crest for the next 2.3 miles and after crossing over Gallo Peak, at 13.4 miles, drops 500 feet into a saddle. In the saddle Trigo Trail No. 185 joins from the west. The path climbs back onto the ridge crest and has its ups and downs along the way to its junction at 16 miles with the Spruce Canyon Trail No. 189 (see Hike No. 15).

If you are tired or having any problems, you may want to take the shortest route to Red Canyon Campground. It is 3.5 miles via T-189 to the campground, 0.7 mile shorter than going by way of Red Canyon Trail No. 89 and

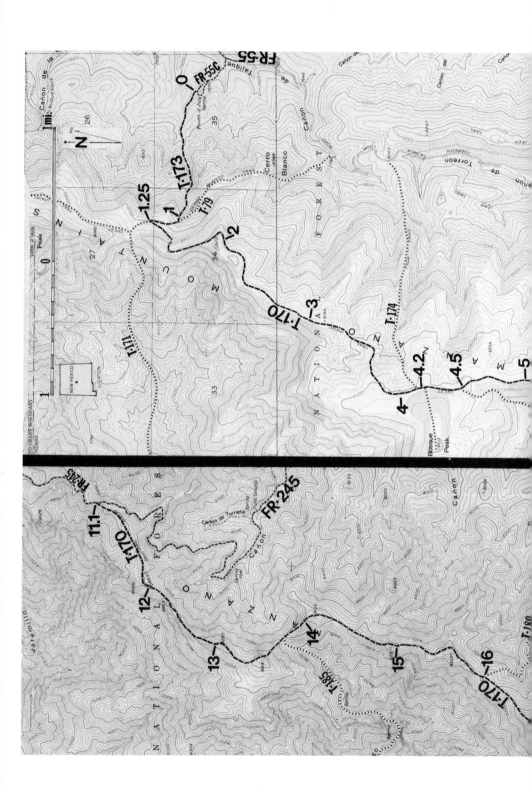

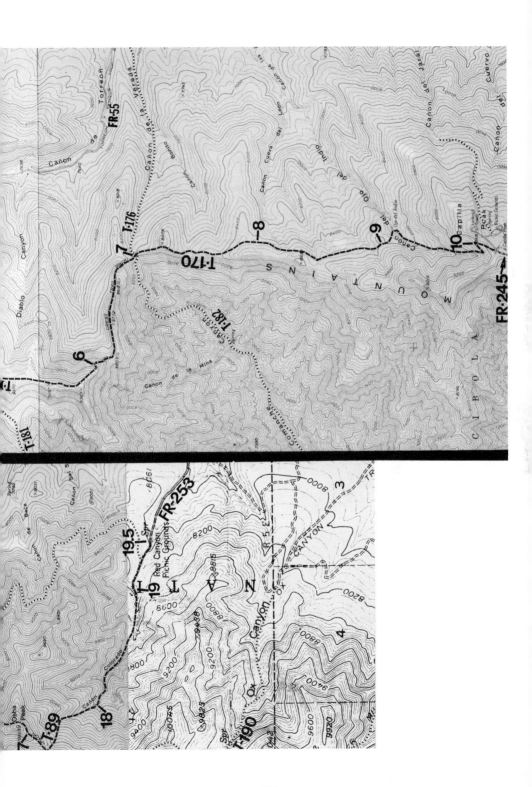

93

avoids the steep climb north of Osha Peak. But you would miss the opportunity of climbing Osha Peak and seeing some nice scenery along the ridge and T-89.

If you continue on the Crest Trail, the 800 foot climb to Osha Peak soon begins. This averages about a 20 percent grade, which is steep. There is a fence alongside the trail briefly. At about 16.9 miles the grade abruptly levels off and there is a sign post (no sign) beside the trail. From this point a faint trail starts southwest to the summit of Osha Peak. Leave your pack here, but take along some water and a snack to add to the pleasure of relaxing on the summit. The trail is soon lost in fallen trees, but continue uphill and the top is soon attained. As from all of the open high places on this hike, the view up here is outstanding. Enjoy the view, because this is the last opportunity you will have on this trip to see in all directions. The hike back to the Crest Trail doesn't take long.

Red Canyon Trail No. 89 junction is 0.4 mile south along the ridge crest at mile 17.2. The 2.3 miles down Red Canyon is a pretty hike and is alongside a little stream at times. See Hike No. 15 for more information about this portion of the trip. Red Canyon Campground, where the hike ends, is at 19.5 miles.

To reach Fourth of July Campground and trail, turn south off I-40 onto N.M. 14 at Tijeras, 17 miles east of Albuquerque. Go south on N.M. 14 for 33 miles to Tajique. Take Forest Road 55 west, from the south edge of Tajique, to the trailhead in the campground. This is 6.5 miles of well-used all-weather road.

For the car shuttle to Red Canyon Campground or Capilla Peak go south on N.M. 14 for 8.5 miles from Tajique to Manzano. To get to Capilla Peak take Forest Road 245 northwest from just north of the church in Manzano. If after a heavy rain you can get across the creek bed at the edge of town, you should be able to make it all of the way to the peak. To get to Red Canyon Campground, take Forest Road 253 southwest from the south edge of Manzano, and follow the signs.

View to the south, of Manzano Mountains Crest,
from near the electronics site south of Capilla Peak.
The high point is Osha Peak.

15 RED CANYON, CREST, AND SPRUCE TRAILS
CIBOLA NATIONAL FOREST, MOUNTAINAIR DISTRICT

Distance: 7.5 miles round-trip
Time: 4 to 6 hours round-trip
Elevation Range: 7,960 to 10,003 feet
Rating: Easy
Water: Only near beginning and end of route, from creek
Seasons: Usually April through December, depending on snow
Topographic Maps: Capilla Peak 7.5', Torreon 15'
Special Map: Cibola National Forest, Mountainair Ranger District, Grid C6

This hike begins and ends at Red Canyon Campground. The basic loop hike is 7.5 miles and should take about 4½ hours to complete. It offers some interesting possibilities for side trips, so if you want to do some extra hiking, allow yourself the additional time it will take.

Red Canyon Campground is reached from N.M. 14, by turning south on F.R. 253 in the southern edge of the small town of Manzano. This road goes past Red Canyon State Park, which is well marked. It is six miles from Manzano to the Canyon Campground by all-weather road, which is well maintained and suitable for any passenger car. The campground has a number of sites with tables in very scenic settings among large coniferous trees, with a small stream nearby. Hand operated pumps provide potable water, and the outhouses are clean and well-kept.

The hike begins and ends at the loop road in the campground and can be made in either direction. The trails on this route are as good as any you will find in a national forest.

This route goes up Red Canyon Trail No. 89 from the campground. It follows alongside and crosses a small stream many times. The only water available on this hike will be from this stream (at the last crossing) or from a less accessible stream near the Spruce Canyon Trail on the way down. You can get water that should be safe to drink at 0.55 mile as you cross to the north side of the stream, the 20th and last crossing.

At 1.71 miles the route is out of the drainage onto a sloping plateau and shortly you will be walking through a forest of very large pine and fir trees. There is a good vista to the east to the campground and the desert beyond (at 1.84 miles). The route is going northwest along here and you should start seeing aspens soon.

The junction with Crest Trail No. 170 is at 2.34 miles just to the east of the ridge crest. There is a sign here for Red Canyon Trail No.

89 (which you have just come up). The Crest Trail has recently been rerouted northeast from this junction. The sign says, "Crest Trail No. 170, Ox Trail (to the southwest) 2 miles, Osha Peak (to the northeast, no distance given because it is nearby), and Trigo Canyon 4 miles northeast." There are other signs on the abandoned portion of the Crest Trail.

If you wish to make the hike to Ox Trail junction two miles south, or to Manzano Peak four miles distant, this is the place to start. The Crest Trail between here and Ox Canyon goes through one area of open meadow and is not traveled enough to keep the grass worn to show a path, so watch for trail sign posts and blazes on trees. If you can't find the trail through here, just keep close to the ridge crest.

At about two miles from the junction, there is a trail fork and two badly chewed sign posts with the damaged signs on the ground. This is the Ox Canyon Trail junction, and that trail goes directly south, and appears to be more heavily traveled than the Crest Trail, which goes southwest. From here you're on your own to Manzano Peak.

Back at the junction of Red Canyon Trail and the Crest Trail, to continue the loop, go northeast o the Crest Trail. In about 100 feet there is a trail sign indicating that the Crest Trail continues in the direction you are going. Soon, Osha Peak (10,003 feet) will be to your left. Look for indications of a trail going up to it. At 2.75 miles the path crosses over to the west side of the ridge in a small saddle. There is a post here, but no sign. From this point a faint trail starts up to Osha Peak to the southwest. The faint path to the peak is soon lost in fallen trees and brush, but getting to the summit, one-quarter mile distant is not really difficult — just keep going uphill. The view from the summit is excellent. To the north you can see Capilla Peak 4.5 miles distant, with the lookout tower, observatory, etc. on it. Note that the ridge between Osha and Capilla Peaks drops quite low, indicating a good uphill climb if you decide to hike to Capilla Peak. Return to the sign post and go north on the Crest Trail.

The long drop in elevation begins here. There is a good view to the north, of the crest and Capilla Peak, and to the west. At 3.6 miles the trail is on the crest and there are many small, good campsites along here and to the north. A fence comes to the trail from the southwest at 4.07 miles and follows north along the trail. Shortly the route is in an open, flat saddle and there are two sign posts (4.12 miles).

This is the Spruce Canyon Trail junction. The sign to the east side of the Crest Trail says, "Spruce Trail No. 189" and also an arrow points along this way to Red Canyon Campground 3½ miles. This is the route you want to take to complete the loop. The sign on the other side of the Crest Trail is down on the ground, but indicates that the Crest Trail goes both north and south from here and Red Canyon Trail is 1.25 miles to the south and Trigo Trail No. 185 is to the north.

Rock cairns and blazes on trees help guide you along the Crest Trail through the grass to the Spruce Trail junction. The Spruce Trail

drops down to the east and is easy to follow. About one-quarter mile below the junction a side trail drops steeply to the left. This one may go down to water, and if you are desperately thirsty you may want to dump your pack and see if you can find water. But, it is less than an hour back to camp from this point, so consider what is best. At about 0.7 mile below the Crest Trail is a good view to the east of the campground and beyond.

The Spruce Trail has a very gentle, constant slope to it. In contrast with the Red Canyon Trail, which follows a stream bed in a shady valley, the Spruce Trail goes along the side of a hill, exposed to the sun but providing many excellent vistas. The surroundings and vegetation are typical of a dry climate.

You are back at the loop road in Red Canyon Campground at 7.52 miles.

As I said earlier, the trails on this hike are excellent, well routed and maintained, with easy grades. If there are any shortcomings at all with these trails it is in the signs, some of which have been damaged or destroyed by age or by bears. But for the alert, reasonably capable hiker this should present no problem. To find out about snow, water or other factors ahead of time, contact the U.S. Forest Service Office, P.O. Box E, Mountainair, NM 87036.

Route follows the southern portion of Manzano Mountains Crest. Note the rock cairn marking the way.

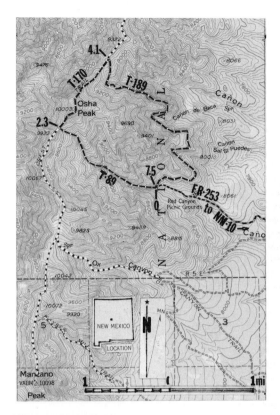

Bears haven't tasted this one yet.

16 OSHA CANYON AND TOLTEC MESA
CARSON NATIONAL FOREST

Distance: 5 to 25 miles round-trip
Time: 3 to 6 days
Elevation Range: 9,200 to 10,400 feet
Rating: Moderate hiking, but requires very experienced route finder
Water: Dependable in most of the streams along the route
Seasons: May through November usually, but depends on snow
Topographic Map: Toltec Mesa
Special Maps: Carson National Forest, Grid 1E-F; Rio Grande National Forest, Grid 9D,E

There are a number of ways to get into this hike. The easiest route to follow is to drive 23 miles on a rough dirt and gravel road. Another is to drive a few miles farther on a rocky all-weather gravel road which arrives at the same place. The way that will appeal to those who like to do something different and out of the ordinary is to ride the narrow gauge railroad from Antonito, Colorado or from Chama, New Mexico to Osier, Colorado, an optional starting place. It is possible to drive to Osier from Antonito, but is not nearly as much fun as the train ride.

This hike is into Osha Canyon (also called Cruces Basin) and on Toltec Mesa. The area is drained by Diablo, Beaver, Lobo, and Cruces Creeks, from the west and south. The basin is open, with scattered forest, due to a big fire that occurred here in the 1880s. There are patches of aspen, firs, etc. that grow at these elevations, above 9,000 feet. Beavers dam the creeks, which have reliable water flowing in them and reportedly 10 to 12-inch rainbow trout. This area is a calving ground for elk and you will see many deer here as well (and hunters too, in hunting season). Wild flowers are particularly plentiful and beautiful in the basin.

There are some unmarked trails in the area, but no marking is necessary, due to the open character of the landscape. Leaders of hikes into the basin should have plenty of experience in route-finding and map reading to minimize the chances of getting lost. It is a real pleasure to wander in the basin, exploring and making camp near the various creeks on an unhurried schedule. You can easily spend a week in here, camping at a different, beautiful spot each night.

The creeks which drain this basin join near where the abandoned jeep road from the south ends. The combined creeks become Beaver Creek. Beaver Creek drops sharply to the east and about three miles from the jeep road end flows into Rio de los Piños. Some of the river bottom between Beaver Creek and Toltec Gorge, along the Piños is privately owned, so be careful about trespassing there. Toltec Gorge is about four miles upstream, and is quite spectacular. The train to Antonito runs along the northeast side of the gorge and passengers can look down into it.

To day-hike into the gorge you can camp at Cruces Creek the night before. From your camp, go northeast up onto Toltec Mesa (there is no trail to the gorge). When you are on the mesa you will see two large rock outcroppings, which are near the canyon. Go between these outcrops and drop down a drainage into the canyon. If you go to the right of them you will get to the river downstream of the gorge and if you go to the left of them you will be upstream of Toltec Gorge. Rio de los Piños, in the gorge, reportedly has trophy-size brown trout in it. The hike into the gorge is strenuous and weak hikers should not attempt it. But the experience is worth the effort for strong hikers.

To get to this hike, go 10.7 miles north of the town of Tres Piedras on U.S. 285, a mile past two picnic tables on the left (west). The road junction is just south of San Antonio Peak, a big rounded mountain that stands alone above the rolling country around it. Turn left (west) on Forest Road 87 toward Lagunitas. Six miles along F.R. 87 you enter Carson National Forest. If you get caught by rain while on this hike you may have to drive out a longer, but better route to Antonito, Colorado via F.R. 87A. The junction of F.R. 87 and F.R. 87A is 22 miles from U.S. 285. Signs here point to Lagunitas five miles west (starting point for Hike 17), and to the right (north) is 87A which goes to Antonito. From this junction continue west on F.R. 87 for 0.85 mile. Immediately after the road makes a 90 degree bend to the left, a jeep road goes north (right) up onto the ridge. This is the road to Osha Canyon on the south end of the hiking area, shown as F.R. 572 on the Forest Service map. Go north on the jeep road 0.1 mile to a gate (be sure to close it after you go through) and continue over the low ridge to descend into Cruces Basin (Osha Canyon). From the ridge you can see the whole basin spread out ahead.

From the ridge the road going downhill is fairly steep and very rocky. A passenger car can make it if you drive to the sides of the worn tracks and avoid or move any rocks that might damage the underside of the car. The jeep road passes a stock water tank (pond) on the left, and comes to another on the right a short distance later. Beside the road adjacent to the second stock tank there is a Forest Service sign prohibiting motorized vehicles beyond this point. I've driven this far with a horse trailer and a couple of horses without any problem. The road beyond the sign has been bulldozed in numerous places to prevent passage of motor vehicles.

Start your hike at the sign. There is plenty of room to park and it is open and fairly level here. Once when I parked here I saw some small golden furred animals scurrying along fallen trees and through the flowers. On closer observation I found that it was a pair of weasels or black-footed ferrets. Deer crossed the road ahead of me as I hiked to Beaver Creek. This is a neat place to hike!

The barricaded road takes you to Beaver Creek at a transition point in the terrain. West, upstream, are open valleys and slopes with scattered clumps of trees all the way to Brazos Ridge. Downstream the valley closes in and the forest gets relatively dense, and continues like this much of the way to Rio de los Piños.

Look the country over before you leave the road, and be sure you can get back to where you started. Use your map and compass and pick out some distinct landmarks on Brazos Ridge and other high places that can be seen from viewpoints in the area to be hiked. This entry point, as you can see on the map, is at the extreme south side of the roughly circular Osha Canyon area. Osier, Colorado, the other entry point, is on the extreme north side of this same area. With ample time you can wander over the whole canyon from either starting place, and from Hike #17 also. This is a super place to explore on horseback too.

The Cumbres and Toltec Scenic Railroad has a narrow gauge steam train that runs from Antonito, Colorado to Chama, New Mexico. Write or call C&TS RR, P.O. Box 789, Chama, NM 87520, (505) 756-2151 or C&TS RR, P.O. Box 668, Antonito, CO 81120, (303) 376-5483 for schedule and price information. The price at this writing is $20 per person. The train runs from both Antonito and Chama to Osier, Colorado where they stop for lunch and then return to the station from which they came. They run five days per week from mid-June to mid-October. You can arrange to ride from either station to Osier for the hike and return at a later date. The trains arrive at Osier at about 1 p.m. which gives you a few hours to hike down to the river and on to your night's camp site. There is a sign by the restaurant building (which was a toll station on the toll road that ran through here about 100 years ago) pointing to Osier Creek.

The hike from Osier down to the Rio de los Piños is about a mile. When you arrive at the river, follow the trail alongside it south to the first drainage that goes up to the west. It is a short, comfortable half-mile up this drainage to a good place to stop and camp, at around 10,000 feet elevation. The next day you can continue up the drainage, cross Toltec Mesa, and drop into Cruces Basin for the next night's camp. There is plenty of country to explore up here. Your return route can be the reverse of the route you came in on, or from Cruces Basin you can go down Beaver Creek, cross Rio de los Piños, and hike up to Sublette Siding to the northeast and catch the train to Antonito. Check this out ahead of time with the train people so they will expect you and you will know when to get there.

Have a good hike, and don't get lost!

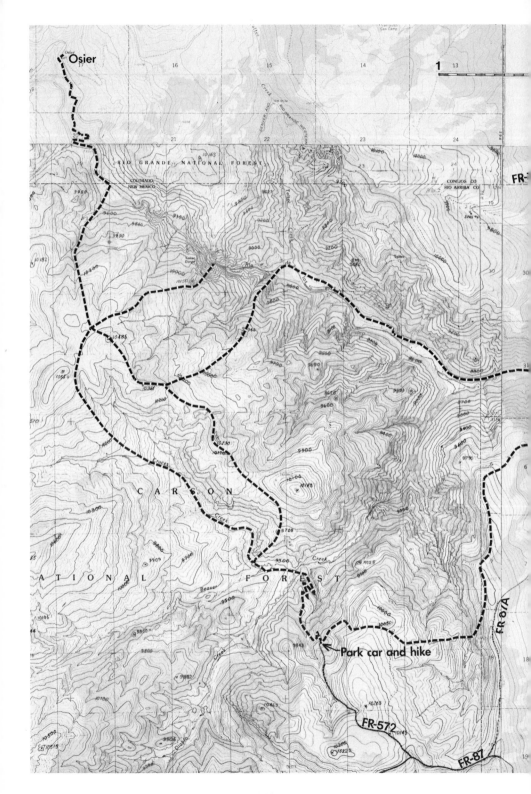

From Osier this sign points the direction to hike.

Sublette siding, an alternate place to catch the train back to Antonito.

17 BRAZOS RIDGE
CARSON NATIONAL FOREST

Distance: 5 miles one-way on Brazos Ridge, or 8 miles to north end of Toltec Mesa
Time: 6 to 10 hours round-trip to end of ridge, 10 to 15 hours round-trip to north end of Toltec Mesa (best to plan to camp a day or two)
Elevation Range: 10,400 to 10,962 on ridge and down to 9,000 feet if you drop off into Toltec Gorge
Rating: Moderate walking. Route-finding requires experienced hiker skilled in use of map and compass
Water: None on ridge, but available in drainages to the east (plan to carry what you will need unless you intend to take time to look for it in the drainages)
Seasons: May through November usually, but depends on snow
Topographic Map: Toltec Mesa
Special Map: Carson National Forest, Grid 1-E

This hike follows northwest along the crest of Brazos Ridge for about five miles and continues for about three miles more northeast on a ridge across Toltec Mesa. You are free to drop off the ridge into the drainages (Osha Canyon) or forested area to the east, at almost any point after the first two miles. This would take you into the same area covered in the Osha Canyon/Toltec Mesa Hike #16.

A trail leads you from the Upper Lagunitas Campground, along the ridge for 0.7 mile, where it disappears. The remainder of the hike is along the ridge crest without an obvious trail.

The hike starts from near the campsite and toilet at the end of the road that loops through Upper Lagunitas Campground. There is no sign, but it is easy to follow the path that goes west-northwest out of the forest and along the exposed side of a ridge. When you re-enter the forest old blazes on trees occasionally indicate a trail has followed along the ridge for some time. The trail from the campground seems to end at a bench mark at 0.7 mile, shortly after entering the forest on the ridge crest. Continue northwest along the crest of the ridge and you cross an old fence line at about 0.9 mile, go over a low peak at 1.1 miles, and drop into a saddle at 1.5 miles. A short distance beyond the low point in the saddle you encounter a rocky four-wheel drive road that you can follow to about mile 4.0. Here the old road curves left and drops down to the west and the hike continues north along the ridge.

There is fairly easy access to water in drainages to the east at about 3.5 and 4.1 miles. It is easier to get down at the 4.1 mile place. You can depart from the ridge at about any point, to camp or explore. From the ridge you can pick out the places you want to hike to — the view up there is excellent.

At about 5.5 miles, at the northern-most high point along the ridge (10,822 feet), the ridge forks. Take the northeast fork, which drops fairly steeply down onto Toltec Mesa. From the mesa you can do your own thing. If you are only day hiking, turn around at the midpoint of your hiking time. Wherever you go, remember how you got there and how to get back to your car. The area is generally open and Brazos Ridge prominent enough that it will be difficult for an experienced hiker to get lost.

To get to this hike, go 9.7 miles north of Tres Piedras on U.S. 285 to two picnic tables on the west side of the road. Turn west on the side road toward Lagunitas. This is F.R. 87. Six-and-a-half miles along F.R. 87 you enter Carson National Forest. The road to this point can be very muddy in rainy weather and if you get caught by rain while on this hike, you may have to go out a longer but better route to Antonito, Colorado. You will come to a junction of F.R. 87 and 87A at 22.5 miles from U.S. 285. The sign here points ahead (west) to Lagunitas five miles, where this hike starts. F.R. 87A, to the north goes to Rio de los Piños, 10 miles, and on to Antonito, Colorado. From the 87/87A junction continue 5.3 miles to upper Lagunitas Campground and the trailhead.

Looking southwest from near the trailhead of Hike #17.

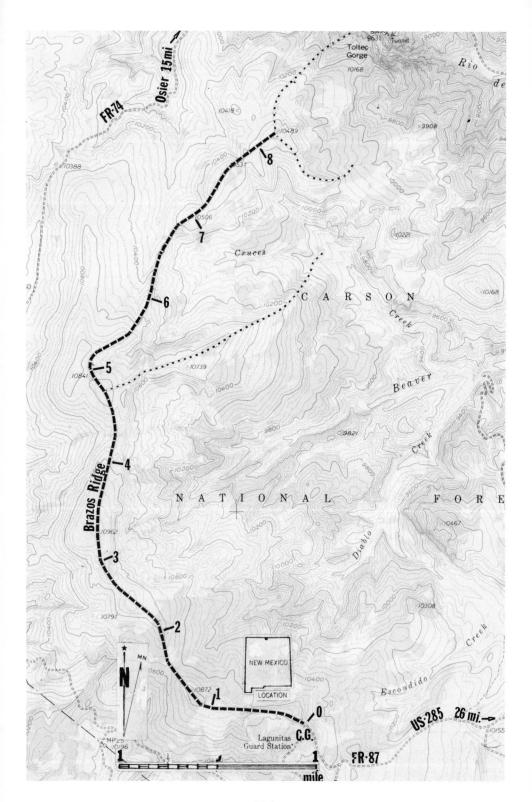

18 RIO GRANDE CANYON TRAIL
RIO GRANDE WILD RIVER

Distance: 6.75 miles one-way, from Big Arsenic Campground to river, along river, and up to La Junta Campground

Time: Big Arsenic to river — 30 minutes, along river — 3 to 5 hours, and up to La Junta Campground — 1 hour

Elevation Range: 7,420 to 6,600 feet

Rating: Easy to moderate. Flat riverside trails, short distances, with short, but steep climbs from river to rim

Water: Big springs at Big Arsenic Campground beside river, below Big Arsenic, and smaller spring at riverside campground below Little Arsenic. Also available at campgrounds along the rim

Seasons: Mid-March to mid-December. Snow may close trail after mid-December and winters are cold. Summers are mild, seldom over 90° F

Topographic Map: Guadalupe Mountain

Special Map: Rio Grande Wild River brochure with map available at Visitor Center. Also "Boating on the Rio Grande Wild and Scenic River" map and classification of rapids

Permit: Required for camping in the canyon when Visitor Center is open, Memorial Day to Labor Day

This is a really good, different, hike. As is the case with most New Mexico hikes, there are a number of optional places to start, end, camp, turn around, day hike, etc. The canyon is quite scenic when viewed from the rim, but this doesn't compare with the thrill of camping and hiking alongside the boiling and roaring wild river.

The Wild and Scenic Rivers Act of 1968 was enacted to preserve the natural state and beauty of our environmental treasures. Forty-eight miles of the Rio Grande from the Colorado border south, and the lower four miles of the Red River, in New Mexico, were among the first to be protected by the act. This hike is in a small portion of these original 48 miles. The hiking trails discussed herein provide access to the canyon in its most scenic part, near the confluence of the Rio Grande and Red Rivers. These trails were built as a 1963 Works Project. They continue to be maintained in good condition, and are used primarily by fishermen.

The change in ecosystems is abrupt, as you drop from the rim to the bottom of the gorge. The rim is dry and generally grassy with sage brush and occasional shrubs. Piñon pine and juniper are scattered or in randomly spaced groves. A few Ponderosa Pine and Douglas Fir can also be found up here. In contrast, a variety of lush vegetation grows along the river. Cottonwood, ponderosa, and willow, along with a variety of bushes, and box-elder thrive there.

A number of trails provide access to the river from the rim. The most upstream trail is from Big Arsenic Springs Campground. The route is 1.75 miles of fairly steep, rocky trail to the big campground by the river. It takes about 30 minutes to go down to the junction with the streamside trail and 45 minutes or more to come back up. The next trail downstream is from Little Arsenic Campground, with a distance and hiking times similar to the previous one. The trail from La Junta overlook goes directly to the juncture of the two rivers. This path is two miles long and takes about 40 minutes to go down and an hour to come back up. Another trail drops to the Red River from El Aguaje Campground. Across the Red River a trail goes to the confluence from Cebolla Mesa Campground.

From Big Arsenic Campground on the rim a trail drops, in an upstream direction, to a series of three-sided riverside camping shelters. The shelters are strung out with five upstream and two downstream from the trail junction. Big springs provide clear, cool water conveniently near the campsites. The next riverside campground is 1.25 miles downstream. There are three shelters and a spring for drinking water here. A half-mile downstream is another campground with four shelters but it has no spring. Campers can get water from the spring upstream or use river water. The campground at the confluence of the Rio Grande and Red River is 1.25 miles farther downstream. It has five shelters, but no spring.

The trail alongside the Rio Grande is very good. It is well constructed and maintained and has little gradient, except at its upstream end. A log across the Red River gives access to an additional mile of trail downstream to Cibola Mesa Campground.

A fisherman's trail on the northside of the Red River follows it upstream for two miles to the trail which comes down from El Aguaje Campground. This trail isn't nearly as good as the one along the Rio Grande because it is the result of repeated use by fishermen and wasn't actually built and is not maintained.

A permit is required for camping along the river when the Visitor Center is open, but none is necessary if you want to hike and camp along the rim. Water is available in all of the rim top campgrounds.

To get to this hike, get on N.M. 3 and turn west 3.3 miles north of Questa on N.M. 378. The sign at this junction says "Rio Grande Wild and Scenic River, Recreation Area, 8 miles." It is 5.5 miles from N.M. 3 to the recreation area boundary and an additional 6.5 miles to the Visitor Center. It is also 6.5 miles from the boundary to Big Arsenic Campground.

One of the riverside shelters in Big Arsenic Springs Campground.

106

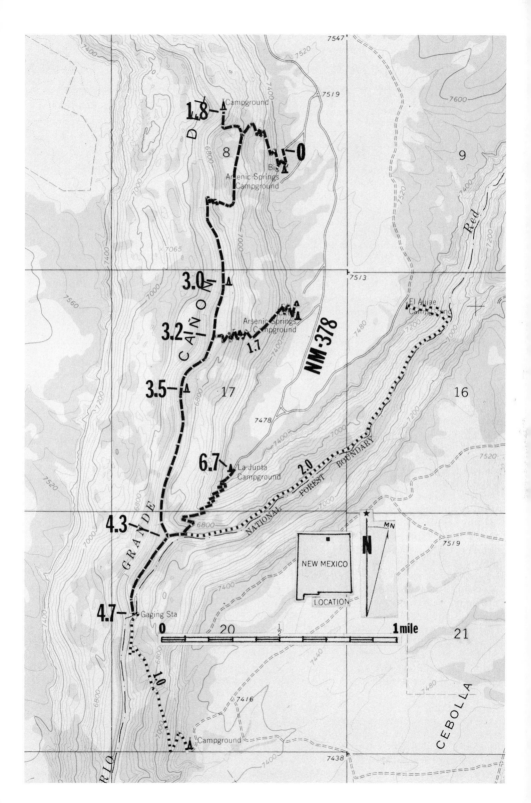

19 RITO DEL MEDIO TRAIL NO. 287
CARSON NATIONAL FOREST

Distance: 8.2 miles round-trip to end of T-287; 19.6 miles round-trip to Heart Lake
Time: 5 to 9 hours round-trip to end of trail; 2 or 3 days to Heart Lake
Elevation Range: 8,040 to 10,680 feet on T-287, up to 12,600 feet to the lake
Rating: Moderate if day-hiking to end of trail; strenuous with pack (need to be experienced
    with map and compass to continue toward Heart Lake)
Water: Route follows a good stream from 2.5 to 4.1 miles
Seasons: April through November usually, but varies with snowfall
Topographic Maps: Cerro, Latir Peak
Special Map: Carson National Forest, Grid J2

This is a good trail which is well-routed and appears to have been heavily used in the past. Because it is so obscure, it is likely used only by local residents. It is a beautiful route that climbs steeply, more than 1,000 feet in 0.7 mile (28 percent grade) alongside a rushing, cascading stream. Though the trail is not shown on a forest map nor topographic map, it *was* marked with a sign at each end and with blazes on trees along the way. I said it *was* marked with signs, because on my last hike here I found that the trailhead sign and one of its posts had been pulled up, apparently by a pickup truck, and taken away. You can't get away from vandals even in the forests (as long as you are near a road anyhow). The path is near or alongside Rito del Medio stream from about 2.5 to 4.1 miles, and beyond if you go up Virgin Canyon.

My last trip in, the trail was torn up in the steep hillside stretches, away from the stream, and here unstable parallel tracks marked the slopes. This is because local ranchers have been driving herds of cattle and sheep up and down the trail. There was a sheep camp in Virgin Canyon and cattle roamed the slopes near timberline. The animals were not any problem, as they were so widely scattered. However, I was reluctant to drink the water from the pretty, clear stream without treating it with chemicals, as I have done in the past.

The hike starts in a small cluster of houses that are El Rito, one mile east of N.M. 3. The gravel road runs east from N.M. 3 and one mile from the highway, in El Rito, makes a 90 degree left turn to the north. You can park your car in the corner between the road and fence. Or, you may want to try to drive to the trailhead, but I'll start the hike distances at the fence corner for those who prefer to walk from here.

Walk north along the gravel road to 0.3 mile where a recently established rough dirt "road" turns off to the east. Follow this road for about 1.2 miles where it T's into a north-south two-track road. Turn right (south) here and go about 0.3 mile. The trailhead is on the left, marked by the remaining post for the trail sign. This is mile 1.8 for those hiking from the fence corner. Just before arriving at the trailhead, openings in the juniper and piñon permit good views to the west of the road to El Rito, N.M. 3, and the broad valley beyond, to Rio Grande Canyon (Hike #18).

The sign which formerly marked the trail said, "Rito del Medio Trail No. 287, State Highway No. 3 2 miles (west), Heart Lake 8 miles (east)." It is difficult to believe that the fence corner where I suggested that you park is only one mile directly west of the trailhead, after the devious route on the dirt roads. The forest boundary fence is less than 100 feet to the west.

On the trail go east toward Heart Lake. At this elevation, the path is through a fairly dense forest of mixed conifer and oak brush. The trail surface is good and the gradient is uphill, but easy, to begin with. About 0.3 mile along the trail you can hear water flowing somewhere to the south. The grade is getting steeper and the surface is rockier, but it is still a good path. It is now passing through the deep shade of a virgin forest of large conifers. Soon the stream approaches the trail and runs alongside it for the remainder of the way, to the end of T-287. The steep, 28 percent grade is experienced between 2.4 and 3.0 miles. It begins to ease at 2.9 miles and becomes almost level at 3.0 miles, and after a short respite resumes a gentle slope upward.

The path disappears in a marshy area at 3.4 miles so watch for blaze marks on trees. Stay to the left edge of the wet area for 30 feet or so to keep your feet dry. About 3.6 miles is an opening in the forest with a slightly steeper grade, and mosquitoes.

The trail crosses an abandoned logging or mining road at 4.1 miles and continues into the forest on the other side. About 150 feet into the dense forest you cross a small stream and come to the trail sign on two posts. It announces, "Jaracito Trail No. 293, Jaracito Canyon (northwest), Virgin Canyon (southeast)." The route to Virgin Canyon is marshy near the sign, but it seems that the trail would be found near the stream that runs up this canyon. It would be about 1.4 miles up Virgin Canyon to Trail No. 82, which would take you to Heart lake, if you want to go there. You can explore to the north or south on the abandoned mine road. To the north it switchbacks for 1.5 miles up the north side of the valley southwest of Virsylvia Peak and abruptly ends

on the slope, south of this peak and west of Venado Peak. From road's end you could, with some scrambling on rocky slopes, get up to the pass between Virsylvia and Venado Peaks and cross Venado Peak to get to T-85. This looks more difficult than via Virgin Canyon.

If you don't want to hike beyond the end of T-287 there are many good places to camp nearby, with plenty of water and firewood.

Be sure to mark where T-287 emerges onto the mine road, as it is not too obvious and you may have some trouble finding it when you want to return. The return trip is downhill all the way, and much faster than the trip up.

To get to this hike, go three miles north of Questa on N.M. 3. Near milepost 31, at the sign pointing to El Rito, turn east on the gravel road. Go east one mile to the 90 degree left turn and park in the fence corner, or follow the directions previously given for trying to drive to the trailhead.

Cabresto Peak as seen from the old mine road on Venado Peak.

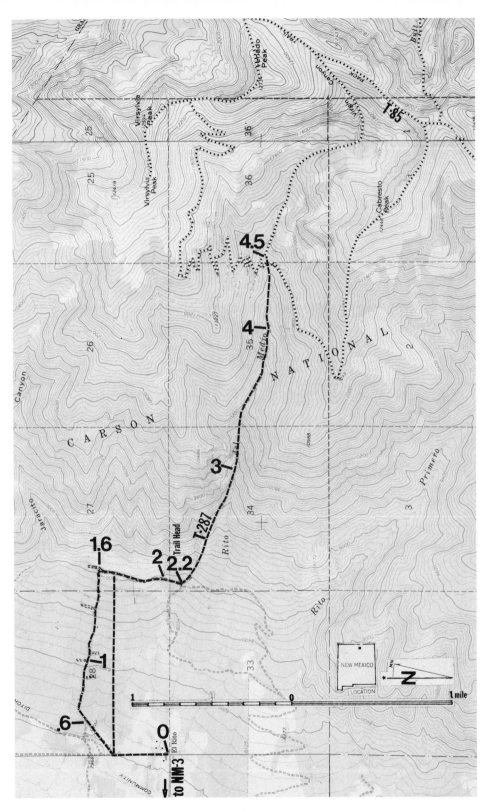

110

20 WHEELER PEAK VIA EAST FORK AND MIDDLE FORK TRAILS
CARSON NATIONAL FOREST

Distance: 19.8 miles
Time: 3 days or more
Elevation Range: 9,400 to 13,161 feet, highest point in New Mexico
Rating: Strenuous
Water: Some along the way, but carry a canteen. None on Wheeler Peak
Seasons: Usually early June through October, but depends on snow
Topographic Map: Wheeler Peak
Special Map: Carson National Forest, Grid K3

If you are looking for a top-notch, spectacular backpack trip, try this one. It takes you through forest and streamside; across rock slides and around a lake lost in the forest; through alpine meadows, along exposed ridges above timberline, and to the summit of New Mexico's highest mountain. When I try to decide which is my favorite backpack trip in New Mexico (I've never reached a decision), this hike is usually one of the candidates.

You should allow a minimum of three days for hiking this route. Some fast hikers may be able to make it in less time, but they will miss many of the activities that make a backpack trip so enjoyable; the relaxing, exploring, fishing, loafing around camp, bird watching, visiting other campers, or whatever you like to do. In fact, four or five days or more would make this an even better trip.

This hike starts in the National Forest parking lot at the confluence of the West Fork and the Middle Fork of Red River, south of the town of Red River. A car shuttle will not be necessary because this is a circular route. If preferred, hikers and packs can be dropped off at the Ditch Cabin parking area, shortening the hike by 2.5 miles for these participants. The driver could then take the car to the Middle Fork/West Fork parking lot, and hike back unencumbered to join the others. This would save a little time and effort and have the car waiting as close as possible at the end of the trail.

The Middle Fork/West Fork parking lot, where you leave the car, is 1.4 miles from the junction of Forest Road 58 and 58A. After you park the car go northeast on F.R. 58 to F.R. 58A, and turn southeast on F.R. 58A. Along the way you pass a number of nice cabins in this valley. The road goes across private land and you must open and close a couple of gates at

2.0 and 2.1 miles from the car. The parking area where you may have dropped off companions and packs is on forest land at 2.5 miles. There is a sign here telling wilderness users to park in this area and, four-wheel drive to continue to Ditch Cabin only.

From here the route gains altitude slowly but steadily to the site of Ditch Cabin, which is reached at 3.0 miles. Fifty yards farther the trail crosses a log bridge and on the other side is a trail sign, "Main Fork Trail No. 56, Sawmill Park 2 miles, Horseshoe Lake 6 miles." Arrows on the sign indicate that both places are in the direction you are walking.

The path crosses Elizabethtown Ditch at 3.5 miles and the grade eases for a while. A trail junction sign at 3.8 miles marks a side trail, "Sawmill Park Trail No. 55, Sawmill Park 1 mile east, Taos Cone 8 miles east." Another sign informs you, "Main Fork Trail No. 56, Horseshoe Lake 5 miles ahead, Lost Lake 5 miles ahead."

The trail surface is still excellent and the gradient uphill, but easy. A small stream crosses from the left, with good drinking water at 5.0 miles. At 5.1 miles the route crosses a nice size stream on a wooden bridge. The water here is plentiful and good for drinking and this is a good spot for a rest stop.

Beyond the bridge the trail has been rerouted. The course it takes from 5.1 to 7.6 miles, as plotted on the map, is only approximate, estimated from my field notes. As I passed through the area I didn't notice the junction with the path that the maps show as Lost Lake Trail (now abandoned). A forest of conifers envelops the trail as it climbs out of the valley with an easy grade. The route crosses a small stream at 5.6 miles and passes a marshy area at 6.7 miles. There is a good view from a rock slide at 6.8 miles that provides an opening in the forest, and another good viewpoint at 7.0 miles looking across the forest to the northeast and to the mountains to the north and northwest.

There is a small bridge at 7.2 miles and a Wheeler Peak Wilderness sign at 7.3 miles. Another wooden bridge down in a small canyon crosses an energetic stream. This marks the camping area at 7.7 miles. After you cross the bridge, there is a good campsite in the trees immediately ahead, or go upstream to camp in the open, grassy areas.

Plan to spend a couple of nights here. There is plenty of good water and firewood and the area is not nearly as heavily used as that around Lost Lake.

Two hundred feet uphill from the campsite and bridge is a trail junction. The left fork takes you up past Horseshoe Lake to Wheeler Peak, which is the way you want to go when you climb the peak. The right fork (Middle Fork Trail No. 91) goes to Lost Lake, and on down to where you left the car. On your hike, after crossing Wheeler Peak and dropping down to Lost Lake, you will return to camp on this trail. A sign on the left, says, "Horseshoe Lake 1 (south), Lost Lake 1 (north)." Another sign pointing back the way you came from says, "East Fork, Red River."

It will be a good day's hike from camp to Wheeler Peak and back, so get an early start. Carry at least a canteen of water per person and if the day is expected to be warm you may need more. To be prepared for the capricious weather on the high ridges carry some warm clothes and rain jacket too. The summit is a good place to spend some time enjoying your triumph, having some lunch, and soaking up the fantastic panorama.

Horseshoe Lake Dam is at 8.7 miles. A sign here says, "Wheeler Peak 3 (ahead), Lost Lake 2 (behind)." There is a good view of Wheeler Peak to the southwest from here. An unmarked trail joins from the left at 9.2 miles. You get a good view of Old Mike Peak across the valley to the south, as you cross the ridge south of Horseshoe Lake. On the south side of this ridge the trail climbs slowly but steadily to the ridge crest just south of Wheeler Peak. The ridge crest trail is reached at 10.1 miles. Turn right to go to Wheeler Peak or left if you want to take a side trip to Old Mike and areas beyond.

Don't miss the turnoff to Wheeler Peak at 10.6 miles. The crest trail passes below the summit on the east side and as soon as it gets on top of the ridge crest again a side trail on the left doubles back to the summit, 250 yards away. You will be well aware that the air up here is thin and will welcome the rest and lunch break on the summit, 13,161 feet above sea level.

When you leave the summit go north on the crest trail. The next peak the route crosses is Mt. Walter, at 11.0 miles. You get a good view of Horseshoe Lake from along here. At 11.5 miles you depart from the trail, which would take you down to Bull of the Woods and Taos Ski Basin (see Hike #21). Follow along the ridge crest (no trail) that goes a little east of north, to the right of the Crest Trail No. 90. At 12.5 miles you will be immediately above Lost Lake. It is a very steep drop, with no trail, so be careful as you work your way down to Lost Lake. The upper end of the lake is at 13.0 miles. A trail takes you around the south side of the lake to Middle Fork Trail No. 91. Turn right (south) on T-91 and return to camp, which you will reach at 14.0 miles.

Spend as many days as you like in this area or at Lost Lake. When you get ready to hike to the car, go north on T-91 past Lost Lake (14.7 miles at the dam). The abandoned Lost Lake Trail is seen to the right at 15.1 miles and 100 yards farther along is a wilderness boundary sign. There is another wilderness boundary sign at 16.2 miles. The route follows near the ridge crest until about 16.5 miles where it starts to switchback and lose elevation more quickly.

At 18.8 miles the trail joins a road which runs alongside a stream; the Middle Fork of Red River. Turn right (downstream). Trail 91 goes upstream at this junction to Middle Fork Lake. A sign here says, "Middle Fork Trail No. 91, Lost Lake 4 (the direction you came from), Middle Fork Lake 1 (upstream, south)."

Follow the road down to the bridge that takes you across stream to the car, at mile 19.8. You will probably be glad it is waiting nearby.

To get to this hike, go to the town of Red River. As you go south out of town the road forks; N.M. 38 goes left and F.R. 58 goes right. Take F.R. 58 and go south to the junction with F.R. 58A at 5.1 miles from the road fork. If you plan to drop off some hikers and packs at the Ditch Cabin parking area, turn left on 58A. If not, continue the additional 1.4 miles to the Middle Fork/West Fork parking lot.

*Horseshoe Lake and the forested valley of the East
Fork of Red River from near the summit of Wheeler
Peak.*

113

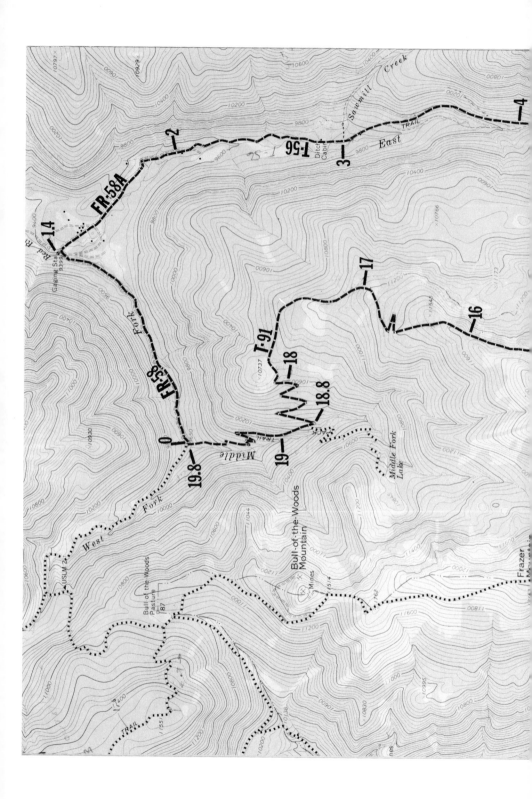

114

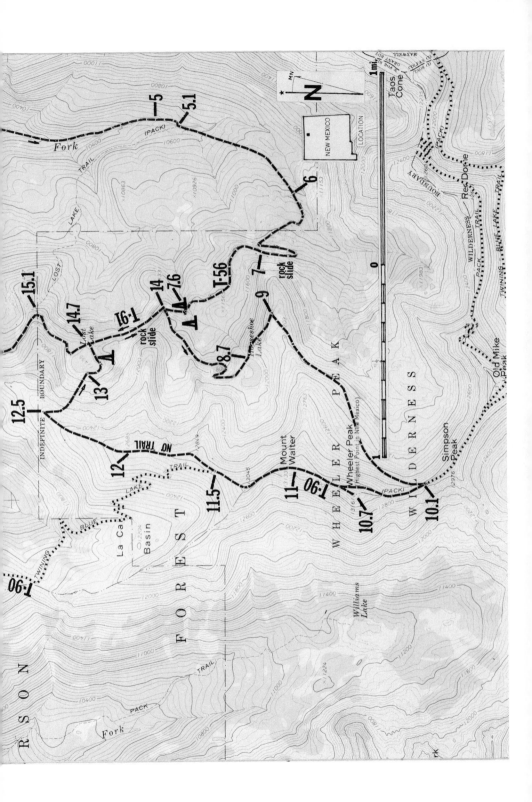

21 WHEELER PEAK FROM TAOS SKI BASIN
CARSON NATIONAL FOREST

Distance: 14.4 miles round-trip
Time: 10 to 16 hours round-trip, with a day-pack
Elevation Range: 9,400 to 13,161 feet
Rating: Strenuous, due to distance and high altitude (good trail-finding skills and map reading abilities needed at lower elevations)
Water: Carry some. Available at 4.7 miles (11,760 feet)
Seasons: Possibly May through October, but depends on snow
Topographic Map: Wheeler Peak
Special Map: Carson National Forest, Grid K3
Permit: None required for day-hiking but is required for overnight

This route makes it possible for you to climb the highest peak in New Mexico in one day, round-trip, though you should spend more time in this enchanting area if possible. This Wheeler Peak hike is a very popular one and is regarded as a must for those people who do much hiking. In spite of its popularity, this route at its beginning (across private land) is one of the poorest marked and confusing in the state. And, it is worse coming down than going up.

The trail surface is good and gradients are generally not too steep. At higher elevations the route gets rocky, but this is to be expected. The scenery is outstanding, with vistas from high ridges above timberline across the varied and interesting country below.

Weather on the mountain is capricious, so be prepared for rain and cold, as well as warm and sunshine. I have seen people well along toward the summit retreating because they didn't bring rain gear or warm clothing. Ultraviolet radiation is intense at high altitudes, so wear protective clothing or use sunscreen if you are prone to sunburn. A companion on one of my climbs wore shorts on a cloudy day, and had a bad burn on her legs before we reached the summit.

On the privately owned land at lower elevations the trail turns, forks, merges, joins roads, departs from roads, crosses roads and roads join, cross, branch, etc. without adequate markings. Comments in the register at the summit indicate that many of the hikers thought they had reached the summit in spite of the trail problems, which they felt were the greatest hardships of the hike. Hikers on the summit swap tales of the experiences they had in trying to follow the route, and the doubts

they had when they were actually on the right track. Need I say more? In spite of these problems, two dozen or more hikers may reach the summit on a summer Sunday. If you have problems, watch for other hikers who can give you assistance. Or, you can use map and compass to set your own cross-country course or to make decisions at trail/road junctions.

The hike starts from a parking lot at the end of N.M. 230 (F.R. 58). The pavement ends just before the road ends at a gravel loop and parking lot. The trailhead is at the left side of a sign at the parking area that says, "Follow colored arrows to Wheeler Peak Trail. Permit required for overnight use only." Please note that there are no colored arrows helping you find the route down, and not nearly enough on the way up.

The following notes may be of some help in getting you to the summit. It is also important that as you proceed on the way up, try to remember the side trails, junctions, roads, etc. so it will be easier to make the correct choices coming down. When you have walked 700 feet up the route from the parking lot, you will have crossed a small stream and some small paths and will come to a section of trail that may be flooded. Keep to the left of the flooded section and rejoin the route higher up, where it is dry again.

You cross an abandoned road or power line route at 0.7 mile and at 0.73 mile is a red arrow on an aspen tree pointing the way to the left (west). There is a trail sign lying on the ground at 0.87 mile, showing Long Canyon Trail going west to Gold Hill 4.5 miles and to Goose Canyon four miles. There is also a "No Vehicles" sign here. Fifty feet farther along is another sign that points ahead to "Bull of the Woods Pasture 1 mile" and "Goose Canyon 4 miles." Follow the route to Bull of the Woods. Another red arrow at 0.94 mile points left (north). Go the direction it points and you will shortly come to a small road. Go left, uphill, on the road. An additional arrow at 1.0 mile points to the right along the road, which turns to the right at this point. There is a second arrow here, on a post nearby, indicating an optional route. Don't take this route, as the trail is an obstacle course of fallen trees, and it shortly comes out on the road again. The road continues a bit north of east, to Bull of the Woods pasture. At 2.1 miles the route flattens out and you see the level green pasture ahead. There is a road junction here, with a small one coming from the right. Turn right (south) on this small road. A sign at this junction says, "Bear Lake Trail No. 90, Wheeler Peak 6 miles (SE), and Bear Lake 10 miles (SE)."

A hundred feet or so east of this junction, toward the pasture, is a sign. It says, "Gold Hill Trail No. 64, Gold Hill 3 (north), Red River City 11 miles north." The Gold Hill Trail has been designated as a portion of the National Trails System, and could be an optional addition to this hike.

Go south on the road toward Wheeler Peak Trail. A couple of hundred feet along, going south, the road forks again. This time take the fork to the left, uphill.

At 2.6 miles, on the ridge crest, there are good views to both right and left. Continue straight ahead (an arrow in a tree to the left points ahead). The road forks again at 2.8 miles and again you go left, uphill. Soon you leave the road and follow the trail, which is easy to follow from here, to the summit.

A post without a sign is passed at 3.6 miles and you enter the wilderness area at 3.7 miles. Along here the trail is on the west side of an open slope and at 4.2 miles it crosses the end of a recently bulldozed road.

A sign on the crest, above timberline at 4.3 miles says, "Bear Lake Trail 7 miles south, Taos Ski Valley 6 miles (north, where you just came from)." There is water in a stream the trail crosses at 5.1 miles, after it drops into a forested area in a high valley. There is good camping here among the trees, with the water nearby. You may be tempted to leave the trail and avoid dropping down to cross the stream by climbing up to the ridge or skirt the valley at

A short side hike on a ridge to the east from the summit ridge will afford this view of Lost Lake on the route of Hike #20.

constant elevation, but it is easier to just remain on the trail.

The trail crosses Mt. Walter, 13,141 feet at 6.9 miles. This mountain was named for H.D. Walker "who loved these mountains." Wheeler Peak summit is at 7.2 miles. It is 13,161 feet, highest point in New Mexico. The peak was "named in honor of Major George M. Wheeler (1832-1909) who, for 10 years led a party of surveyors and naturalists collecting geologic and biological, planimetric, and topographical data."

Don't spend too long on the summit and have to negotiate the lower portion of the trail after dark. When the weather is pleasant and clear, the temptation to linger and enjoy the magnificent scenery and the feeling of being on top of the world may win over your better judgment to leave soon. A better plan would be to camp at Bull of the Woods or in the forest by the stream at 5.1 miles. This would permit you to spend more time on the summit, and/or hike on over to Old Mike Peak, and to explore the Gold Hill Trail, etc.

Your return trip will take about half as long as the climb if you retrace the route you came up. By looking over the terrain between the summit and Twining (where you parked the car) you may decide to make the return more directly, cross-country. If you decide to try this, be sure you will be able to navigate when you get down into the forested area.

To get to this hike, go about 3.5 miles north of the center of Taos on N.M. 3 and turn north onto N.M. 150/N.M. 230 (F.R. 58). Follow this road 15 miles to Twining (Taos Ski Valley). The hike starts at the parking area at the end of this road.

This summit ridge drops down to the north to Bull-of-the-Woods meadow, in the valley, at the extreme right.

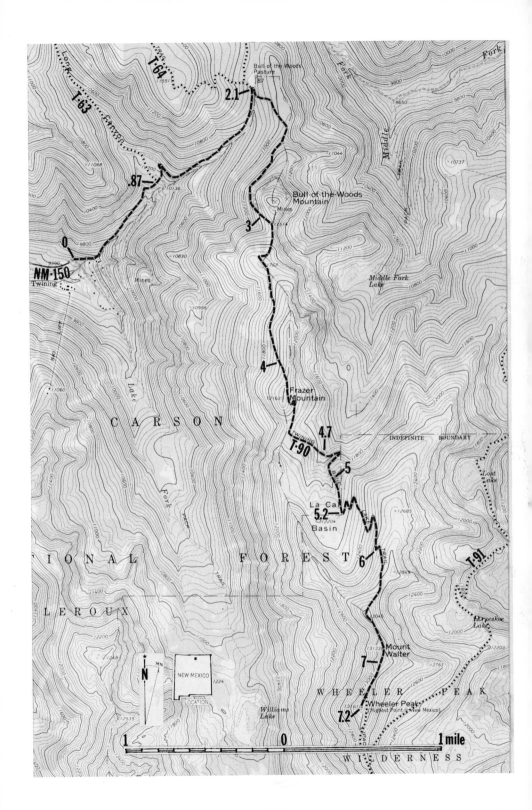

22 BORREGO, RIO NAMBE, AND RIO CAPULIN TRAILS
SANTA FE NATIONAL FOREST

Distance: 8.71 miles round-trip
Time: 4½ to 6 hours, day-hiking, longer with pack for camping overnight
Elevation Range: 9,200 to 7,680 feet
Rating: Moderate
Water: Rio Nambe and Rio Capulin are reliable sources, but must be treated
Seasons: April through November. When F.R. 150 is closed by snow at higher elevations you
  can try it from the west and near Tesuque (don't hike in hunting season, October and
  November)
Topographic Map: Aspen Basin
Special Map: Santa Fe National Forest, Grid J7

This is a nice hike through forest and along stream side that gets you away from civilization, but is only a 30 minute drive from Santa Fe. Leave the car at the sign under the power line on the ridge. The trail sign there says, "Trail 150, Rio Nambe 1¾, Rancho Viejo 3."

From the trailhead go north on Borrego Trail No. 150. It is wide and well used, with some rocky places. The path is through a coniferous forest and goes rather steeply downhill all the way to Rio Nambe, 1.71 miles distant.

At the trail junction beside the stream there are signs giving directions and distances to various places. Go left, downstream, on Rio Nambe Trail toward La Junta. There are a few river crossings along the way. The stream bed has willows and oak brush, in addition to conifers, growing near the stream. Fishermen may want to try their luck in both streams. You travel 1.43 miles from T-150 to Rio Capulin and T-158. There is a nice open area for camping where the streams join, at 3.14 miles.

From the confluence of the streams, T-158 goes upstream (northeast) along the north side of Rio Capulin. A path crosses the stream to the south side at 3.29 miles, but it would be best to continue on the north side for another three-quarter mile or so. After the path enters a clearing at 4.1 miles, it fades away and this is a suitable place to cross to the south side.

The path on the south side takes you past some log cabins that are situated on a broad, grassy terrace well above the stream bed. This portion of the valley is privately owned, so leave the cabin remains alone. At 4.66 miles is part of another cabin. To the north, across the stream, are some low, sandy hills. In the edge of the forest at 4.67 miles, a short distance past

the last cabin, is the junction with T-150. Two trail signs mark the routes and give distances to various places. Go south on T-150, unless you want to take an optional route farther upstream.

Borrego Trail No. 150 is well-traveled and easy to follow. The route south is dry, and at times hot. It passes through ponderosa and oak brush, up over a ridge and down to Rio Nambe at 6.9 miles. When you get to Rio Nambe turn right (west) and go about 0.1 mile downstream to close the loop at 7.0 miles. The 1.7 miles south on T-150 to the car is all uphill.

To get to this hike from Santa Fe take N.M. 475 (Forest Road 101), the route to the ski basin. About 13 miles out of Santa Fe turn left (north) on F.R. 102. This gravel road forks 3.1 miles after you leave the pavement. Take the right fork, which is F.R. 412 and go 1.9 miles to a confusing intersection. Do not take the road to the right unless you want to visit the remains of Aspen Ranch. Parallel routes go north, the direction you should go to get to the trailhead. A few yards past the intersection there is an Aspen Ranch sign on the right. About 0.7 mile north from the turnoff to Aspen Ranch the road comes to the trail sign on the ridge, under the power line. The road makes a sharp turn to the right and continues. Be sure you get on the trail, and not on an old mine or logging road 100 feet or so to the east.

This is a beautiful area. Enjoy your hike.

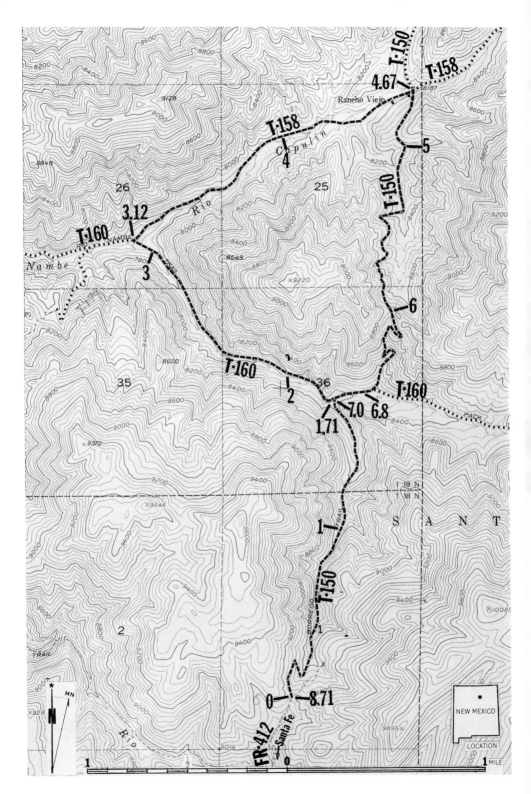

Remains of a log cabin (on private land) which
overlooks Rio Capulin. The junction of T-158 and
T-150 is in the trees beyond.

23 WINDSOR TRAIL TO SANTA FE BALDY PEAK
PECOS WILDERNESS
SANTA FE NATIONAL FOREST

Distance: 14.7 miles round-trip
Time: 6 to 12 hours
Elevation Range: 10,200 to 12,622 feet
Rating: Easy to moderate
Water: At 2.5 miles in Rio Nambe and at 3.5 miles in East Upper Nambe
Seasons: Usually April through November, depends on snow
Topographic Maps: Aspen Basin, Cowles
Special Maps: Santa Fe National Forest, Grid J7; Pecos Wilderness Guide
Permit: Required for day-hiking and for camping in Pecos Wilderness

This is a popular hike that takes you to the top of one of the highest peaks in the state. It is quite scenic, with conifer and aspen forests at the lower levels and open grassy slopes above timberline, near the summit. The unforested summit gives the feeling of being on top of the world, with big vistas in all directions.

The hike along Windsor Trail No. 254 starts at the Santa Fe Ski Basin parking lot. There are good signs here, marking the way along Trails Nos. 254 and 251.

At the beginning the trail is wide and well-maintained. It is relatively steep for the first half-mile to the Wilderness Boundary, near the top of the ridge at about 11,000 feet. The vegetation along this section of the route is predominantly fir mixed with aspen stands, and occasional meadows. From the Wilderness Boundary, the trail is level or slightly downhill to Rio Nambe, at 10,600 feet (2.6 miles). You probably won't see Trail No. 403 that forks to the left at 1.5 miles. From here the route remains at about constant elevation on the north slope of the mountain and crosses another fork of the river in a relatively flat area, at 3.8 miles. From the river the route climbs and turns north. At 4.3 miles there is a sign post marking the junction with Nambe Trail No. 160, which goes to the left (west). Two hundred feet or so beyond this junction the Windsor Trail turns sharply from a NNW direction to southeast. Shortly the terrain flattens in an old burn area with scattered 20 foot high firs around. This is about the 4.5 mile point and there is good camping in many places near here. This is about a half-mile from the water in Rio Nambe and is close to an intermittent stream to the north, which makes this an ideal place to spend a night or two. It is an easy hike from the campsite to the ridge

(5.0 miles) which takes you directly to the summit of Santa Fe Baldy.

To get to the summit, depart from the trail on the crest of the ridge. It is obvious when you are there because the trail continuing east starts downhill and you can see that there is no other ridge in that direction that is as high up as you are. Turn left (north) from the trail (5.0 miles) and follow the crest of the ridge all the way to the summit, two miles distant and 1,500 feet higher (7.2 miles).

The summit and much of the upper portion of the ridge are without trees. This provides excellent vistas in all directions, and on the summit you can see the whole Pecos Wilderness to the north and east.

This trip can be a day-hike for most people, who are in reasonably good physical condition. It should take eight to 10 hours, not including the time you spend on the summit, or long stops along the way. If you plan to lunch at the top, be sure to take along some warm clothing to protect you from the cold wind which usually is blowing up there. You should also be prepared for rain, particularly in late summer.

Inquire at the Siler Road office of the Forest Service south of town in Santa Fe for camping rules, and get your permit and maps of Santa Fe National Forest and Visitor's Guide to Pecos Wilderness. Permits are required for camping in Pecos Wilderness and may be required for day-hiking too. All lake basins in the area have been closed to camping in recent years.

To get to this hike take N.M. 475, F.R. 101, from Santa Fe to the Santa Fe Ski Basin. Just prior to arriving at the ski basin, signs mark the trail, which departs in a north-easterly direction.

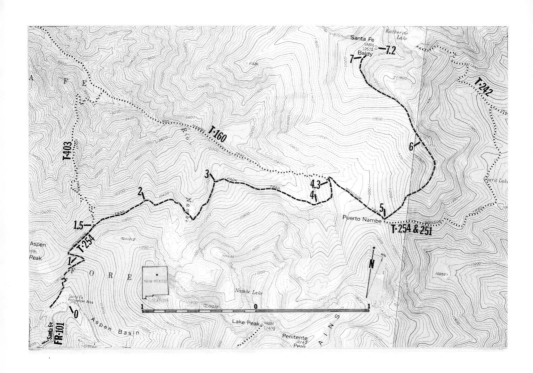

Santa Fe Baldy from Windsor Trail at Nambe Creek Lake. Photo by Joe Repa.

24 FOREST ROAD 150
SANTA FE NATIONAL FOREST

Distance: 13.2 miles round-trip (you can shorten it if this is too far)
Time: 5 to 9 hours round-trip, or you can camp along the way or at the top
Elevation Range: 10,000 to 12,040 feet
Rating: Easy
Water: Two places, three-quarter mile and 2.5 miles
Seasons: All — hike when there is no snow; cross-country ski when there is
Topographic Map: Aspen Basin
Special Map: Santa Fe National Forest, Grid J7

This trail is significant for a number of reasons. It is very popular in aspen season (late September) when the leaves are turning, because it provides such good access to view the fall colors. It is an excellent cross-country skiing trail because it is along a wide path (roadway) with good gradients. It is near the city of Santa Fe, on a good road that is kept open all year. And, it is a good, scenic hiking route.

The hike starts adjacent to Aspen Vista Picnic Area parking lot. It has a locked gate and only vehicles going to the radio transmitter tower are permitted on the road. The route starts in a mixed forest of conifers and aspen, and continues in this type forest for a half-mile. The forest then becomes predominantly aspen. The aspen forest continues for about 1.5 miles. This is the area that is so popular in late September.

After the large aspen forest, the vegetation for the next three-quarters mile or so consists primarily of fir trees. The fir forest is followed by one to 1.5 miles of relatively open ridge, with only scattered trees. The remainder of the route is through intermittent patches of conifers and open areas along the high ridge.

The route is essentially working up the side of a mountain to radio transmitter towers. It passes the top end of a ski lift near the top of the mountain.

There is water at three-quarters mile in a stream which crosses under the road in a culvert, and again at 2.5 miles, near the edge of the aspen forest. There are good campsites all along the way, including the top of the mountain.

There are many view points to the west of the Jemez Mountains and the Rio Grande Valley. From the top you can see in all directions. You look over the Pecos Wilderness to the northeast and to the south to see the Sandia Mountains.

To get to this hike, take N.M. 475 (F.R. 101) out of Santa Fe toward the Santa Fe Ski Basin. At about 13.5 miles from the city, turn off to the right, into Aspen Vista Picnic Area parking area. Leave the car there. The hike starts at the locked metal gate adjacent to the picnic area.

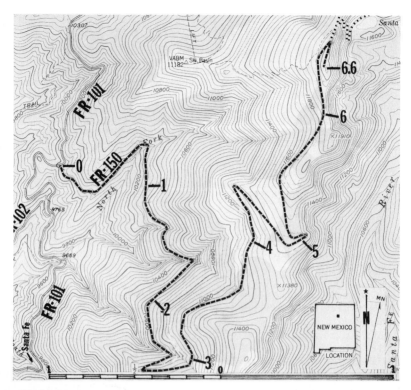

Forest Road 150 provides excellent year-round outdoor experiences. In the fall, particularly, this is a favorite route for many Santa Fe area residents to hike and view the brilliant foliage of the aspen trees. In winter and early spring it affords excellent skiing.

25 ELK MOUNTAIN, PECOS WILDERNESS AREA
SANTA FE NATIONAL FOREST

Distance: 7.8 miles one-way
Time: 6 to 9 hours up, 4 to 7 hours down; plan to camp overnight
Elevation Range: 8,600 to 11,661 feet
Rating: Moderate to strenuous
Water: As noted
Seasons: Usually May through October, but depends on snow
Topographic Maps: Porvenir, Honey Boy, Rociada, Elk Mountain
Special Maps: Santa Fe National Forest, Grid 7L, 8M; Pecos Wilderness Sportsman's Map
Permit: Required for remaining overnight in Pecos Wilderness

It is a scenic drive on a good road from Las Vegas into the Sangre de Cristo Mountains for this hike. Camping is permitted at the trailhead, but Porvenir Campground back down the road a piece (9.0 miles) is better, with facilities. In case you decide to camp at the trailhead, there are a few nice places a short distance up the trail, alongside the stream. If you camp here, or any place else, take care and don't pollute or litter.

Trail 216 starts from the small, circular parking area at road's end. The route follows the stream up Gallinas Canyon for 2.5 miles, crossing it 14 times in that distance. Signs at the trailhead inform you that permits are required to enter Pecos Wilderness Area, and Burro Basin is four miles, Elk Mountain is seven miles. The path is fairly narrow in places, but is good hiking and easy to follow. It will be a challenge to keep your feet dry if there is much water in the stream. Typical of the Pecos Wilderness, the area is usually moist and the vegetation green and abundant, and the streams are dependable sources of water.

There are good campsites at many places along the way, and you should plan to use some of them. The hike would be more enjoyable if you take two or three days, rather than making the strenuous rush up and back the same day. At the beginning, Gallinas Canyon is rather narrow, but it opens up some at about two miles, and the grade continues to be easy. The trail departs the stream at 2.5 miles and becomes steep, going up out of the drainage to the top of the ridge. You cross the ridge crest just before the three mile point and then begin to drop into Burro Canyon.

The trail crosses the stream at 3.6 miles. This is the last dependable place to get drinking water, so get what you will need for the remainder of the trip. Fifty yards beyond

the stream are a couple of trail signs. One, pointing northwest, the way you want to go, says, "Burro Basin Trail 216, Elk Mountain 2." The other, pointing the way you just came from, says, "Burro Basin Trail 216, Gallinas Canyon 1 — Valley 7."

The trail beyond the signs is difficult to follow as it passes through a grassy and sometimes marshy meadow. A few posts help mark the way. Be particularly observant on your return to this place because the trail going from the meadow to the signs, in the trees, is not easy to see and you will be so intent on following the path through the grass (it continues downstream) that you will miss the turn. A small pile of brush across the path in the grass should alert you to look for the turn. When you look around you should see the signs, to the right toward the stream. Remember, the return route turns to the right just as soon as you come to the trees at the downstream end of the grassy, marshy area.

Continuing, the trail ducks back into the forest at 4.17 miles, and climbs rather steeply to the north to its junction with Trail No. 218 at 4.55 miles. Signs at the junction say, "Trail No. 216, Burro Canyon ½, Gallinas Creek 4½ (the direction you just came from)" and "Trail 218, Skyline Trail 1½ (to the left, where you are headed), Harvey Ranch 4 (to the right)." At 4.95 miles, the route crosses a jeep road. If you go left on this road you quickly come to a couple of interesting log cabins. If you continue on the trail instead, you will miss the cabins. The jeep trail turns to the right just beyond the cabins and the trail joins it at 5.04 miles. It appears that the trail might cross the jeep road at 5.04 miles, but the path that continues soon plays out. Follow the jeep road another 40 yards to where it crosses another jeep road. Turn left on the other road and remember this intersection so you won't miss it on the return trip. If you need water, there is a small stream from a spring downhill to the left of the road about 60 yards at about 5.2 miles.

The road you are on goes through a gate at a fence line, and joins Skyline Trail at 6.52 miles. There is a nice campground in the forest to the right. Trail No. 251 goes to the north through the campground. Don't be surprised if you see a vehicle here, because four-wheel drives and pickups can drive on Skyline Trail to this point, and on up toward the summit. Turn left, uphill, just after you go through the gate and follow the two-track up the ridge. You are getting close to timberline here, so much of the remainder of the route is through open, grassy meadows, skirting the clumps of trees. At 6.86 miles you are in the open area and have a magnificent view to the west of the mountains on both sides of the Pecos River Valley. Santa Fe Baldy is to the WNW and Cowles is in the valley midway between you and the distant mountain. To the northwest is Pecos Baldy and farther north along the same ridge are the Truchas Peaks. You are looking over an area that surely must be one of the most beautiful parts of New Mexico.

There is a splendid area for camping (no water) in the open forest on the ridge at 6.93 miles. A barricade across the road at 7.22 miles limits vehicle travel beyond this point to those going up to service the microwave tower on the summit of Elk Mountain. The trail crosses through a fence to the left. You can follow the

trail, which shortly joins the road and follow the road as it takes the long way to the summit. Or, it is shorter and is easy going to cut cross-country, SSE, to the ridge top and pick up the road on its final switchback to the top. At 7.52 miles the road makes a 90 degree switch to the left. The summit is attained at 7.78 miles. The view from here is enchanting, with the previously mentioned peaks to the northwest, and Hermits Peak (Hike #26) to the east, and plenty of other fine scenery in between.

Trail Nos. 218 and 251 and Skyline Trail (the road) offer some optional hikes if you can spend the extra time, with a base camp set up near the junction of whatever route you hike. There is no water along the Crest Trail No. 251, to the north, so be sure you carry plenty if you make this hike.

To get to Hike #25, start in Las Vegas from U.S. 84 (I-25). Get on N.M. 65 going northwest from Las Vegas. Finding N.M. 65 in Las Vegas isn't as easy as it could be, but there are a few signs. The road distances were measured from the central plaza in the northwest part of downtown Las Vegas. Go northwest on N.M. 65 from the plaza and follow signs to El Porvenir. At 5.1 miles go left to N.M. 65/F.R. 263 toward El Porvenir, and go left again at 13.7 miles. You have a choice of directions at 15.9 miles, depending on your immediate plans. To get to the trailhead go left on F.R. 263 and continue to road's end at 22.7 miles. If you want to camp at nearby Porvenir Campground before making the hike turn to the right on N.M. 65.

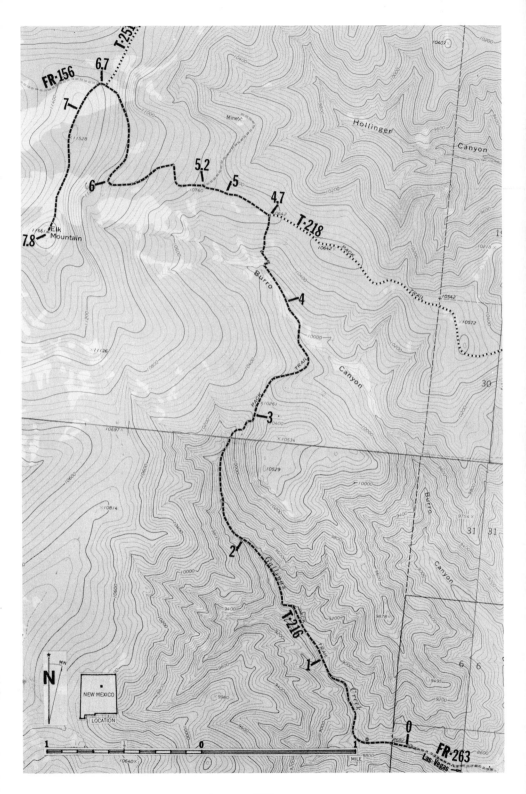

Time has taken its toll of these once-comfortable log houses, which can be seen at 5.0 miles on this hike.

View west-northwest from the summit of Elk Mountain. Pecos Baldy is to the left and Truches Peaks are right of center, on the horizon.

26 HERMIT'S PEAK
SANTA FE NATIONAL FOREST

Distance: 13.4 miles plus side hikes
Time: 7 to 14 hours
Elevation Range: 7,510 to 10,250 feet
Rating: Moderate
Water: Yes, as indicated
Seasons: Usually May through October, but depends on snow. Trail No. 233 gets less snow, so would open earlier and close later than No. 219
Topographic Maps: El Porvenir, Rociada
Special Maps: Santa Fe National Forest, Grid 7M, 8M; Pecos Wilderness Sportsman's Map

Trail No. 219 takes you into the typical lush, green well-watered Pecos Wilderness. The Hermit Peak portion offers a change of environment to the drier, piñon-juniper forest.

This hike starts at Porvenir Campground. There is plenty of room to leave the car here, and you can stay here before and after the hike. It is 0.3 mile back to the trailhead, along the road, from the campground. The trail sign here says, "Trail No. 219, Porvenir Canyon, Bollinger Canyon, Beaver Creek."

The route goes northwest up Porvenir Canyon along the southwest side of the stream. Occasionally you get a glimpse of sheer red cliffs on the southeast side of Hermit Peak, and can see where Porvenir Canyon narrows.

The first stream crossing, at about one-half mile, is via a good log bridge. The next crossings are on logs and rocks. There are good campsites in the large flat, open forest area by the stream, with a good view of the cliffs and peaks. There are shelters with tin roofs here, at 0.95 mile. Also, there are the remains of a log cabin with fireplace. The trail so far has been wide, well defined, and easy walking.

There is a natural rock shelter to the right of the trail at 1.6 miles which could offer shelter from the weather. A small waterfall is on the other side of the trail from the shelter. At about two miles there are many good campsites at intervals. There is a good campsite with a small waterfall and swimming hole at 2.4 miles at the fifth stream crossing. You enter Pecos Wilderness Area (vehicles prohibited sign) at 2.6 miles. The trail is still very good, with an easy grade, at 3.0 miles, and you cross the stream for the 10th time. Soon the canyon gets very narrow and steep-walled, giving you

a closed-in feeling. You cross the stream for the 20th time at 4.0 miles, and the canyon widens at 4.1 miles at the 22nd crossing. Shortly there are good campsites along the stream in the flat, green valley floor. A log fence with a gate crosses the path at 4.5 miles.

The trail is out of the rock-walled canyon and into a V-shaped, forested valley at 4.4 miles. You come to the junction of Trail No. 219 and Trail No. 247 at 2.6 miles. Signs say, "Trail No. 219, Hollinger Creek (west-northwest), Elk Mountain 10 mi. (WNW)" and "Trail No. 247, Beaver Creek (north), Skyline Trail 8 mi. (north)." The junction is in a wide, flat place in the valley, and an extremely good place to camp.

Take Trail No. 247 north, up the valley. The grade is still gentle and the path is fairly distinct in the grass and flowers, thanks to its use by cows. So far it has been a pleasant hike, with beautiful surroundings, good trail and easy going.

At five miles the route is still in the valley, but not for long. There are blazes on some trees at 5.1 miles. A post in a big pile of rocks at 5.3 miles marks a trail fork. Trail No. 214 continues up the valley. Take Trail No. 247 to the right, up the hillside toward Trail No. 223 on top of the ridge. You leave water behind here and won't find any more until you get to Hermit Spring, on the far side of the peak, so fill up. This uphill portion of No. 247 appears to be fairly new and is easy to follow, but the grade is steep. It averages 21 percent from T-214 to ridge crest and is a constant uphill pull.

The trail tops out on the ridge at 6.2 miles. There are two posts here at the intersection with Trail No. 223. One post doesn't have a sign on it, but the sign on the other one says,

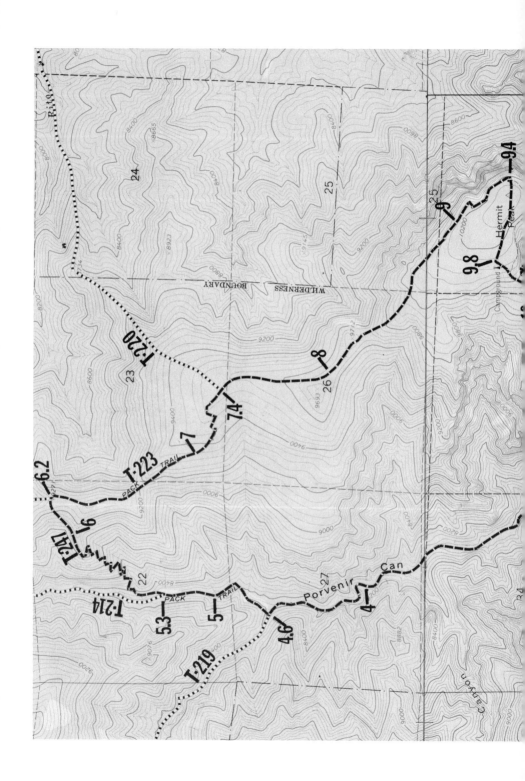

132

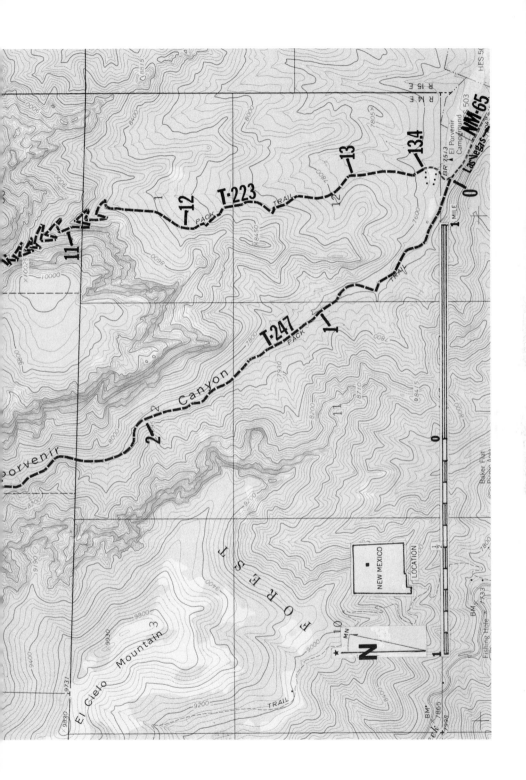

"Sapello Creek (north), Beaver Creek and Hollinger Canyon (back the way you just came from)."

Go south on the ridge on Trail No. 223. You cross through a fence and shortly the trail becomes rather indistinct in spots, at about 6.4 miles. Continue south on top of the ridge.

There is a trail sign at 7.4 miles which says, "Trail No. 223, Hermit's Peak 2 mi. (southeast), Lone Pine Mesa 4 mi. (NW), Beaver Creek 2 mi. (NW where you just came from)." Another sign points north to "Trail No. 220, San Ignacio 6 mi." Continue southeast along the ridge on No. 223, and just past 8.0 miles is a small, open saddle which would be a good campsite if you needed to stop here (there is better camping on Hermit's Peak).

At 9.4 miles you are on a big flat area near the top of Hermit's Peak, and there is a sign by the trail with an arrow pointing southwest to Hermit's Cave. Dump your pack here or nearby and walk east to the edge of the mesa at the top of the high, sheer cliffs and take in the big view. Good campsites are everywhere near the summit of the peak.

If you want to visit Hermit's Cave, it is a 0.9 mile side trip, if you don't make a wrong turn or two. The route is a bit hard to follow in places, making the cave difficult to find. From the sign with the arrow, go southwest on a wide trail to the edge of the mesa, back up about 100 feet, and go right (west) on a small trail that goes downhill. A quarter of a mile from the first sign with an arrow is another pointing to Hermit's Cave. You will soon start seeing large wooden crosses, standing and fallen, that reportedly were erected by a religious group.

It is reported that the religious Penitentes still crucify and flagellate members of their cult. This all dates back to the Penitent Hermit who supposedly lived in the cave (or another cave that is reported to be up here also). He knew herbs and helped the Indians when he came down from the mountain every few weeks for supplies and to doctor the people. He was murdered by marauding Indians from another area. The cave doesn't appear to be a good place to camp.

On return to the first Hermit's Cave sign go west about 100 yards to a trail sign, "Trail No. 223, Beaver Creek 4 mi. (north), Lone Pine Mesa 6 mi. (north)." Continue west. There is a large cross nearby, and more along the way. The trail is very wide, heavily used, and quite rocky. About 0.4 mile from the cave sign you come to a concrete and stone box with a metal lid. A sign says, "Hermit's Spring." There is good, cold water inside. A short distance down the trail is another sign, "Trail No. 223, El Porvenir Campground 4 mi." The trail down is very rocky and heavily used. About 0.6 mile below Hermit's Spring another small spring flows across the trail. You cross this trickle a couple of times in the next half-mile. A wilderness boundary sign is encountered between the two stream crossings at 11.1 miles. Trail gradient eases some at about 12.0 miles.

The route forks at 12.75 miles. Go left, and at 12.9 miles you are alongside a stream. This hike ends at Porvenir Campground at 13.4 miles.

To get to this hike, go to Las Vegas on I-25/U.S. 84. From U.S. 84 get on N.M. 65 in Las Vegas. This isn't easy, so you will have to turn northwest on N.M. 3 and go to about the second red light, going uphill. Watch signs carefully, as one points left to N.M. 65. The route passes a park in the center of town, which is the point to measure driving distances from. Go northwest on N.M. 65 and follow signs to El Porvenir. At 5.1 miles go left and at 13.7 miles take the left fork on F.R. 263/N.M. 65. At 15.9 miles keep right on N.M. 65 to El Porvenir and continue on N.M. 65 to the campground (18.4 miles).

134

The dark gash in the cliff, on the left, is the entrance to Hermit's Cave.

27 MILLS CANYON
KIOWA GRASSLAND UNIT OF PANHANDLE GRASSLANDS

Distance: Up to 6 miles one-way upstream or 13 miles downstream (3 miles from canyon rim to campground at river)

Time: Depends on distance hiked; at 1½ miles per hour average speed, the 26 mile trip downstream and back would take about 17 hours without any long stops (this should be at least a two day trip)

Elevation Range: 5,200 feet upstream, 5,100 feet at campground, 5,000 feet downstream, and 5,800 feet on the canyon rim

Rating: Easy to moderate, depending on distance; easier on horseback

Water: The river always has water, but it is sometimes muddy; best to bring your own

Seasons: All, but you can be cold in winter; snow closes the road at times

Topographic Maps: Beaver Canyon, Mills West, Canyon Colorado

Special Maps: U.S. Dept. of Agriculture's "Panhandle National Grasslands" (Kiowa National Grasslands)

Mills Canyon is one of those pieces of public land that almost nobody knows about. Chances are that if you see anyone else in the canyon when you are there, they will be local residents who came there to catch the catfish (reported to be big and numerous) in the Canadian River, which made the canyon. This is a good place to plan to stay a few days and explore and hike around, and be alone. To make certain that you'll be alone, bring plenty of insect repellent, as there are times when you may need it. As you approach the canyon, through rolling, rough ranch land, there is no indication of what lies ahead. Mills Canyon is steep-walled in many places, about 700 feet deep, and possibly a mile wide in the portion encompassed by the grasslands. The road does not provide a dramatic view from the canyon rim. It works its way down a side canyon and is probably halfway down to river level before you can see into the canyon. But even from this elevated position, the road affords an impressive view of the canyon's rugged beauty, both upstream and down.

The county has a contract with the federal government to maintain the road into the canyon when it needs it, about once a year, but there may be times when it is passable only by a pickup or four-wheel drive. I've done it a couple of times in Volkswagen Rabbits without any problems, so I feel that most passenger cars can make it if the driver just takes it easy and moves or avoids the rocks that might damage the underside of the car. Before you attempt to drive into the canyon, check the road by walking down it a short distance.

The worst places are usually in the first quarter mile or so, going in, and they will be harder to negotiate coming out, so look it over and use good judgment. A week or more may pass before anyone happens along to help you if you have car trouble.

From the canyon rim the distance to the turnoff to the campground is about 2.9 miles and it is 0.2 mile farther along to the turnoff to the ranch house and stage station ruins, and another 0.1 mile on to where the road crosses the river. If you are tempted to drive across the river on the good concrete low water crossing, try walking it first to check water depth, and always be alert for flash floods when crossing the river. The road continues another 1.1 mile downstream on the west side after the crossing.

As you start down off the mesa, ponderosa, piñon, juniper, and oak are growing at the upper levels of the side canyon. Farther down there is scattered juniper and oak and a variety of flowers and grasses. The floor of the canyon is relatively flat and has scattered groves of trees. There is a Forest Service Campground with tables and outhouses in a large grove of scattered trees beside the river. Access to the river is restricted in many places by dense riverside stands of tamarisk, but the river is easily accessible from the campground. The valley is quite scenic, and much of the grasslands has been recommended for designation as wilderness.

Man-made structures of interest in the canyon are the old two-story stone Mills Ranch House and the nearby adobe Butterfield Stage

The Mills ranch house, which is near the stage station.

This is about all that is left of the old Butterfield Stage Station in Mills Canyon.

Station. The setting for these structures is enhanced by a large amphitheater in the red sandstone cliff behind them. Mills had an apple orchard on his ranch, and an interesting item outside the ranch house is a big metal fruit dryer.

Road 600 (see grasslands map) goes into the canyon, across the river, and up the west side of the canyon to the mesa on that side. This must have been the old Butterfield Stage route. One of the long-time residents of Mills told me of a stage holdup in the canyon in which a person was killed and the stage destroyed. He said that if you knew where to look there were still pieces of the stage to be found. And, he added that after the killing many old-timers would not spend the night in the canyon because they believed that the person killed in the holdup had been seen as an apparition similar to the headless horseman.

There are no hiking trails in the canyon, but the floor is relatively flat, and is easy walking in most places. It would be wise to hike in long pants through the deep grass and weeds. Swarms of deer flies and mosquitoes at certain times of the year also mandate that you have long pants available. When the river is low you can hike along the sand bars in the river bed. Public land extends along the river for about six miles to the north and 13 miles to the south. The road goes a little over a mile each direction from the campground and beyond this the only access to the canyon is by hiking or by horseback, which also would be enjoyable.

To summarize the do's and don'ts for this trip, to make it safe and enjoyable, you should bring the supplies and equipment you would normally bring and observe the usual safety precautions, in addition to the following items: Bring all of the water you will need, even though there is water in the river, as it may be muddy if the river is up. Look at the road into the canyon before driving it. Check the weather, as a rain could wash out places in the road, or make it temporarily muddy. (A shovel would be handy for fixing holes and washes in the road.) Beware of flash floods in the river. Have the capability for hiking the three miles out of the canyon plus 2.5 miles to the nearest ranch house in case of car trouble. Have long pants and insect repellent available in case you need them.

Don't let all of this scare you away from Mills Canyon. It is a very interesting, scenic and isolated place to come to and stay awhile. It has a lot to offer.

There are two ways to get to the road that goes down into the canyon. The easiest and most direct route is to get on N.M. 39 and go north to the town of Roy and continue north one mile past the turnoff to Mills. Turn west (left) on the dirt side road that is about 200 yards south of mile post 126 on N.M. 39. This side road has a stop sign at the highway. There are a few houses and ranches along the way. Go west 6.2 miles and you will have to go through a gate either to right or left. There is a sign that says, "Kiowa Grasslands Unit 90, Primitive Road — Not Maintained — Hazardous to Public Use." Turn right and (after closing the gate) proceed into the canyon, observing the previously mentioned precautions. You could have turned off N.M. 39 near mile post 125 near Mills and from the road junction southwest of town take the road that goes north. This road takes you to the gate and the Kiowa Grasslands Unit 90 sign.

A view upstream in Mills Canyon.

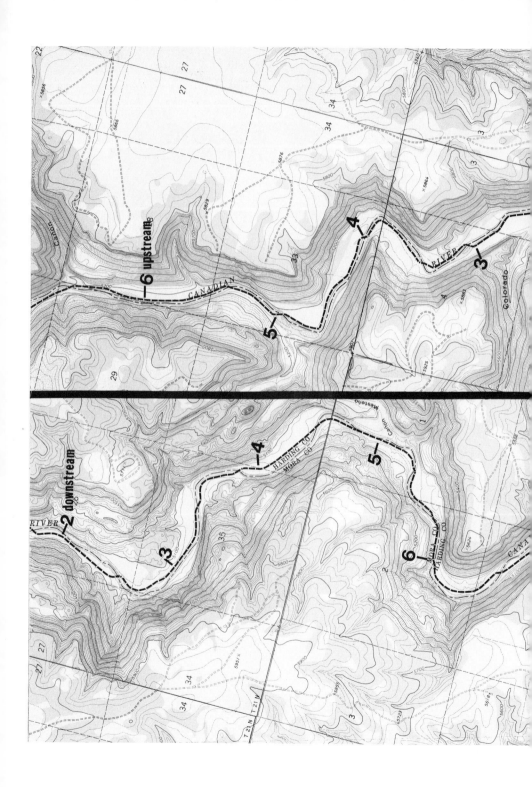

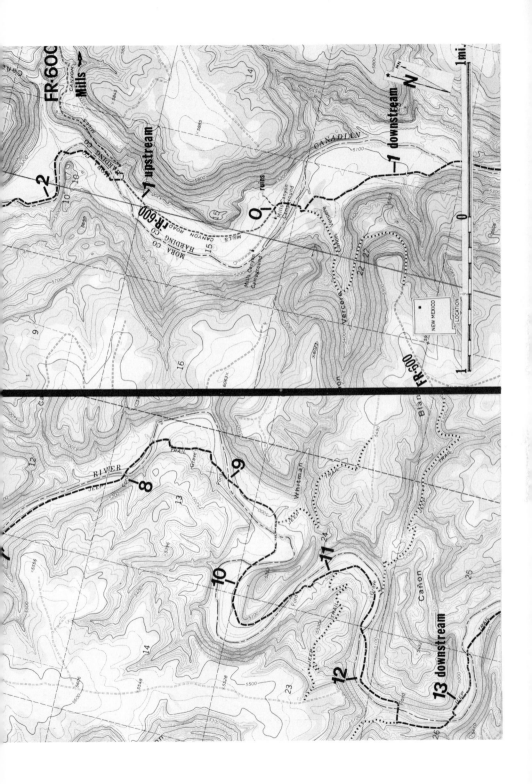

28 PADILLA TRAIL
LINCOLN NATIONAL FOREST, CAPITAN MOUNTAINS

Distance: 4.7 miles one-way to Trail No. 60 junction or 7.8 miles to Crest Trail No. 58
Time: 5 to 10 hours round-trip to Trail No. 60 junction, 9 to 15 hours round-trip to Crest Trail No. 58 (jeep road No. 56)
Elevation Range: 6,660 to 7,280 feet at Trail No. 60 or 9,800 feet at Crest Trail
Rating: Strenuous — Rocky but easy to follow and slight gradients to T-60; steep and rocky to Crest Trail
Water: No reliable sources; small, intermittent stream at Hinchley Canyon
Seasons: Year-round to Trail No. 60, May through October to Crest Trail
Topographic Maps: Capitan Pass, Capitan Peak
Special Maps: Lincoln National Forest, Grid D-3

The first mile of this route takes you uphill from Forest Road 338 to Padilla Trail No. 59. It follows an old road which has washed badly, leaving a very rocky path much of the way. About 550 feet are gained in this part of the hike.

You join Padilla Trail No. 59 at the end of the old road north of a clearing in the forest. The 3.7 miles along Trail No. 59 are essentially level, with few variations in elevation exceeding 60 feet above or below where you join it. There is a Trail 59 sign at the end of the old road marking the route, and the path is quite distinct, though it was probably more heavily used at some time in the past. The surface is generally good, though there are some rocky places.

The path is scenic with much of it through a fairly dense mixed forest of piñon, juniper, ponderosa and oak. Occasionally there are Trail 59 signs to reassure the hiker he is still on the correct route. Bears seem to like the taste of these signs, because some of them are broken and disfigured with large tooth marks. The forest toward the west end of the route is more open, affording good views to the south toward Sierra Blanca. There is a small intermittent spring by the trail in Hinchley Canyon, 3.0 miles along the hike. Don't count on getting water here though; carry what you'll need. There are many good campsites along this portion of the route in level, open spots in the forest. A fence and metal gate cross the path at 3.7 miles.

The junction with Mitt & Bar Trail No. 60 is at 4.7 miles, and Trail 59 ends here. Trail No. 60 comes up from F.R. 57 and goes up to the Crest Trail. A fast hiker can get to the T-59/T-60 junction in less than 2.5 hours, but why hurry? It may take a slow hiker five hours.

If you wish to continue up to the Crest Trail on T-60, it will be a 2,500 foot climb in three miles, which is about a 16 percent average grade. After you reach the Crest Trail, it is another mile and 400 foot climb to the 10,179 foot summit on the crest east of the T-60 junction.

The Crest Trail where T-60 joins it is actually jeep road No. 56. About a half-mile to the east the road ends and Crest Trail 58 begins. Chances are slim that you would see a vehicle up here. Allow yourself at least three hours to go from T-59 up to the Crest Trail, and at least a half-hour more to get to the summit to the east. The hike along the crest is enjoyable, with good views to north and south.

Study your map and decide how much distance you want to hike. A fast hiker with a light load could make it from Padilla Ranch House to the summit on the crest and back in a strenuous 12 hours, but the average hiker should plan on making a two or three day trip of it. Take plenty of water; at least 1½ gallons per person per day in hot weather.

To get to this hike take U.S. 380 between Roswell and Carrizozo. Turn north off 380 near mile post 94, which is about 4.1 miles west of the village of Lincoln, or 9.3 miles east of the town of Capitan. You turn north onto F.R. 57, which isn't marked as such, but there is a sign that says, "Salizar Canyon, Baka Campsite" marking the turnoff. There are two side roads at this turnoff. Take the left road, which crosses the stream. Follow F.R. 57 northeast for 2.2 miles to its junction with F.R. 338, which branches off to the north (left). Go north on F.R. 338 for 1.2 miles, where it turns 90 degrees to the left (a small two-track continues north at the turn). Follow F.R. 338 for one-half mile to the west to the trailhead.

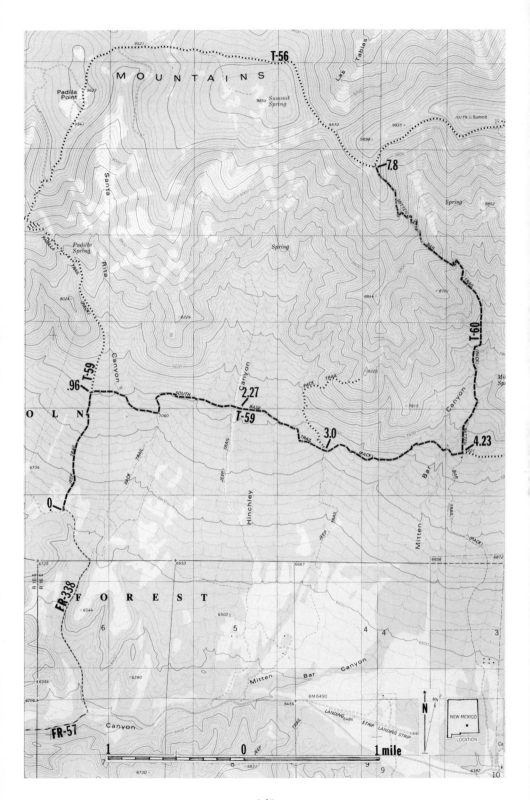

143

The trailhead is not marked and is not obvious. The trail goes north from a point about 100 feet west of a F.R. 338 sign on the south side of the road, and about 150 yards east of the Padilla Ranch House. Go north to a gate in an east-west fence, and you join the very rocky jeep trail which takes you up the mountain side to the hiking trail No. 59.

An alternate hike would be to join Trail No. 59, but go north on it for three miles to F.R. 56 along the crest, and to Padilla Peak. Or, this could be made as a loop by walking east on F.R. 56 to Trail No. 60 and down it to Trail No. 59 and back to the start.

The hike starts here and follows a rocky, abandoned jeep trail to the lower slope of the mountains, which the route skirts, to the right.

Padilla ranch house, near the trailhead.

29 CAPITAN PEAK
LINCOLN NATIONAL FOREST, CAPITAN MOUNTAINS

Distance: 14.2 miles round-trip
Time: 4 to 7 hours to summit, 3 to 6 hours back down, plus time to enjoy it
Elevation Range: 5,280 to 10,083 feet
Rating: Moderate to strenuous
Water: None
Seasons: May through October usually, but depends on snow
Topographic Maps: Arroyo Serrano West, Arabella, Capitan Peak, Kyle Harrison Canyon
Special Map: Lincoln National Forest, Grid E3

Hiking in the Capitan Mountains is a very pleasant experience. These mountains rise abruptly above the surrounding rolling ranch land, providing many distant vistas through openings in the trees. The extensive forest through which the trail passes provides welcome shade on warm afternoons and attenuates the chilling wind when temperatures drop. This hike follows a scenic route through the forest and along ridges to the summit of the highest mountain in the range, Capitan Peak. The main drawback to hiking in these mountains is their complete lack of water, after the snow has all melted. The necessity of carrying water adds to the burden carried by a hiker, but the weight of two or three days' water should not be a deterrent to making this trip. In moderate temperatures, carry at least a gallon of water per person per day, and on warm days 1½ gallons will be required. The higher you camp in the Capitans the better the camping, as a rule, with larger trees and more open forests, cooler temperatures, and more level campsites. The forest near the summit is my favorite area to camp on this hike, when the weather is good.

This can be a moderately strenuous day-hike, a moderate overnight backpack trip or a portion of a more strenuous trip, longer in duration and distance. A look at the Forest Service map will reveal a number of routes that could be added to this hike to make it longer and even more interesting.

The trailhead is well marked with a large brown and white sign on the left (south) side of Forest Road 130 about 3.8 miles from N.M. 48. This sign announces, "Capitan Peak, Trail No. 64." A nearby sign beside the trail says, "Summit Trail No. 58 — 6 miles, Capitan Peak 7 miles." The trail is excellent nearly all the way, though near the beginning it is overgrown with weeds on the hillside above some

of the cabins that comprise Pine Lodge. The first part of the path is not used so much because the majority of traffic appears to start from road's end in Pine Lodge.

While hiking this good trail, it is possible to get off the path onto a few lesser used or "abandoned" routes that are still blazed and are used by hunters and those like me who want to see where they go, and by others who mistakenly take them instead of the main trail. Some of these will be noted in more detail later.

At 0.3 mile the trail turns 90 degrees right and crosses a small stream bed. A nice trail goes to the left alongside the stream bed. This is the route Hike #30 takes to Michallas Canyon, so turn to the right along the wider path. The hike continues along the hillside above the cabins in Pine Lodge. The last cabin is passed close by at 0.53 mile where the trail turns sharply left. After you make this turn you should see a prominent blaze mark on a big Alligator Juniper beside the trail ahead.

There is a T-64 sign beside the trail at 0.56 mile and another at 0.99 mile. The hiking surface is excellent, with switchbacks easing the climb up the mountain side. There is a short, steep place at 1.1 miles.

Be careful at 1.54 miles, where the trail is going uphill with a small drainage to the left, and makes a sharp turn to the right. A fairly distinct trail continues straight ahead, up the drainage, and blaze marks on the trees make you think that you are still on the correct trail. This was probably a part of the original Capitan Peak Trail, which was later bypassed with switchbacks easing the grade. This "abandoned" trail will be somewhat difficult to continue on because it has fallen trees across it, and disappears in places. But it cuts 0.6 mile off the distance to Capitan Peak, and rejoins the regular route at 2.93 miles (2.3

miles by the old route). If you think you are on the main trail and begin to encounter fallen trees or disappearing places in the trail, turn around because you have taken a wrong turn, or more likely, missed a turn.

There is another place to be careful with a side trail. At 3.01 miles the main trail switches left and a small trail continues straight ahead up the ridge crest. I came straight down the ridge crest one time by passing about a mile of gentle switchbacks on the main trail, and this may be the trail I was on that rejoined the main one. I'm not sure, so don't try this one. The main trail is excellent through here, so stick to it.

The ridge crest that the route is following begins to level off at 3.7 miles. The path has been switching back and forth across the crest when the slope is steeper, though a well-used trail running straight up the ridge continually crosses the switchbacks. After the grade eases there is only one path along the crest. There is a T-64 sign at 3.8 miles near the top of a lump on the nearly level ridge crest.

In a clearing at 4.38 miles, on the crest, a bear-chewed sign tells you that the mountain to the east is Sunset Peak, 9,320 feet high. Nearby is a large circle of big rocks, painted yellow, in the clearing. I assume that it is an aerial survey marker. There is another T-64 sign at 4.71 miles. Aspen are becoming more plentiful.

Summit Trail No. 58 is joined at 5.18 miles. The route you want to follow doubles back to the right, at the junction. Signs here tell you, "Pancho Canyon Trail No. 62 (south), Capitan Peak Trail No. 64 (north, the way you just came from), Road 536 3½ miles (south), Road No. 130 — 6 miles (north, where you left the car)" and "Summit Trail No. 58, Capitan Peak 1½ miles (west), Seven Cabins Trail No. 66 — 5 miles (west), Pierce Canyon Trail No. 61 — 5 miles (west)." These are some of the optional routes to explore if you have the time, water, and desire to do so. This would also be the place to cross over to Sunset Peak, via a saddle, if you want to climb it.

The route crosses a big rock slide at 5.66 miles, which makes a big opening in the forest that provides an excellent view to the north and east. You can see Pine Lodge down below, and much of F.R. 130.

The path has leveled off and is paralleling timberline in the edge of the forest at 6.95 miles, when you come to a sign, chewed and broken by bears. The sign points up the open, grassy slope to the left, to Capitan Peak. Leave the trail here and head uphill along a faint path in the flowers and grass. A hundred yards or so uphill is a fence corner and above this is an odd-looking V-shaped roof, which collects snow melt and rain water for the Forest Service cabin one-fourth mile downhill. I disturbed a Golden Eagle which was apparently feeding near the water collector on one of my trips here.

The summit of Capitan Peak is attained at 7.13 miles, and it is a glorious place, with impressive views in all directions. Plan to spend some time here soaking up the sunshine and the view. It is definitely worth the effort it took to get here! I found swarms of Ladybugs on some of the rocks and the sign post on the summit, as I did on Osha Peak in the Manzano Mountains and other peaks in New Mexico.

On return to the place where you departed the trail, you may wish to continue on T-58. There is a T-58 sign a few hundred feet farther along. The Forest Service cabin is to the left of the sign, above the trail at timberline. You will probably want to visit the cabin briefly to satisfy your curiosity about it. If you do, please don't bother anything.

If you camp near here, or plan to continue west on T-58, you will be interested in distances to the other trails. It is about 3.5 miles west to the junction with Seven Cabins Trail No. 66. It is possible that you would want to hike down this trail to the North Base Trail No. 65, turn east on it and follow it back to your car. I haven't hiked this loop, so can't comment on features or trail conditions. At the T-58/T-66 junction T-61 goes to the south down Pierce Canyon. Four miles west of the junction with these trails, T-58 is joined from the south by Mitt and Bar Trail No. 60 (see Hike #28). This junction is near the end of jeep trail No. 56, which is a continuation of Summit Trail No. 58 to the west, to the Capitan Pass Road.

There are many optional hikes which can draw you back to the Capitan Mountains many times. Be careful during hunting season, as this is a popular area for hunters because it is the habitat for deer, elk, bear, and wild turkey.

You get to this hike from N.M. 48, 32 miles north and east of the town of Capitan, or about 55 miles west from the center of Roswell. Turn off N.M. 48 south onto F.R. 130. The turnoff is (or was before a section of the road toward Roswell was rerouted and paved) near mile post 42 on N.M. 48. The sign by the highway says, "Pine Lodge 5, F.R. 130." A short distance along F.R. 130 the road appears to go straight ahead, with a heavily traveled rutted, rocky road turning off to the right. Turn right, as the road that goes straight ahead soon ends at a gate. The road is rough, rutted, very rocky in places, but is frequently used by all sorts of passenger cars, pickups, four-wheel drives, etc. Drive sensibly and you should not have any trouble. The trailhead is on the left (south) side of F.R. 130 about 3.8 miles from N.M. 48. A short distance farther along the road is the cluster of cabins of Pine Lodge.

Capitan Summit Trail runs west along this ridge from near the Forest Service cabin, lower left, to beyond the summit, upper right.

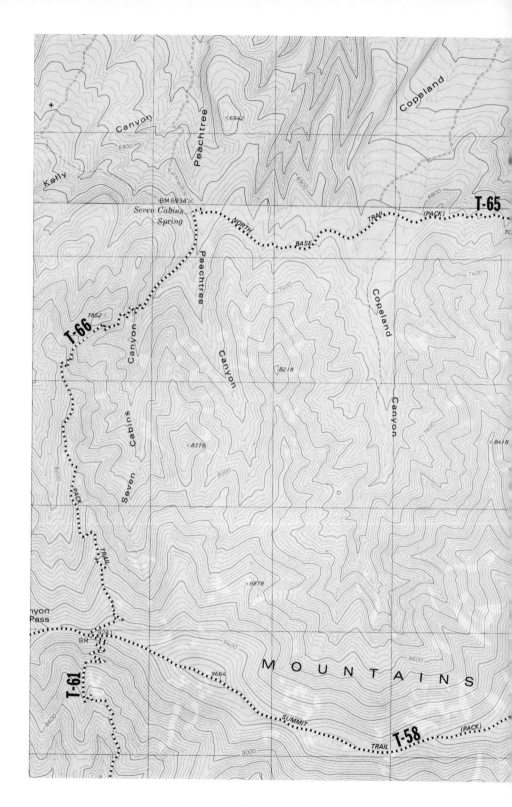

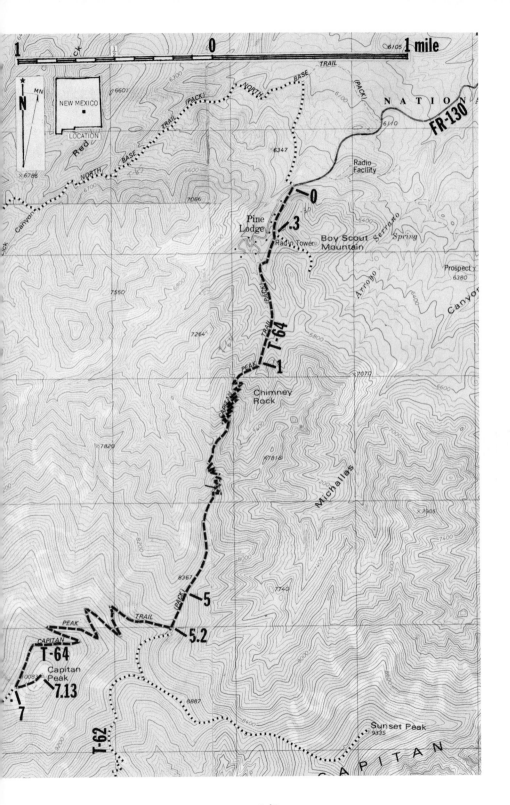

Glimpses of chimney rock from points both below and above it. View looking north.

Smokey Bear's relatives must like the taste of this sign, which points to nearby Capitan Peak summit, 10,083 feet.

30 MICHALLAS CANYON
LINCOLN NATIONAL FOREST, CAPITAN MOUNTAINS

Distance: 4.2 miles round-trip
Times: 3 to 5 hours round-trip, but it is a good overnight trip
Elevation Range: 6,280 to 6,680 feet
Rating: Easy hiking, but difficult route finding
Water: Fairly reliable in Michallas Canyon, but carry some anyhow
Seasons: All, but don't try it in snow
Topographic Maps: Capitan Peak, Arabella
Special Map: Lincoln National Forest, Grid E3

If you do not want a long, strenuous hike, but want to get to a peaceful, secluded, and pretty place for camping or for picnicking this may be the one for you. On this hike you climb only 400 feet above the trailhead to cross a ridge and drop back to about the same elevation as you started from. The remainder of the hike loses elevation very gradually. The distance to the suggested camping area is only 2.1 miles.

It appears that this route was, at some time in the past, a wide, frequently used trail. Some of the trees with blaze marks remain along the way. A few dead trees with blazes are still standing. Many must have fallen and decayed, because there are few blazes marking the portion of the trail that passes through the juniper and piñon area. After the route goes into the pine forest, it becomes quite distinct most of the time, though fallen trees frequently block your way.

The trailhead is well marked and the route easy to follow. But, as the path traverses a hillside, weeds have found it is the only flat place in which to grow. At 0.3 mile the main route, to Capitan Peak (hike #29), branches sharply to the right. Your route goes slightly to the left alongside a dry stream bed. A hundred yards or so up the way, the trail crosses to the right side of the wash and continues to follow it up to a saddle between two small peaks. On the left hand peak (northeast) is a microwave tower, which you will be able to see for much of the hike. There are a number of paths among the juniper and piñon trees here in the saddle, but angle across it to the right and you should see the trail emerge and drop down to the right (south). The route soon levels off and curves left, as it circles the head of a broad valley.

When the trail leaves the hillside at the head of the valley and goes onto a rough, but somewhat level area through which a number of steepsided, rocky gulleys pass, the path disappears. This is the juniper and pinon area mentioned previously, and you must be very alert to find any blazes or signs of a trail. It might be best to mark the route you take, temporarily, as you search ahead for marked trees. If there are other hikers with you, consider stationing one person at the last identified place on the route as you explore ahead for another section of trail or blaze mark. Mark the return route as you proceed, in some temporary way, such as bits of plastic ribbon tied to tree limbs or small piles of rocks at frequent intervals. Only those hikers who are experienced in trail finding should attempt this hike. This short portion is a challenge, and the return trip will be more difficult if you have not adequately marked the way, because there are even fewer blazes marking the way in this direction. But, you should not get lost because in the difficult area you can always see the microwave tower on the small peak beside the trail where you crossed over the saddle.

There are some nice views at points along the way, particularly in the difficult-to-follow portion. After you get on the distinct trail in the pine forest, your scenery will be confined to the immediate surroundings. You cross a succession of low ridges and gulleys before coming to Michallas Canyon. The stream in this small, green canyon appears to be a fairly reliable place to get water, but it may not be adequate as summer progresses or in periods of drought, so you should carry along all of the water you anticipate needing. Michallas Canyon is at 1.8 miles and there is good camping just before you get to it and even better camping a short distance beyond it. Dump your pack at the stream and look over the areas near it before deciding on the best spot. Camping in this area will be a really nice experience and you will enjoy relaxing in the cool, shady, green streamside environment. You should plan to hike the trail beyond camp, because maps indicate that you may encounter an abandoned road within the next mile or so, which would open up a route for further exploration. I haven't done this yet, but look forward to doing so.

There is a side hike that you might be interested in, and it is easy to find. After you drop from the saddle (0.54 mile) beside the microwave tower and proceed along the hillside, you cross a dry wash which comes down from the right at 0.85 mile. Continue toward Michallas Canyon for another 150 yards or so and there will be a ridge to your left with a drainage on each side. You can depart the Michallas Canyon Trail and walk out to the end of this ridge and drop down into the drainage below. Go to your right, downstream, along the drainage. This route takes you through a mixed forest of pine and deciduous trees, and is quite nice to hike through. Be sure and flag your route so you can find your way back to the trail. If you continue down this drainage for about a half-mile you will come to a spring. Some of the spring's water flows through a screen which strains it before it flows into a black plastic pipe. This pipe runs downstream about 200 yards to a forest road. (I have driven to this point, but nearly became stuck in sand on the steep hill when I tried to return to F.R. 130.) This is a nice place for a rest or a picnic. From this spring you can return to the Michallas Trail or continue downstream to the road. If you want to return to the trailhead you can go to your left up this road 0.7 mile to F.R. 130. Go left on F.R. 130 for 0.1 mile to the trailhead.

To get to this hike go 32 miles north and east of Capitan, New Mexico or go about 55 miles west from the center of Roswell on N.M. 48. Turn south off N.M. 48 near mile post 42 onto F.R. 130. A sign at the turnoff says, "Pine Lodge 5, F.R. 130." F.R. 130 is rough and rocky, but passenger cars travel for 3.9 miles regularly to Pine Lodge. If you take it easy, and avoid the larger rocks and potholes, you shouldn't have any problem with the road.

The trailhead is on the left (south) side of F.R. 130. A large brown and white sign says, "Capitan Peak, Trail No. 64." Hike the trail 0.3 mile to a fork where this hike turns left, alongside a dry stream bed.

The route passes through this juniper, piñon, oak and other low vegetation before it drops into the pine forest along Michallas Canyon.

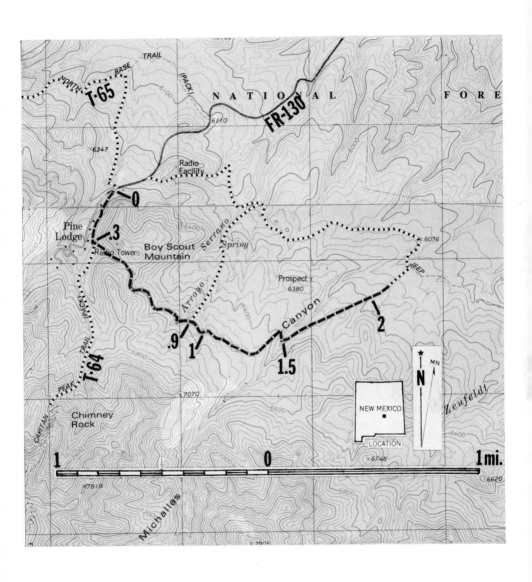

31 YUCCA CANYON TO LONGVIEW SPRING
CARLSBAD CAVERNS NATIONAL PARK

Distance: 2.75 miles one-way
Time: 3½ to 6 hours round-trip, but plan to spend a day or two
Elevation Range: 4,500 to 5,950 feet
Rating: Moderate
Water: Longview Spring, Dog Pen Seep (check at headquarters to confirm)
Seasons: All. Can be hot (100°F) and dry in summer, cold (0°F) and windy with light snow in winter, and windy and cold in the spring
Topographic Maps: Grapevine Draw 7.5′ and Carlsbad Caverns West 15′
Special Maps: Lincoln National Forest, Guadalupe District, Grids 6E, 6F; Carlsbad Caverns National Park Guide; maps available at headquarters
Permit: Required for overnight camping, not for day-hiking. Obtain from headquarters or write Superintendent, Carlsbad Caverns National Park, 3225 National Parks Hwy., Carlsbad, NM 88220. Ground fires are not permitted in the park. Use containerized fuel

The good trail to the mesa top follows Yucca Canyon most of the way. This hike starts in a desert environment and takes you to a grassy plateau with scattered Alligator Juniper, Mexican Buckeye, Big Tooth Maple, Piñon Pine, and occasional madrone, Texas Walnut, Ponderosa Pine, and Chinkapin Oak. Yucca Canyon trailhead is at the end of a primitive road, but the trail sign is a short distance away, across Yucca Canyon.

From the trailhead sign the trail goes up the left (south) side of the drainage. Along most of the route the trail is well prepared and is easy walking, with easy gradients. But, wear long pants because the desert plants, such as White Thorned Acacia, Sotol, yucca, Agave, cactus, and many others, are sharp and scratchy, and overhang the trail. Vegetation in the canyon also includes Oak Brush, Bear Grass, and many grasses and colorful flowers. At 0.8 mile the path crosses to the north side of the stream bed and soon crosses back to the south side. A short distance later it recrosses to the north and goes up some stone steps that have been built by the park service. The route is fairly steep and rocky along here.

At about 1.8 miles the trail tops out rather abruptly on the mesa. A fenced plant study enclosure is in the path, so the trail turns a bit to the left and follows west (WNW) along the south fence to the west corner.

This fence corner is significant because you turn here to go to Longview Spring, or can angle left to follow the faint, cairned route that skirts around the head of West Slaughter Canyon (Hike #32). Turn to the right at the fence corner and parallel the fence to the northwest until you see the small park service

cabin. The route to Yucca Ridge/Longview Spring departs from the old log cabin ruins near Yucca Ranger Cabin.

Longview Spring is nearly due west from the cabin. Piles of rocks (cairns) mark the way. Start west from the cabin, following the cairns as the route they mark curves to the right (northwest) and drops into a shallow canyon. In the canyon, about a quarter of a mile from the cabin, turn left and proceed west along the drainage. You soon come to some old stone walls of a corral and some other structure. Just beyond, on the north side of the canyon is a seep with water dripping over a ledge. This is Dog Pen Seep and could be a good campsite. It is an interesting place and there is nearly always water available here.

The trail continues west from the seep, along the left (south) side of the canyon, which quickly gets deeper and deeper. The path is soon following along a wide ledge above the canyon and below the crest of the ridge it is on. At the end of the ridge the path turns left, continuing on the ledge. Before you get to the spring you pass an old fresno and a plow that were used for building an earthen tank for livestock watering. A few hundred feet farther south in a lush, green patch of vegetation is a pipe (broken) with a stream of cool, clear water trickling out. This is on the end of the ridge which protrudes into broad and deep Slaughter Canyon, affording a grand 180 degree view of the rugged country below and across the way. More water is flowing from the next terrace below. These terraces offer plenty of level area for camping, and with the ample water flowing nearby, the isolation, and outstanding scenery, who could ask for more? You must camp at least 200 feet from the spring.

If the directions for finding Longview Spring via Dog Pen Seep sound confusing, the following directions for a more direct route may help you. From the cabin go directly west (magnetic), following along the crest of the ridge. You may have to thread your way through patches of Lechuguilla, which demands your respect, so take care how you step. There are deep canyons on either side of this ridge and Longview Spring is at its western tip. The spring is about 50 feet down and it is rather precipitous getting to it from directly above. For this reason, well before you get to the end of the ridge, you should go to the north side and work your way down to the trail on the ledge, which is quite visible from above. The trail will take you on around to the spring.

To be sure that camping is permitted here, inquire at Park Headquarters when you get your permit. I've been told that the spring never dries up completely; that there is always at least a trickle of water. But, I suggest that you carry ample water to get you back to the car comfortably, during a long dry spell.

If you prefer to make camp someplace else, level space near Yucca Cabin is almost limitless. Much of the surface is rocky, but this whole area is covered by patches of thick grass and the scattered trees provide welcome shade. Take care with stoves and lanterns in the grass because fire could spread quickly if not properly contained.

To get to Yucca Canyon and Longview Spring Trail, go southwest from Carlsbad on U.S. 62-180. At 18.5 miles you will come to the intersection with N.M. 7 which goes to the Caverns and Park Headquarters, where you should get your permit to hike. After getting your permit, continue southwest on U.S. 62-180 for 5.6 miles to the turnoff to New Cave and Slaughter Canyon. This road is paved for 6.2 miles then it becomes good, all-weather gravel. Turn to the right at the end of the pavement and follow the signs toward New Cave. At 10.1 miles from U.S. 62-180 you cross a cattle guard and enter the national park. When you cross this cattle guard, immediately turn left on the two-track road that follows the fence line. There are some small washes and some rocks that will be hard on a low-slung or heavily loaded car along this road. It is 1.9 miles from the cattle guard to the trailhead at the end of the two-track road.

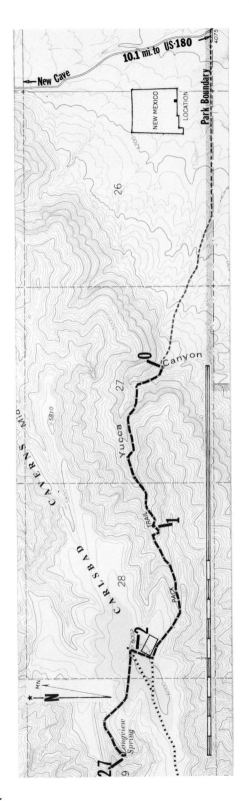

Fresno and plow were apparently used to distribute soil and to prepare a garden on this ledge. Longview

Spring, beyond the fresno, provided the irrigation water.

32 SLAUGHTER CANYON RIM
CARLSBAD CAVERNS NATIONAL PARK

Distance: 23.8 mile circuit
Time: 2 or 3 days
Elevation Range: 4,200 to 6,733 feet
Rating: Very strenuous and requires experienced trail finder
Water: Available at Longview Spring; carry what you will need for first 19 miles
Seasons: Fall is best; winter can be cold (0°F) and windy with light snow; spring cold and windy; summer hot (100°F) and dry
Topographic Maps: Grapevine Draw, Serpentine Bends, Queen, Gunsight Canyon 7.5'; Carlsbad Caverns East and Carlsbad Caverns West 15'
Special Maps: Lincoln National Forest, Guadalupe District, Grid E6, F5 and F6; small map on park information folder
Permit: Required for overnight, write or phone if you wish to get one ahead of time (available from Caverns Headquarters)

If you are looking for a long, scenic route through a semi-desert landscape, try this one. Chances are that you will see no one else from the time you leave the New Cave Trail until you arrive in the vicinity of Longview Spring, 18 miles later. The route, after climbing out of Slaughter Canyon onto the rim, follows an open ridge crest all the way around the head of the canyon. This lofty route provides you with continuous views of the canyon, surrounding mountains including the Guadalupes, and of the desert beyond.

In the spring the wind often makes this hike something less than pleasant, though there are some perfect days too. Summer days can be hot and dry, causing hikers to consume large quantities of water, which they must carry for the first 19 miles. Summer nights and mornings are cool, compensating somewhat for the higher afternoon temperatures. Winters can be cold and snow can obscure the trail, but weather forecasts can usually predict when bad weather is on the way. With proper clothing and equipment, winter hiking here can be enjoyable. But fall is the best time of year for this hike. Temperatures and weather are likely to be nearly perfect, and there should be plenty of water at Longview Spring. To be safe though, always check the weather forecast to be sure nothing bad is on its way, regardless of the season.

On this hike the topography varies from very rocky stream beds at beginning and end, to forested ridge crest with undulating sections and level stretches, all scenic. There are many nice places to camp along the way.

This hike starts at the parking lot for New Cave, and heads into the mouth of Slaughter

Canyon along an old abandoned road that is now blocked to vehicular traffic. The old road sometimes becomes very obscure, but the path to New Cave is easy to follow. At one-half mile there is a sign pointing back to the parking lot. Near this sign the path to New Cave continues ahead and the old road, which you want to follow (very faint through here), drops down to the right into the stream bed. From here on follow the cairns (piles of rocks) up and across the broad and rocky drainage. The cairns are so numerous, most of the way, that you should have no trouble keeping the route in sight. A time or two when the path crosses the wash you may have to stop and scan the area ahead for the next cairns, but they are always there. While following the old road along the right (east) side of the main drainage, you cross a wash that comes in from the right, at just past 1.0 mile. The old road and trail cross this drainage and turn to the right to follow up along its north side. The trail crosses this drainage six times and the seventh time it drops into the canyon, it stays in until it comes to a rock ledge which spans the stream bed. When it rains and water is flowing, it pours over the ledge as a small waterfall, and has scoured out a basin in the solid rock below the falls, which holds water. This rock basin, called a tinaja, can hold water for days or even a few weeks after the stream has stopped flowing. If you walk up the stream bed, from here for 100 yards or so, and look up at the canyon wall to the right (east), you should see the large entrance to Goat Cave immediately above you. A permit is now required for entering the cave, and if you are interested in caves, you should ask about this when you get

The route along Slaughter Canyon rim provides almost continuous views into the rugged canyon.

This sign points to Longview Spring (Hike #31).

your hiking permit. You may want to enter Lower Painted Grotto which you might possibly find on your way out of Slaughter Canyon, near the end of this trip. No permit is required for entering it.

On the west bank of the stream bed, at the rock ledge and tinaja, is a sign that says, "Putman Canyon 7 miles (west), Ridge Road 4 miles (west)." This sign is at 2.8 miles from the parking lot.

Follow the trail up the slope to the ridge crest. The steep part of the climb eases at the 3.0 mile point, near a fire scarred tree. From this position, high on the side of the canyon, you can see Goat Cave entrance in the opposite wall near the canyon floor. Progress is much easier from this point on and the crest of the ridge is attained at about 3.5 miles.

On the ridge the route is quite easy to follow. Scattered pine and juniper add their color to the landscape, and provide some sometimes-welcome shade. The trail surface is less rocky up here, and when the weather is good, hiking conditions, landscape, and scenery combined will make the next 16 or more miles a very rewarding excursion. In a saddle on the south side of the ridge, at 5.3 miles, is a large, level, forested area to your left (south) which appears to be a very good place to camp. There is no water here and few hikers will want to stop and make camp this early in the day, but it is a nice area. Soon after passing this forested area the route crosses the ridge crest and maintains a fairly level gradient along the side of a hill to another saddle, at 5.7 miles.

A two-track road, F.R. 201 joins from the north, and the hike follows this route, known as the "Guadalupe Ridge Road," along the crest of Guadalupe Ridge for the next seven miles. There is a sign alongside the path where it joins the road that tells you, "Headquarters 11 miles (north along the road), Putman Canyon 5 miles (south along the road)" and another sign pointing back the way you just came from says, "Slaughter Canyon 3 miles." The distance to Putman Canyon is more like four miles instead of five.

There are quite a few ups and downs, large and small, in the route before you arrive at Putman Cabin at 8.6 miles. This is a small, 10 x 20 foot cabin, built and maintained by the park service. Emergency water is sometimes available from a barrel here, but don't plan to refill from it because there may not be any. When there is water in the barrel, it may not look very potable and will definitely need purification. You may want to camp in the vicinity of the cabin (it is one of the designated camping areas, though you may camp any place you wish). The ridge along here is gently rolling and the cabin is on a high place, providing excellent views; you can see Yucca Cabin and Longview Spring from here if you know where to look. This is about the midpoint between the start and Yucca Cabin and is a good place to stop for those who want to break a three-day trip up into approximately equal distances each day. There is deep grass and an open oak, pine, and juniper forest near the cabin and along the ridge beyond, which makes a pleasant setting. No wood collecting or campfires are permitted in the park.

West of Putman Cabin the ridge continues its undulations and the forest gets dense. Ponderosa become more numerous and on a warm afternoon they give the forest an aroma of vanilla milkshake. A high hump on the ridge is crossed at 12.0 miles. There is an old railroad car and a nearby concrete or steel tank that were used to store water for livestock. Water was apparently hauled up here in a tank truck. The topographic map calls this Munson Reservoir.

The hiking trail departs Guadalupe Ridge Road (F.R. 201) at 12.6 miles. The trail turns sharply left and almost reverses direction. A USGS bench monument is in a pile of rocks on top of the small hill that is on the inside of this sharp turn. This hill, 6,733 feet, is the highest point on the hike. F.R. 201 continues west and eventually joins paved N.M. 137. The trail now follows an old, faint road to about 13.8 miles, where the road departs downhill to the left into the upper end of Slaughter Canyon. Continue along the ridge crest.

On departing F.R. 201, the trail goes east through the forest for 0.3 mile and then turns to the southeast. It re-enters the national park at 14.2 miles. The trail gradually loses altitude from the road junction until it reaches a saddle of 14.9 miles. At some time in the past a trail went from this saddle to the south, down into Double Canyon, but no longer is discernible. In this saddle there is an old Ponderosa Pine with a couple of signs attached to it. One is a park service sign and the other is a very old Forest Service sign that was put here well before this area was taken over by the Park Service.

The trail climbs rather steeply out of the saddle onto the ridge crest and from 15.5 miles to Yucca Cabin at 18.6 miles is almost

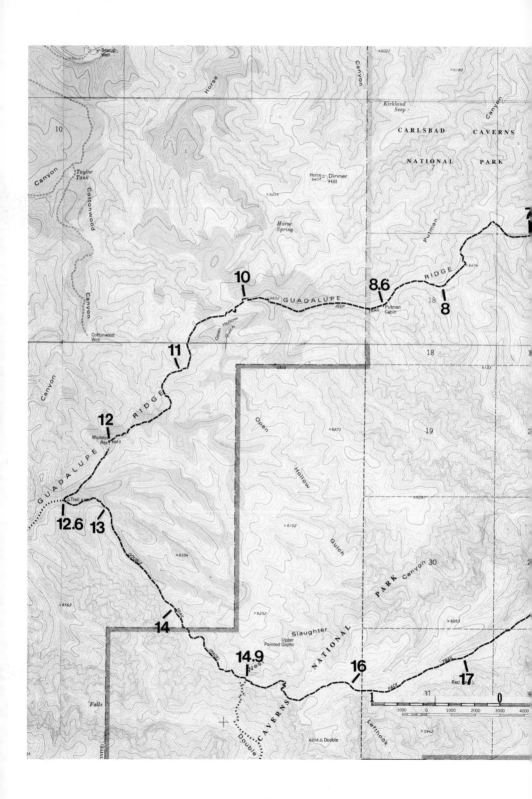

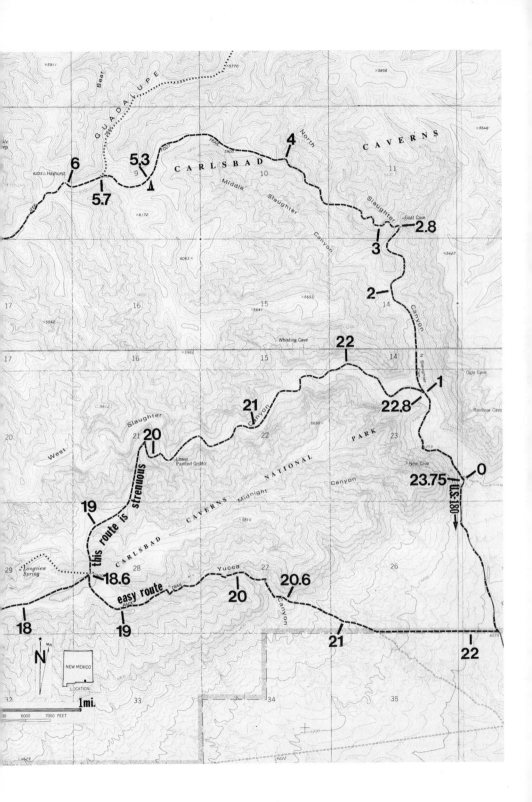

level, with only minor variations from the 6,000 foot elevation. The path is difficult to follow along much of the level section, with a few cairns marking the way, and some pieces of trail visible. Stay on the ridge crest and you should keep finding the patches of trail. At about 18.3 miles you come to the chain-link fence around a vegetation study enclosure. Go left along the southwest side of the fence and you should soon the Park Service cabin to the northwest.

Yucca Cabin is at 18.6 miles. It is in the midst of an extensive level, grassy (and rocky), open forest. The forest is primarily juniper and piñon with occasional madrone and ponderosa, and cactus. This is a pretty and spacious area for camping. You could camp here and carry water from the springs that are less than a mile away. Or, better yet, you can camp on the ledge near Longview Spring. This is a spectacular place with dramatic views of Slaughter Canyon and the far rim. The only restriction is that you must camp at least 200 feet from the spring. The disadvantage of this site is the extra distance you must carry your pack. See Hike #31 for detailed directions to Dog Pen Seep and Longview Spring.

There are two optional routes from the cabin to the New Cave parking lot. The easiest route is to go from the cabin down Yucca Canyon Trail to the two-track road (see Hike #31 for details of this route) 2.0 miles. It is a 1.9 mile hike along the two-track road to the gravel road that goes 1.2 miles to the parking lot. The total distance via this route is 23.8 miles. The Yucca Canyon route takes three to four hours to hike from cabin to car. Parking a car at Yucca Canyon trailhead before starting the hike would shorten the overall distance to 20.7 miles, cutting 3.1 miles of walking and about two hours time off the last leg.

The other route from Yucca Cabin to New Cave parking area is by way of Slaughter Canyon. It is about the same distance as the Yucca Canyon route, but is much more strenuous and takes a tiring five hours or more to negotiate. If you are already tired or behind schedule at the cabin I suggest that you don't take this way down. It is not recommended in hot weather either. But, if you are strong and want to do some more exploring, try it. You start from the cabin and go almost directly north and follow the crest of a ridge that runs down into Slaughter Canyon. Continue following this ridge as it swings northeast, then back to north. Instead of following the ridge all the

way to the floor of the drainage you can drop off to the right (east) when you see a good opportunity to get down into the drainage. Follow the rough, rocky, brushy canyon floor downstream (basically east) to join the trail you started the hike on. This junction will be at about 22.8 miles. Turn to the right (south) on the trail and follow it 1.0 mile to the parking lot. Total distance this way is 23.8 miles. This route takes you near Painted Grotto, which is not located where the map shows it to be. No permit is needed for entering the grotto.

To get to this hike go southwest from Carlsbad on U.S. 62-180. If you have not obtained your permit for overnight camping in the national park take N.M. 7 to Carlsbad Caverns Headquarters. Also, while there ask about condition of the springs and about camping near them. Get permission to enter the caves along the way, if you are interested. You can purchase topographic maps here also.

From the N.M. 7 junction continue southwest on U.S. 62-180 for 5.6 miles to the turnoff to the right (west) to New Cave and Slaughter Canyon. There is a sign marking this turnoff and other signs mark the way to New Cave. The road to New Cave, which is paved for the first 6.2 miles, is a good all-weather route. Follow the New Cave signs and at 10.1 miles from U.S. 62-180 you cross the cattle guard into Carlsbad Caverns National Park; 1.2 miles farther along in the New Cave parking lot, with porta-potties nearby.

Take plenty of water; and, enjoy your hike!

162

33 SITTING BULL FALLS
LINCOLN NATIONAL FOREST, GUADALUPE DISTRICT

Distance: One-half mile round-trip to falls; 1.9 miles one-way to canyon rim
Time: One-half hour round-trip to falls, but plan to stay there a while; 2 to 3 hours round-trip to canyon rim
Elevation Range: 5,250 to 5,500 feet
Rating: Easy
Water: Available at picnic area and at spring
Seasons: All
Topographic Maps: Red Bluff Draw, Queen
Special Maps: Lincoln National Forest, Guadalupe District, Grids E4, E5

This is an easy day-hike to a beautiful desert waterfall, to the source of its water, and to the canyon rim above the spring. It is an easy walk of less than a fourth of a mile on a paved path to the foot of the falls. The falls are best seen in the morning when they receive front illumination. Sitting Bull Falls is a popular spot for local people from the Carlsbad area, particularly on spring and fall weekends and holidays. The majority of the visitors enjoy the falls from below, though many hike around to the area above the falls where there are many small cascades and clear pools on the terraced plateau. These are as pretty as the high falls and give the opportunity to wade and explore the many streams and pools amid the lush, green aquatic plants and colorful, wild flowers. A few visitors continue upstream to the spring, which is a nice secluded place to sunbathe on the grass beside the clear, rushing stream. The spring is encased in a concrete and metal box and some of the water is piped down to the picnic area and restrooms. Not many people hike beyond the spring to the canyon rim for the big view over the valley and surrounding countryside. Almost no one hikes beyond the canyon rim on Trail No. 68 to N.M. 137.

Sitting Bull Falls is a very pretty place and I think everyone would enjoy seeing it and day hiking around the falls and canyon. It is not a place to backpack, because the area is so small. Camping is not permitted in the falls picnic area, but the land for a few miles in each direction is public National Forest (see the forest map for boundary information) and there are places to camp nearby.

The trail to the foot of the falls starts from the southeast corner of the parking lot, goes through the picnic area, and continues around to the open, grassy area which affords a

number of vantage points for viewing and photographing. The hike to the top of the falls and beyond starts at the parking lot. It goes uphill across the road from the point where the road enters the parking lot. The path is fairly rocky and moderately steep as it climbs the 200 feet up to the plateau above the falls. There are nice, large restrooms near the parking and picnic area but they have been completely wrecked by vandals.

There are a few optional ways of hiking this trail. One is to hike the 3.8 miles on Trail No. 68 from N.M. 137 to the falls parking area. T-68 starts from N.M. 137, 14.0 miles southwest of the junction of F.R. 276, the road to Sitting Bull Falls, and N.M. 137. There is a sign on the right side of the road (north) marking the two-track road that is the beginning of T-68. The road follows a fence north for about 1.6 miles, where it curves to the right, at a corral. The trail leaves the road and continues north through the corral and through the forest for 0.3 mile where it is near the canyon rim to its left. The trail turns left and drops over the rim at 1.9 miles, which is the midpoint of this hike. From the canyon rim there is a good view of the valley above the falls and the rough country beyond. From the canyon rim the path drops into the small, brushy canyon and proceeds downstream 0.7 mile to the spring. Less than 100 yards before you get to the spring there is a small rock shelter on the east side (right) of the trail, 15 feet to the side and 12 feet above. You may want to spend a few minutes looking around the shelter before continuing to the spring. Below the spring paths become more numerous, dividing and crossing, so that staying on the main route becomes a problem. But you can't get lost. In fact, you should take a side trip to your right (east) to look over the attractive area above the falls before continuing to the parking area. This is a nice hike, as described here, but since it is so short and the same route can be hiked by starting at the parking area and hiking up and back down, it may not justify the 21.7 mile one-way car shuttle.

To get to this hike go 24 miles south of Artesia or 12 miles northwest of Carlsbad on U.S. 285 to the junction with N.M. 137. Turn southwest on N.M. 137 and go 31 miles to the well-marked turnoff on F.R. 276. Sitting Bull Falls is 7.7 miles from N.M. 137, on F.R. 276.

A travertine deposit has been built up by Sitting Bull Falls as the dry desert air evaporates the mineral laden water.

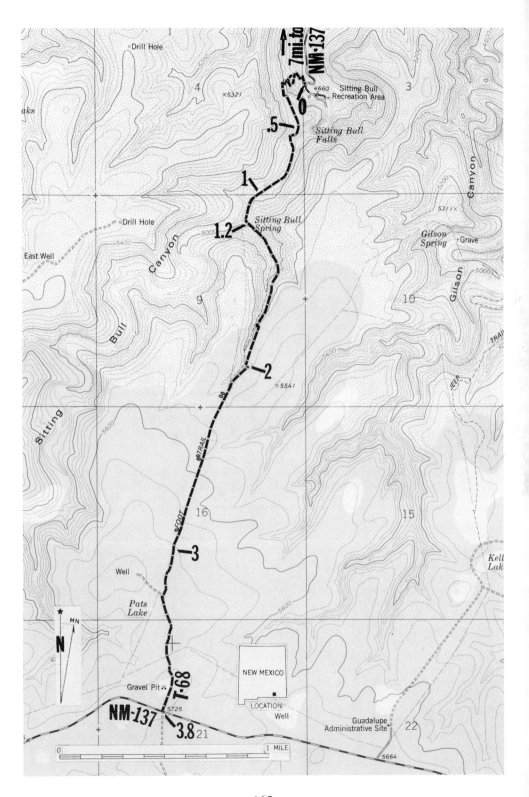

Drill Hole

4

×5321

7mi. to
NM·137

4660
Sitting Bull
Recreation Area

3

.5

Sitting Bull
Falls

Canyon

1

Drill Hole

1.2

Sitting Bull
Spring

53⁄1×

Gilson
Spring   Grave

East Well

5400

5000

Gilson Canyon

5000

9

10

Bull Canyon

5400

2

×5541

TRAIL

JEEP

Sitting

5600

007 TRAIL

16

15

007 TRAIL

3

Kell
Lak

Well

Pats
Lake

5600

MN

N

Gravel Pit ×

T·68

NEW MEXICO

NM·137

5725

3.8   21

LOCATION
Well

Guadalupe
Administrative Site

22

0   1 MILE

5664

165

34 WHITE MOUNTAIN CREST TRAIL — WHITE MOUNTAIN WILDERNESS

LINCOLN NATIONAL FOREST

Distance: 18.0 miles; car shuttle required or walk an additional 5.6 miles
Time: 2 or 3 days backpacking
Elevation Range: 7,500 to 10,400 feet
Rating: Moderate to strenuous due to distance and pack weight; trail is easy to follow
Water: Reliable sources along the route as noted
Seasons: Usually May through November, but depends on snow
Topographic Map: Nogal Peak
Special Map: Lincoln National Forest, Grid B4

The Crest Trail is an ideal trip for just about any hiker. There is ample drinking water at intervals along the route. A number of side trails go back down to Forest Road 107 in the event that it is necessary to cut the trip short. The route takes you through a variety of beautiful scenery and surroundings. There are oak and pine forests at lower elevations and conifer and aspen forests higher up, with lush, flower bedecked ridges and peaks above timberline. Ridge top and hillside paths provide impressive distant views, and stream-side walking in the forest brings you close to the clear, cascading water and the variety of shrubs, flowers, and trees. The trail is well defined and easy to follow all the way, and the surface is very good, though rocky in places. Signs mark all of the junctions, point directions, and give distances. This hike is popular with backpackers, and deer and elk hunters on horseback use it too. I have hiked parts of it on snowshoes in the deep snow of early spring and it is beautiful then.

This hike starts at the Crest Trail No. 25 sign near the cattle guard on F.R. 108 and it crosses the ridge crest, 8,700 feet, east of Nogal Peak and south of Nogal Canyon. A car shuttle or key exchange will be necessary unless you hike the 5.6 miles between here and South Fork Rio Bonita Campground. This extra distance isn't too bad if you haul your pack up here and dump it, take the car back down and park it, then hike back up the road unencumbered. Up at the trailhead you can leave a car in a wide area alongside the jeep road just northwest of the cattleguard on F.R. 108.

From the cattleguard walk west for about 0.3 mile up the jeep road, which parallels and crosses a fence that runs up the ridge crest. The trail goes left (west) where the jeep road makes a 90 degree turn to the north. Before it enters an oak thicket, the route is marked with

a Wilderness sign and a Crest Trail No. 25 sign.

This dense forest of small oak trees envelopes the trail at the beginning. The oaks apparently make a good habitat for deer because I've seen some on the trail or in open places in this area each time I've hiked here, except during hunting season. The trail emerges from the dense oak near the top of a low cliff about 1.2 miles from the start, and the view from here is outstanding. Nogal Peak towers above, to the northwest, and Bonita Valley is spread out below to the south. The Rio Bonita system drains the entire area within the ridges traversed by this hike. From this viewpoint you can follow the course of the Crest Trail as it goes west onto the ridge that runs southwest from Nogal Peak. The route continues to follow this ridge as it slowly curves to the south and eventually to the east, encircling Bonita Valley. Lofty Sierra Blanca Peak can be seen to the south beyond and above the ridge to the south.

From the trailhead the path follows a generally constant elevation as it cuts along the slope on the south side of Nogal Peak. At 2.0 miles the trail goes from the mountain side onto a ridge that is the southwest flank of the peak. Here Trail No. 54 branches back north to go past Nogal Peak. Less than 100 yards farther along, Trail No. 54, which comes up Tanbark Canyon, to the southeast, joins the Crest Trail. Almost opposite Tanbark Canyon Trail is Water Canyon Trail No. 53, to the northwest. Signs here at this junction say, "Water Canyon Trail," with an arrow pointing northwest, and, "Crest Trail, Road No. 108 2 (where the trail starts), Argentina Canyon Trail 2¼ (southwest, the way you want to go)."

The route follows along the ridge crest to the southwest, passing through alternating forest and meadow. After crossing over a ridge at 2.2 miles the trail drops rather steeply to

Spring Cabin, on Doherty Ridge. The spring is nearby. Camping is not permitted within 100 yards of the cabin, but there is an excellent site in a grove of large pine trees, nearby.

The White Mountain Crest Trail follows on or near the crest of the scenic White Mountains, which encircle the basin drained by Bonito Creek.

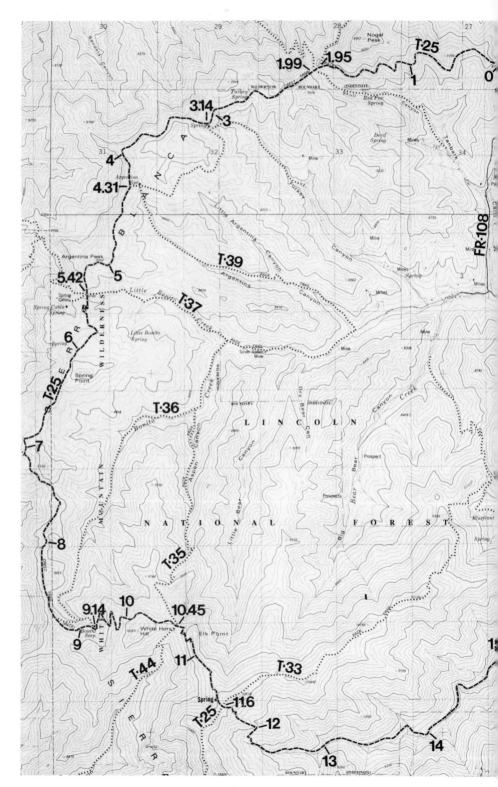

168

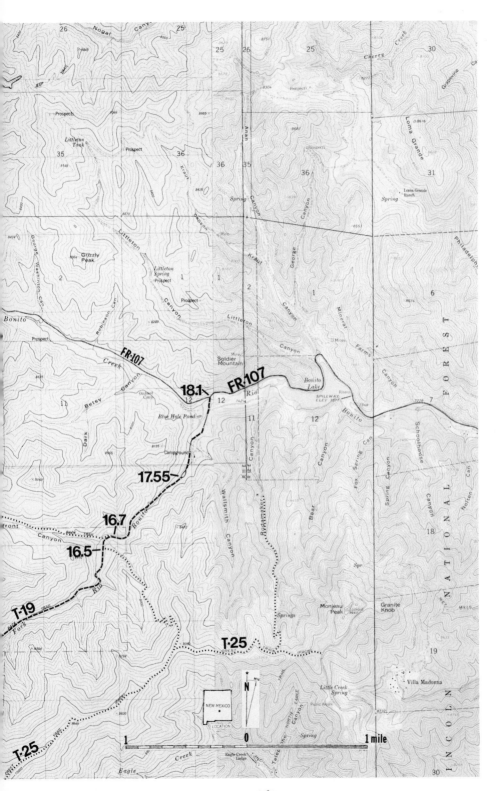

cross a small drainage. In the drainage to the left of the trail is an old pipe with water trickling out. From the spring the route climbs slowly, through open forest and meadow and crosses to the desert side of the ridge at 3.3 miles.

A junction with Argentina Canyon Trail No. 39 is reached at 4.3 miles. A sign here informs you, "Argentina Canyon Trail (arrow pointing southeast)." Another says, "Crest Trail (arrows south and north), Doherty Ridge Trail 1¼ (south), Little Bonito Trail 1¼ (south), Water Canyon Trail 2¼ (north)."

The path runs downhill into an open saddle at 5.4 miles. Signs here tell you, "Crest Trail (northwest and southeast), Bonito Trail 4 (southeast, the way you want to go), Argentina Canyon Trail 1¼ (northwest)," and "Little Bonito Trail (T-37, to the east), Doherty Ridge Trail (T-50, to the west)." It is 2.6 miles down T-37 to the end of F.R. 107.

This is a choice area in which to spend the first night of a three-day hike. There are springs to either side of the Crest Trail here, and plenty of space for camping. The Doherty Ridge Trail provides a nice side trip. A Forest Service cabin with nearby spring is 0.3 mile down Doherty Ridge Trail. The cabin is in a fenced enclosure, along with a shed and an outhouse. There is a trickle of water in a small canyon just southeast of the cabin. The main spring is in a fenced area a short distance upstream, with a water trough just outside the fence, and a pipe to carry water somewhere. Camping is not permitted near the cabin, but 100 yards before you get to it is an excellent place in a grove of big ponderosa on an elevated flat area between two drainages.

There is a good spring in the head of Little Bonito drainage. This one is closer to the Crest Trail and sometimes has a greater flow than the one near the cabin.

To continue, proceed south across the grassy saddle into the trees and switchback to the right up onto a ridge and continue south, uphill. The climb tops out at about 6.1 miles in a hillside forest. There is a gate across the trail at 6.35 miles. Please keep it closed. You will see a variety of spruce, pine, and fir in the forest along here, with patches of aspen.

The trail is atop a bare ridge at 7.6 miles, with a big forested valley below, to the left (east). The route goes across the right side of a big, bald hill on the ridge and is in another saddle at 8.1 miles. The trail ahead can be seen switchbacking up the side of a high, unforested

mountain to the east. At 8.6 miles there is a trail and a Trail No. 36 sign to the left of the Crest Trail about 30 feet but no visible junction nearby.

At 9.1 miles there is a trail sign, with the wide Bonito Trail visible across the small canyon below. The sign says, "Crest Trail (north-south), Aspen Trail 1½ (ahead, south), Little Bonito Trail 4 (behind, north), Doherty Ridge Trail 4 (behind)."

There is a spring a few yards northeast of this sign, with a good stream of water flowing from a pipe. Three hundred yards beyond the spring the trail switches sharply to the right and continues to switchback up the grassy mountain side. Annoying nettle stings bare legs along here and along much of the remainder of the trip. The route goes over a high shoulder at 9.9 miles, with good views in most directions.

In a saddle east of the high peak there is a trail junction and signs that point to, "Aspen Trail (No. 35, north), Three Rivers Trail (No. 44, south)," and "Crest Trail (east-west), Blue Front Trail 1¼ (east), South Fork Rio Bonito Trail 1¼ (east, where you are going), Bonito Trail 1½ (west, where you just came from)."

The trail continues along the ridge crest in the saddle and goes to the right where it switchbacks up through a mixed forest into an aspen forest. At 10.95 miles there is a good tree-sheltered campsite on the ridge crest. From the campsite the trail drops into a small open saddle and then climbs up a high, grassy slope. The scenery gets better the higher you go! In October when aspen and oak leaves are turning varying shades of yellow, the mountains seen from here are gorgeous, with brilliant patches of color. There is a small spring flowing out of a short piece of pipe alongside the trial, just to the right, at 11.5 miles. This is surprising because it is so high, with very little area above it to collect water. Just beyond the spring, at 11.6 miles, is a trail junction. This is where this hike leaves the Crest Trail and starts its six mile descent along the South Fork of Rio Bonito. Signs here say, "South Fork Rio Bonito Trail (east, where you want to go), Blue Front Trail (east)," and "Crest Trail (south and northwest), Lookout Trail 2 (south), Three Rivers Trail 1¼ (north-west), Aspen Trail 1¼ (northwest)," and less than 100 feet east, down the trail, "Bluefront Trail (east), South Fork Campground 6 (east, where you should have left a car)," and "Southfork Rio Bonito, Trail No. 19."

There is a space for camping along the top of a narrow, forested ridge at 12.0 miles. An obvious trail proceeds along this ridge, but fades away when it goes into the dense forest beyond the campsites. Do not go this way, as this must be the Bluefront Trail No. 33. Trail No. 19, which you should take, switchbacks sharply to the right just as you come onto this small ridge, and continues to switchback down the slope to the stream below. From here on the hike is along the South Fork of Rio Bonito.

While you are hiking alongside Rio Bonito you will find some small streams that pour down the steep slope to the left, at 13.0, 13.75, and 14.7 miles to provide good drinking water. There are many fine places to camp at intervals along the way, and the cascading stream will relax you and sing you to sleep. The trail crosses the stream nine times before you get to some trail signs at 16.5 miles. These signs tell you, "Bonito Trail No. 19 (you are on it), Peacock Trail No. 818 (to the right, southeast), Monjeau Lookout (right)," and "Crest Trail 5 (where you just came from), Bonito Dam 3 (it is 1½ miles from this sign to the car parked near F.R. 107)." A trail forks back sharply to the left, upstream, at 16.6 miles. A sign here says, "Bluefront Trail." There is a Wilderness sign at 16.7 miles.

The trail ends at pavement in the campground at 17.5 miles, but since the campground is closed much of the year, cars must often be left down near F.R. 107, at 18.0 miles.

To get to this hike, go north out of Ruidoso on N.M. 37/48, or go south from Capitan on N.M. 48, to where N.M. 37 turns west. Go west on N.M. 37 for 1.2 miles to the fork where F.R. 107 goes left to Bonito Lake. Turn left on F.R. 107 and go west for 6.5 miles to the junction with the side road to the left (F.R. 107C) that goes to the South Fork of Rio Bonito Campground. You will need to leave a car at the gate or the parking area near road's end after dropping hikers off at the trailhead.

From the turnoff to South Fork Campground, go west 2.3 miles on F.R. 107 to its junction with F.R. 108. Turn right (north) on F.R. 108, which goes up Tanbark Canyon. Along the way you pass the sites of Parson's hotel (now burned), a restaurant, and a mining camp. Keep to the right at the fork 0.8 mile along F.R. 108. Ignore other side roads, and follow F.R. 108, which turns sharply left and switchbacks just above the old boilers and rows of concrete footings on the left about 1.5 miles from F.R. 107. F.R. 108 crosses the cattleguard at the trailhead 5.6 miles from the South Fork junction or 3.3 miles from F.R. 107.

The high country through which the Crest Trail passes. The steep peak in the center is Nogal Peak, as seen from the southwest.

171

35 WHITE SANDS HIKING TRAIL
WHITE SANDS NATIONAL MONUMENT

Distance: 2 miles round-trip
Time: 1 to 2 hours round-trip, but plan to camp overnight
Elevation Range: 4,000 to 4,025 feet
Rating: Very easy
Water: None; carry what you will need
Seasons: All. Hot days and cool nights in the summer; can be cold in winter
Topographic Maps: Holloman, Point of Sands 2
Special Map: For longer hikes get Lake Lucero, Lake Lucero NE, Tres Hermanos Topos
Permit: Required; obtain at Monument Headquarters; monument entry fee is $1 per car
Special Warning: Reflections from the sand are as bad as from snow or water, so wear
sunglasses and protective clothing to prevent sunburn and eye problems

This is really a special hike! The distance is only a mile each way, across not-quite snow white sand dunes. Its short distance and negligible elevation changes make it within the capability of anyone who can walk this far. Kids of all ages enjoy hiking and playing in the sand. Be sure to wear adequate protective clothing and sunglasses.

The National Monument is on U.S. 70/82 between Alamogordo and Las Cruces, 14 miles southwest of Alamogordo. When you arrive at White Sands go into headquarters to get your camping permit and ask any questions about the hike, including optional day hikes beyond the campsite. While in headquarters take time to see the displays and information about the monument.

Three miles into the monument from headquarters, stop at the nature trail, on the left. The 45 minutes or so that you spend on this short route, using the guidebook, observing the plants, insects, tracks, etc. will add greatly to your enjoyment of the longer hike and camping trip.

Parking for the hiking trail is at 4.8 miles from headquarters on the left (south) side of the road. The pavement ends just beyond this place. Park your car in the area provided and climb to the top of the nearby dune, to the southwest. Near the top of this dune is a post with #1 on it. From here you can see post #2 nearby. Post #3 is SSW beyond a low place in the dunes and may be a bit difficult to see, due to its distance and a few small trees growing in the sand near it. There are 10 such posts along the way marking the route. All the others are easier to see than post #3. These posts are necessary because wind shifts the sand and obliterates tracks often, and hikers could lose the way unless they navigated with a compass (and know which way to go). The route takes

you over packed sand dunes (with an occasional spot of soft sand) and down across the flat, grassy interdunal areas.

Near post #10, in the interdunal flat, is a sign telling that this is the camping area. This is a nice, secluded place with a flat area which winds some between the dunes, providing privacy for a number of small groups. It would not be often that you would find anyone else camping here though. It might be more exciting to sleep atop a nearby dune, particularly by full-moonlight. If you want a campfire, bring your own wood and don't burn any of the brush or wood that you find around camp. Check with headquarters about campfires when you get the camping permit. Also ask about disposing of human waste.

If you wish to make additional, extended day-hikes, you should check with headquarters when you get your permit. It is a nice hike to Lake Lucero, for example, but may take you onto White Sands Missile Test Range, so be certain that it will be all right. On return from a longer hike you may miss the campsite, so plan ahead how you will orient yourself to find it.

Camping in the White Sands is a unique experience, particularly by full moonlight. The reflective sand makes night seem almost as bright as day. If there is no wind, the silence is overwhelming, broken only by the call of an owl or other night bird or the howl of a coyote in the distance.

Always bring a tent if you plan to camp in the dunes. If the wind is not blowing, you may not need it, but in case of wind you definitely will. In either event, you will be picking sand out of your hair and teeth for the next three weeks. When the wind is blowing, there is something restful about the tick-tick of sand grains against your tent. You must try it!

Scant rainfall and shifting sands necessitate development of extensive root systems by trees, such as this cottonwood.

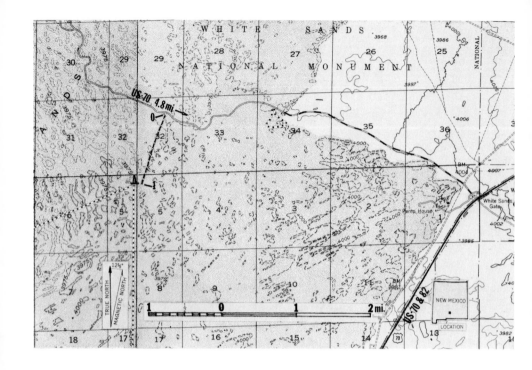

Cottonwood trees with the primitive camping area nearby, in White Sands National Monument.

36 INDIAN HOLLOW
ORGAN MOUNTAINS

Distance: 2.5 miles one-way
Time: 1½ to 2½ hours one-way, but plan to stay a couple of days
Elevation Range: 5,680 to 6,700 feet
Rating: Easy to moderate hiking; return route hard to find initially
Water: Indian Spring is dependable; carry a canteen for the hike
Seasons: All
Topographic Maps: Organ, Organ Peak
Special Maps: None

Indian Hollow will have more appeal to the experienced hiker than does Pine Tree Circle, which is the most popular hike in the Organ Mountains. Indian Hollow is off the beaten path and has plenty of space for primitive campsites, with a reliable water source nearby. Even though it provides an excellent wilderness camping experience, this is a relatively short hike. The camping area is very attractive, in an open forest, among ponderosa, juniper, piñon, small hardwoods, oak, and mountain mahogany. Sugarloaf, an isolated monolith, and the jagged wall of Organ Needles tower above camp, enhancing the scenery and providing interesting day-hikes and challenging rock climbs. There is usually a good stream running by the base of Sugarloaf, with a couple of other intermittent ones flowing into it.

This hike starts from the loop road at a point just east of Aguirre Spring Campground. It is marked with a sign that says, "Pine Tree Circle Trail, hiking time 3 hours." On the trail, take the left fork which goes basically south.

The path maintains a gentle, but relentless gradient, and has an excellent rock fragment surface. It is well-used, easy to follow, and is well-maintained. The route passes through a variety of environs, including low brush, large boulders, small green patches around springs and along small streams, and through mixed forest.

At the beginning the trail starts toward the south, but shortly begins to wind around as it works upward. There is no problem in following the route along Pine Tree Circle Trail up to the point at 1.58 miles where a less prominent path branches to the left to take you to Indian Hollow. Before arriving at this junction, the main trail proceeds north angling up the west slope of a ridge. The trail turns to the right, onto the ridge crest and doubles back to the south along the ridge at 1.56 miles. At the point where the trail arrives on the ridge, the crest is level to the north (left) and a short trail takes you to an excellent viewpoint. From here the trailhead is visible and a panorama to the north from east to west. Sugarloaf can be seen to the southeast.

From where the trail arrives on the ridge crest follow it for 120 feet to the south to the less prominent path that branches 40 degrees to the left. The left fork takes you toward Indian Hollow.

The Indian Hollow trail climbs up the ridge and presents you with some nice views to the east. Hiking gets steeper, with a brief section of ball-bearing loose gravel just before the route drops over the ridge crest. The faint path drops slightly as it leaves ridge crest to skirt, at about constant elevation, the head of a valley to the left, at 1.76 miles. Deer trails make following the correct path somewhat difficult, but look ahead and behind and try to maintain a fairly straight and level route along the curving hillside. The route arrives on the crest of the next ridge at 2.0 miles. At this point look back over the route you have just traversed and make some mental notes so you can return the same way. A compass bearing on Sugarloaf or a small heap of rocks here on the ridge would help establish your present position.

From here on the ridge you can drop down into Indian Hollow and head for Sugarloaf, looking for water and a good campsite. From your camp you can day-hike up the drainage into the saddle beside Sugarloaf. The more energetic may also want to climb up into the high places around the Needles to the south. Of course, it's no sin to be just lazy and loaf around camp if you prefer.

When you break camp and head back to the

175

car, take care in returning to the place where you arrived on the nearest ridge crest. Try to return by the route you followed on the way up. If you lose the way, the tendency is to climb too high while skirting the head of the valley and miss the trail altogether. If you can't find the trail, don't panic: just head northwest, crossing a couple of rocky stream beds and ridges and keep going until you come to Pine Tree Circle Trail. Turn to the right on this trail and it will take you back to the trailhead.

Indian Hollow is an excellent hike. It is not far from El Paso and is close to Las Cruces, but is not heavily used.

To reach the trailhead, turn off I-10/25 onto N.M. 70 and go east for 14.7 miles to the well-marked turnoff. Follow the paved road south for 5.9 miles to Aguirre Springs Campground. There are other hikes available from here too (see Hike #37).

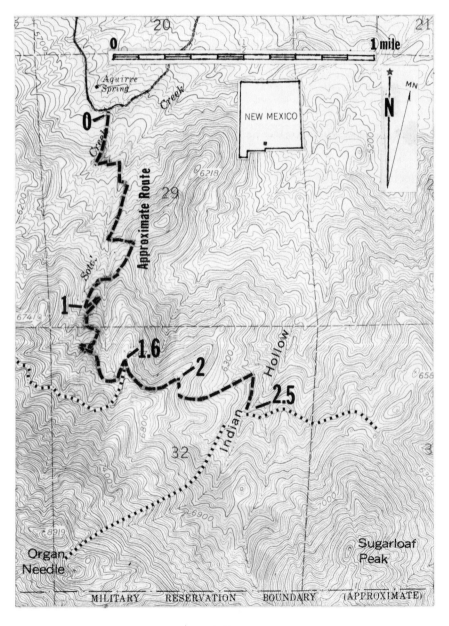

This hike affords excellent views of the steep, jagged Organ Mountains. Organ Needle, not visible in this view, is near the center of this photo.

The route to Indian Hollow follows the excellent Pine Tree Trail for 1.6 miles before departing to the left. Pine Tree Trail, which is a loop that returns via a different route, is a moderately easy day-hike. There is a primitive camping area about midway along the loop.

*Looking east across Indian Hollow. Sugarloaf
dominates the view.*

37 BAYLOR PASS
ORGAN MOUNTAINS

Distance: 5.8 miles round-trip
Time: 3 to 6 hours round-trip
Elevation Range: 5,620 to 6,390 feet
Rating: Easy
Water: Carry what you will need
Seasons: All; summers can be hot and winters cold
Topographic Maps: Organ, Organ Peak
Special Maps: None

On the paved loop road, the first trail sign you come to when you drive into Aguirre Spring Recreational Site is the one marking the Baylor Pass Trail. This sign says, "Baylor Pass Trail 4½ mi., Hiking & Riding, Horse Trail, No Bikes."

The trail is well-used, with an excellent surface. The gradient is constant, but not too steep. Scattered juniper, piñon, and small oaks grow along the route to just below the pass. The surroundings are quite green along this part of the route, much of the year. Red granite formations are scattered among the trees and some are so large that they are barriers that make the path take devious routes around them, adding variety and interest to the hike. The trail works up the northeast-facing slope, and the higher you climb, the bigger the view to north and northeast. There are many good viewpoints along the route, but near the top of the climb, at 1.6 miles, where the path turns southwest to go over the pass, is an outstanding place. This is a good rest or picnic spot, in addition to its being the best viewpoint along the way.

Baylor Pass is a grassy and sometimes windy, saddle in the mountainous ridge. A fence along the ridge crest crosses the trail, with a zig-zag pass through, at 2.0 miles. A sign here points to a designated camping area nearby. This makes a good place to camp, though it is popular with scouting groups and you may have some lively company. Many day-hikers turn around at the pass, but I would recommend this whole trip as a day-hike if you don't want to camp overnight.

As you cross the pass, you look west down a large valley, which in the distance is joined by a smaller drainage from the left. At this junction the valley curves right, to the northwest. A small, usually dry, stock pond can be seen at the confluence of the drainages. You can see this dry basin much of the time as the trail wanders down the valley to it. The dry pond offers the flattest, brush-free place to camp in this valley and is near an intermittent spring.

The trail on the south side of the pass is steeper and has a gravel surface that is slippery in places. The route winds around and is not nearly as good as the path on the north side of the pass. When you arrive at the dry stock pond (2.9 miles) plastic and metal pipes can be seen running from the pond up a small drainage to the east, to a spring. The area near the pond and spring is a nice, quiet, remote place for camping or picnicking. It would appear that the spring flow was much greater in the past, when the pipes were installed, than it is now. When it is flowing, the spring provides excellent drinking water. This is a genuinely desert setting, with few trees and predominately desert vegetation.

To get to the trailhead, exit from I-10-25 onto N.M. 70 near Las Cruces and go east for 14.7 miles to the well-marked turnoff, south, to Aguirre Springs Campground. Turn south on the paved road and go 5.9 miles to the recreation area. The trail sign is on the right, almost opposite the small, stone stable below and to the left of the loop road.

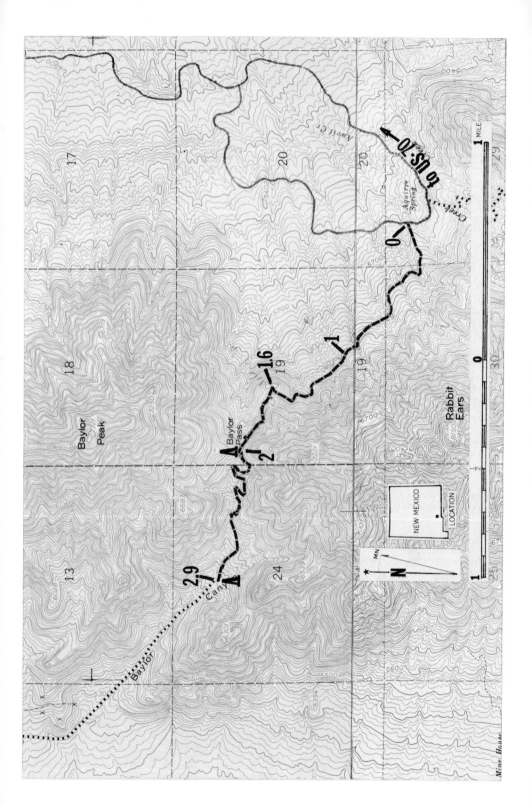

CLANTON DRAW TO GERONIMO SURRENDER SITE
CORONADO NATIONAL FOREST

Distance: 18.94 miles, loop route

Time: Two days or more; with a light pack and lots of luck, I made this hike in less than 12 hours, but didn't have time to enjoy the solitude and scenery

Elevation Range: 4,700 to 6,100 feet

Rating: Strenuous; requires extremely experienced trail finder and map reader (rough trail much of the way and long distance)

Water: Reliable in East Skeleton Creek at Surrender Site. Plenty in drainages during rainy seasons, usually mid-July through September and January through March. Check with Forest Service or carry enough

Seasons: All year, but summer afternoon temperatures can exceed 100°F and in winter nights can get down to 0°F, but these are extremes (deer hunting in November and javelina in February)

Topographic Maps: Apache Arizona-New Mexico covers the hike; Animas Peak, Guadalupe Canyon, Cienega Springs adjacent areas

Special Map: Coronado National Forest (Dragoon Mountains), Grid D6

Any hiker who goes to the Peloncillo Mountains in New Mexico's Coronado National Forest for the first time has a pleasant surprise in store for him. These mountains are well off the beaten path, situated in the extreme southwest corner of the state (and a bit of Arizona too). From the location you would expect the whole region to be hot, arid desert — but it is not. As you approach the Peloncillos, low, sparsely timbered hills are most apparent, with a hint of higher, forested country in the background. Forest Road 63 (Geronimo Trail) leads quickly into the inner mountains, which to the north of the road are densely forested with juniper, pine, oak, and Arizona Cypress on the slopes. Along the streams there are juniper, pine, sycamore, willow, and Arizona Walnut. During the wet seasons many of the streams are flowing with a trickle of crystal clear water and dotted with numerous small pools. These quickly dry up when the rains cease. To the south of F.R. 63 the mountains are generally lower, less steep, and not so densely forested.

It is advisable to contact the U.S. Forest Service office in Portal, Arizona (zip 85632) for current weather and water conditions. Also, for $1, the map of this area (Coronado National Forest, Dragoon Mountains) is available. This map shows roads, trails, major drainages, public land boundaries, etc.

The forest map shows a few roads going from N.M. 338 to the forest boundary, but only F.R. 63 gives access on the east side of the forest. F.R. 63 takes you into Clanton Draw

(Blair Well Road or Geronimo Trail) at the midpoint of the forest, and again at the south end near Cloverdale. From Cloverdale the road takes you to the Cloverdale Forest Service Cabin. You can walk two miles west from the cabin into Guadalupe Canyon, or four miles northwest to Guadalupe Peak.

To get to this hike from Interstate 10 and U.S. 80, go 12 miles west of Lordsburg or five miles east of where U.S. 80 joins I-10, to N.M. 338. Turn south on N.M. 338 and go south through Cotton City and Animas. About 25 miles south of Animas turn west on F.R. 63, Geronimo Trail. Go west on F.R. 63 for 7.1 miles to the National Forest boundary. Two miles inside the forest boundary is Black Water Canyon trailhead (Hike #39) on the south (left) side of the road and the National Forest Clanton Campsite is at 2.5 miles on the north (right) side. Clanton trailhead is on the north side of the road at 3.1 miles from the boundary.

Near a small grove of sycamore trees at the confluence of South Skeleton and East Skeleton Creeks, Geronimo and his band of renegades surrendered in March, 1886. At 10.6 miles on this hike you arrive at this historic place. A sign nearby, alongside the abandoned road proclaims that this is the Geronimo Surrender Site. The exact place of the surrender is not precisely known, but it was nearby if not here. A gravel road comes to here from U.S. 80 in Arizona, but the portion in the National Forest is badly washed and rocky in stream crossings. Signs near the Surrender Site sign prohibit motorized vehicles beyond this point, but a washed-out road continues up East Skeleton Canyon for 3.5 miles to Deer Canyon Trail. The road along East Skeleton follows the route of the old Skeleton Wagon Road which was used about 1880. Skeleton Canyon was used as a main artery trail by Indians and Mexicans traveling to and from Mexico long before the road was built. This area has quite a bit of history.

The hike to this historic place begins at the Clanton Trailhead on F.R. 63. Clanton Trail goes almost directly north from the road, up Clanton Draw, over a low pass and fence at .44 mile, and down to Whitmire Canyon Trail. This first portion of the route is fairly well marked with cairns and can be followed by a moderately experienced trail finder. The junction with Whitmire Canyon Trail is at 1.24 miles. There is plenty of flat area alongside Whitmire Creek, beneath the big trees, providing excellent camping for those who only want to hike this far. Signs on metal fence posts mark the route at this junction.

From Clanton Trail the route goes west (left) up Whitmire Creek, crossing from side to side. Numerous excellent campsites will be found all along this drainage. Occasional old blaze marks on trees, or rock cairns, are reassuring that you are on the trail. At 1.8 miles the drainage forks, with a rocky point in between. The larger fork is from the southwest (left) and a sign points this direction for "Whitmire Trail," but don't go this way. Follow the smaller branch (right) to the west. Another sign here points back east where you came from to "Salt Canyon." An arrow on this sign points west to "S. Skeleton," which is where you want to go. Follow the stream bed to the west to another fork at 3.1 miles. There is a low, flat bank between these forks. This time go left along the drainage to the southwest. The trail leaves the stream bed many times and returns to it, so watch for rock cairns or blazed trees marking the route. At 3.25 miles the trail is back in the stream bed, which is scoured, bare rock. The main drainage is going west and a small branch goes left. The trail has been in the trees on the left, but rock cairns can be seen on the north (right) side and there is an obvious trail going up the barren, rocky slope, getting well up on the hillside. The trail drops back down to cross a side drainage from the right, but look for rock cairns because they are going to take you up the hillside away from the stream. The cairns go almost due west and the stream is curving to the southwest. If you have trouble following the trail at this point, just head for the saddle to the west. There is a trail junction in the saddle at 3.55 miles. A north-south trail runs along the length of the saddle and when you get to it turn right (north) and follow it to trail signs at the north end of the saddle. A sign here says, "Canyon ⅛ mile (east), Salt Canyon 3 miles (east), Ranch Headquarters 5 miles (east)." Another sign has an arrow pointing south and another, on the ground, points north.

There is a terrific view of the Chiricahua Mountains to the WNW from here. Go north on the west side of the ridge and soon the trail is dropping fairly steeply to the northwest, alongside an old fence. There is a gate in the fence at 3.86 miles. A trail sign here, badly chewed by bears, says, "East Skeleton (south, the way you want to go), Chalk Canyon (north)." The upper portion of the sign is obliterated by teeth marks. There is also an arrow pointing back up where you just came from. This sign says, "Whitmire Country." Don't go through the gate toward Chalk Canyon. Take the route to the south. This is the portion of trail that is shown looping south on the map. The worst going on the hike is down this drainage. Long pants are almost a necessity through here because of the catclaw, manzanita, bear grass and other scratchy brush. Low limbs snag your pack. At 5.09 miles there is a sign pointing southwest (downstream). It says, "Outlaw Mountain, Geronimo Pass, Whitmire Country, Salt Country." Don't take the trail going southwest! Take the fork to the right (northwest) to Skeleton Canyon. The trail stays high above the drainage, which curves around to the northwest. It is a little difficult to follow the trail through the juniper at 5.5 miles, but there are a couple of signs bolted to trees and some rock cairns which help. Soon you can see down into a big drainage to the west. There is a dam with a nice pond behind it, in the stream bed to the NNW. The trail is rocky, but well marked with cairns, and drops almost straight west into the big drainage. Cross to the west side where you can see a major trail from above, and there are some trail signs. This is South Skeleton Canyon and the pond with the concrete dam in the drainage is shown on the Forest Map.

Signs here say, "East Skeleton Canyon (southeast), Whitmire Canyon (where you just came from)," "South Skeleton (the main

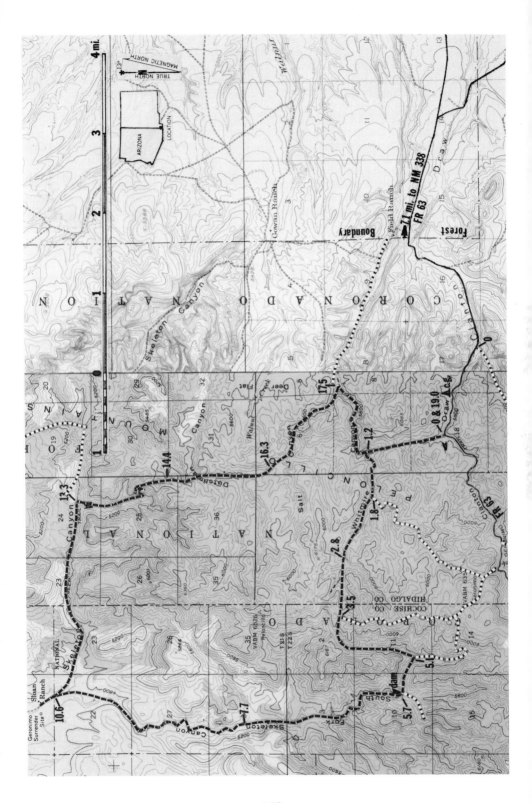

trail you are now on, north-south), U.S. Road 5 (north)," and "Starvation Canyon, Cowboy Area (south)." Along here the trail is very wide and distinct, compared to the terrible trails you have been over. This junction is at 5.68 miles.

Go north on the trail. The dam and lake are at 5.76 miles and from here to the Surrender Site is easy. Just follow the drainage and keep on the trail as it crosses from side to side. Few good campsites will be found between the pond and Surrender Site. Water in Skeleton Canyon is not reliable in the dry seasons. The trees become fewer and farther between as you progress north and from 7.6 miles on the surrounding country is quite open.

Geronimo's Surrender Site is reached at 10.65 miles. This would be a good place to spend the night on a two or three-day trip. There should be water in East Skeleton, but if there isn't and you are desperate, there is a ranch house less than a half-mile along the road to the north. There are a couple of signs here. One sign, with arrows pointing south, says, "Skeleton Canyon, South Fork Skeleton (south), Fairchild Allotment 3½ (south)." The other, with arrows pointing east says, "New Mexico State Line 1¼ (east), Devil's Kitchen, Old Ranger Sta. 4, Animas Valley 7."

The route goes east from here, up East Skeleton Canyon on the old road. There is a gate at 11.84 miles and this may be the New Mexico State Line. A sign beside the road on the right, at 11.91 miles says, "Dead End Road 2 mi." There is another fence at 12.10 miles and to the north against the canyon wall is a concrete "cabin" built over the entrance to a mine. The canyon gets progressively narrower and at 12.80 miles there are some interesting rock formations on the cliffs to the north of the road.

Pine Canyon Trail goes south from the road at 13.32 miles. Turn to the right and follow this "trail" up the canyon. There is some sort of concrete construction on the east side of the canyon mouth, and the canyon is blocked by a concrete dam a short distance upstream. The dam and pond are shown on the Forest Service Map. Go to the left of the dam and work your way along the steep bank above the pond. The faint trail is in and out of the drainage, usually on the left, as it continues upstream. At about 13.7 miles the trail is up on the east side of Pine Canyon, which is getting precipitous on both sides. The route gets farther from the canyon and crosses a couple of side drainages

from the east, as it works higher up the hillside. At 14.16 miles the trail is very distinct and is going up the steep hill to the east, through trees and manzanita brush. The trail switchbacks to the north at 14.20 miles and passes beneath a large squared off rock formation projecting out above the forest on the hillside slightly below the ridge crest. There is a gate in a fence on a shoulder of the high ridge at 14.42 miles, and the view from here is excellent. From here you can see South Skeleton and East Skeleton drainages, Geronimo Surrender Site, and lots of country beyond. Follow along the fence, heading south. The path goes into a saddle where there is a trail sign bolted to a limb of a small, forked pine tree (14.8 miles). The arrow points southeast down the east side of the saddle. The trail is hard to follow here as it drops east into a forested drainage. If you lose the trail, angle south as you go down the slope and you should encounter the path as it goes south along the slope, at about constant elevation. Follow this trail south and you should arrive on a ridge at the head of the canyon, at 15.02 miles. There is a sign in the saddle here that points back to the north to "Pine Trail."

From the sign the trail goes south at about constant elevation along the brow of a hill. A rock cairn or two mark the route along the way. The route crosses a small canyon at 15.15 miles. It is difficult to find, but the trail runs south along the west side of the canyon up above the stream bed.

At 15.37 miles the trail is well defined along the floor of a canyon, still going south. A little side drainage comes in from the east (left) and beside it on a big pine tree is a sign that calls this "Dutchman Canyon." The trail is in Dutchman Canyon, going south, upstream. A little way up the canyon there is sometimes a small amount of water. The trail stays in the steep-sided canyon for a while then goes up out the left side, over a shoulder then drops back into the canyon, crosses it, and goes up the right side into the trees.

There is a big juniper growing in the stream bed at 16.00 miles that has a blaze marking the trail cut into the bark on its north (down-stream) side. A forked juniper a few feet farther along has blazes on both north and south sides. There is an orange arrow (sign) pointing south in a tree on the west (right) side of the drainage at 16.05 miles. A nearby rock cairn marks where the trail goes steeply up the hillside to the west. The trail is almost impossible to follow up the grassy slope, but a rock cairn or two will reassure you that it is there. Angle southwest up the slope to a broad and fairly level ridge top. A small, isolated juniper at the top has a blaze mark on it. Follow the ridge top to the southeast until you see two metal fence posts with signs on them, at 16.33 miles. One sign says, "Dutchman Canyon" and has an arrow pointing to the northeast, where you just came from. The other sign points south to "Salt Canyon Trail." There is no indication of a trail from here to Salt Canyon, but that is where you want to go. Just go south and drop into the canyon. You should find the trail parallel to the drainage on the hillside, at 16.41 miles. The trail drops down to the canyon floor at 16.58 miles, and nailed to a tree is a sign with a white arrow pointing back up the way you have just come from. There is a beautiful campsite near this sign. It is flat and grassy, with big trees around, and sometimes there is water in the stream beside it.

Two metal fence posts with signs mark a major trail junction at 16.63 miles. One sign says, "Salt Canyon Trail (and points both west, the way you just came from, and east), Dutchman Canyon (west), West Skeleton Canyon (west)." The other sign says, "Whitmire Canyon (south, the direction you want to go), Geronimo Pass (south)." Go south, in the drainage, and you soon see a three-trunked pine tree with blazes on it, on both sides. An orange trail sign on the west (right) side of the drainage points to the east, at 16.90 miles indicating that the trail leaves the drainage here. The trail goes steeply up the east side and

over a shoulder and drops into a canyon. The trail is rocky going up the slope and disappears on top. Look carefully and you will see it down to the SSW on the slope. It holds constant elevation, then gradually drops some, but stays above the west side of the stream bed. Going gets rough and rocky in places. Cairns mark the way, continuing south and crossing some side canyons, but staying out of the main stream bed. At 17.45 miles the trail drops down into the stream bed just as it joins Whitmire Creek, which runs east-west. Three trail signs are on metal posts alongside Whitmire Creek at 17.53 miles. One, pointing north, the direction you just came from, says, "Dutchman Canyon, Salt Canyon, Skeleton Canyon." Two signs parallel to Whitmire Canyon, pointing east-west, says, "Whitmire Canyon (east), Ranch (east)," and "Geronimo Pass (west), S. Skeleton (west)." The hike along Whitmire Canyon to the west is easy, along a broad, flat bank under big shady trees.

Clanton Draw Trail joins Whitmire Canyon at 17.78 miles, completing the loop. Turn left (south) here, go up the slope to the saddle, at 18.18 miles, and down Clanton Draw to the road, which you reach at 18.94 miles.

This has been a beautiful, but tough trip, with many doubts about the route. It needs to be used more. The only use it gets is by the forest ranger who put it in and who rides it occasionally on horseback.

If you feel you are qualified to make this hike, don't pass up an opportunity to do so — preferably when there is water in the drainages. It will be a rewarding experience.

This sign is a cottonwood grove at the juncture of Skeleton Canyon and the South Fork of Skeleton

Canyon is near the place where Geronimo surrendered in 1886.

Skeleton water hole and dam in South Skeleton Canyon, at 5.7 miles.

39 BLACK WATER CANYON
CORONADO NATIONAL FOREST

Distance: 2.0 miles one-way, plus optional hikes
Time: 2 to 4 hours round-trip for basic hike (take time to explore more)
Elevation Range: 5,440 to 5,620 feet
Rating: Easy to moderate
Water: Carry what you will need; it is sometimes plentiful, but unreliable
Seasons: All year, but summer days are hot, and winter can be cold
Topographic Maps: Animas Peak, Apache (Arizona-New Mexico), Guadalupe Canyon, Cienega Springs
Special Map: Coronado National Forest (Dragoon Mountains), Grids 6E, 7D

This hike is to Blackwater Hole, a stock pond behind a concrete dam in Blackwater Canyon. It is a nice hike, particularly when there is water in the stream. This country is open enough that a hiker who can use map and compass should be able to explore this area extensively without becoming lost. Refer to the accompanying map for additional hikes that can be made as extensions to this one.

Bird watchers should be particularly interested in the area from Guadalupe Spring south to Guadalupe Canyon. Guadalupe Canyon is reputed to have the largest number of bird species of any place in the USA. This is because it has many species found elsewhere in the states, plus some species that come north to here from Mexico. Birds seen here include: Band-Tailed Pigeon, Gray Crested Jay, Bridled Titmouse, Bushtit, Hepatic and Western Tanagers, Dusky Capped and Ash Throated Fly Catchers, Black Headed Grosbeak, and Zone Tailed Hawk.

The trailhead is 1.8 miles inside Coronado National Forest from the east boundary cattleguard on F.R. 63, Coronado Trail. There is a trail sign on the left (south) side of the road, but it is difficult to see when approaching from the east because it is hidden by a tree.

This two-mile hike to Black Water Hole is an easy one. It follows the drainage upstream to the south, with slight elevation change, and few obstacles. A person with a moderate amount of experience should have no difficulty in following the route. An old, abandoned two-track is visible cutting across the inside of bends in the stream bed most of the way.

For the initial 100 yards or so, to the stream bed, the route is along a well-used two-track, but after the first creek crossing it appears that no vehicle has driven the route for a long time.

The trail follows the drainage, crossing from side to side as the stream meanders through the valley.

At times there is plenty of clear water running in the stream, which adds greatly to the pleasure of the hike. Typical of drainages in Coronado National Forest there are numerous excellent places to camp on the low, flat benches on the insides of the numerous bends, where there are many large trees and sometimes a carpet of grass. There will be signs of cattle along the way, particularly near the permanent water sources.

At 2.0 miles is a concrete dam across the drainage with a pretty little lake backed up behind it. This is Black Water Hole. On the west side of the pond the valley is flat and grassy (and rocky) with a few nearby live oak trees providing shade. This is an excellent place to camp. The surrounding hills are low and dotted with scattered juniper and other small trees, which makes this quite different from the scenery found on hikes to the north of F.R. 63. This is still a very pretty and interesting hike.

The experienced hiker will not be content to turn around at Black Water Hole. The forest map shows additional trails to the south and to the west, which will likely lure you on. Many of these trails are not marked, and are difficult to sort out from the cattle trails. At times it is easier to use the map and navigate cross-country directly to points of interest, such as the pond on Miller Creek and the one on Lion Creek, and Guadalupe Spring, etc. The country is open enough that it is easy to follow the ridges, cross the valleys, and maintain a fairly straight-line route.

There is an easy route to follow that gets you up out of Black Water Canyon to continue to places of interest to the south and west. The

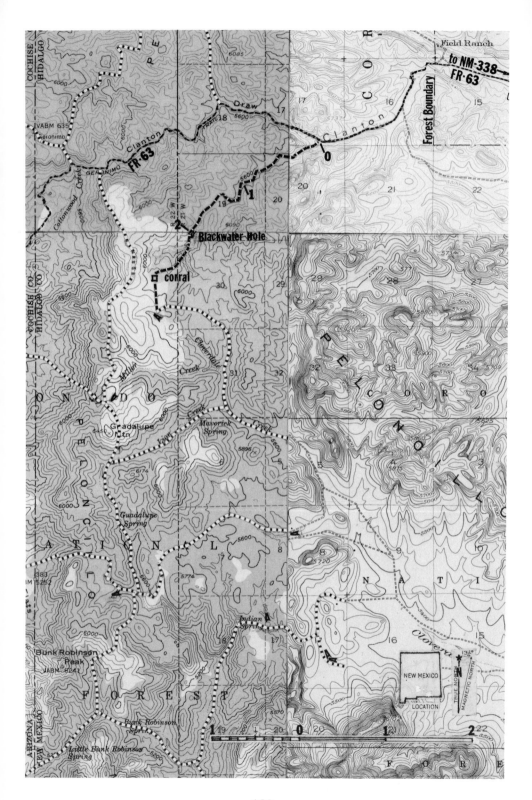

point to leave the canyon is marked, but will require close attention. About one-half mile upstream from Black Water Hole the trail runs along the south side of the drainage, a bit above the stream bed. The alert hiker should see a blaze mark on a large juniper beside the trail as the path is dropping down to cross a small drainage coming down fairly steeply from the left (south). Just across this side drainage the trail turns south and follows up the west side of this drainage.

This trail tops out in a relatively flat, high area surrounded on east, south and west sides by a low, brushy ridge. The trail takes you into a large corral with a metal outhouse size shed at one corner. From the corral, head west and in about a quarter of a mile you will cross a trail that runs north-south along the ridge crest. From here you are on your own because I haven't hiked this trail.

It is about 1.8 miles south along this trail to Guadalupe Mountain and 1.3 miles beyond the mountain to Guadalupe Spring. If you plan to do some birding in Guadalupe Canyon, six miles south (as the crow flies), you may want to start your hike at the Cloverdale Forest Cabin, but you should be able to get there on this trail if you are prepared for the long round-trip.

To get to this hike from I-10, go 12 miles west of Lordsburg and turn south on N.M. 338. Go south on N.M. 338 through Cotton City and Animas and 49 miles south of the interstate turn west on Geronimo Trail, F.R. 63. Go west on F.R. 63 for 7.1 miles to the National Forest boundary. The trailhead is on the left 1.8 miles inside the forest boundary. It is advisable to contact the U.S. Forest Service office in Portal, Arizona (zip 85632) for current weather and water conditions. The map of Coronado National Forest, Arizona Dragoon Mountains, Gila and Salt River Meridian, is also available. It shows roads, trails, major drainages, and other planimetric information and is very helpful when making this hike.

Black Water Hole, looking downstream.

189

40 MYERS CABIN, VICKS PEAK & SAN MATEO MOUNTAIN
CIBOLA NATIONAL FOREST, MAGDELENA DISTRICT

Distance: 6.1 miles one-way to Myers Cabin
Time: 4 to 7 hours to cabin and 3 to 5 hours return; allow two days for up and back, plus a day
  or two for day hikes up Vicks Peak and San Mateo Mountain
Elevation Range: 7,400 to 9,400 feet at cabin, 10,252 feet on Vicks Peak
Rating: Moderate to strenuous, depending on load, temperature, and hiker's physical
  condition
Water: Nave Spring, Myers Spring, and San Mateo Spring (carry some too)
Seasons: Usually April through November, but depends on snow
Topographic Map: Vicks Peak
Special Map: Cibola National Forest Magdelena District, Grid F9

The novice hiker will probably classify this hike as strenuous because of the steep and sometimes hot climb of 1,700 feet in the first 2.25 miles. This steep climb takes you from the juniper and piñon forest of the dry lower elevations to the aspen, pine and fir forest in the mountains. Nearly all of the route in the mountains is through fairly dense forest, with occasional viewpoints.

The trail starts at Springtime Campground, near the head of Nogal Canyon. The path is wide, easy to follow, and well-maintained, but is rocky in places and the 16.1 percent grade (average) is unrelenting. At the beginning the trail is near the floor of Nogal Canyon, but soon climbs the steep slope out onto the equally steep side of the mountain. At the higher elevations there are some grand views to the east over lower foothills and the arid regions beyond, with distant mountains to contemplate. Switchbacks take you up the steeper places and you arrive rather abruptly to a level saddle between two small peaks. This is a one and a half to three-hour climb, depending on your load and physical condition, and is the most strenuous part of the hike. Much of the climb is exposed to the sun until mid-afternoon and in warm weather even the experienced hiker will admit that it is hot and steep going. The climb levels off in the saddle at 2.25 miles, for which one and all will be thankful. There is a large triangle of white (painted) rocks nearby, which is apparently an aerial survey marker.

The trail junction where you turn left is at 2.29 miles and is well-marked with two signs beside wide and easy to follow T-43 which you have been on up to this point. The signs says, "Shipman Tr. No. 50 (southwest, the way you want to go), Nave Spring 2¼, Forest Road 377

7 (in the same direction)" and "Apache Kid Trail No. 43 (north-south), San Mateo Lookout 2 (north), Blue Mountain 7 (north), Springtime Campground 2¼ (south, where you just came from)." If you need water you can continue a half-mile north on T-43 to San Mateo Spring. An excellent optional hike would be the one north on T-43 to San Mateo Lookout Tower atop San Mateo Peak and on north to Apache Kid Grave Site and beyond to Blue Mountain, the turnaround point for Hike #41.

Turn left (southwest) on T-50, which is also a good, well-marked route, though not nearly so wide and heavily used as T-43. Along some portions of this route there are T-50 signs every hundred yards or so to reassure you that you're on course.

The trail crosses over a ridge at 2.57 miles and begins to drop rather steeply. The route bottoms out in a nice flat-floored valley with plenty of shady places to camp under large trees, at 3.00 miles. There is a trail junction here, with a side trail going down the valley to the west. Signs say, "Milo Trail No. 49 (west), San Mateo Canyon 4 (west), Forest Road No. 76 6 (west)" and "Shipman Tr. No. 50 (north-south), Apache Tr. No. 43 1 (north), San Mateo Lookout 2½ (north), Forest Road No. 377 6 (south)." Part of the Shipman Trail sign has been chewed by bears.

The trail climbs from Milo Canyon until it crosses a saddle in the ridge at 3.61 miles. Occasional openings in the forest provide views back to T-43 and to the west toward Gila Wilderness, in the distance. The route crosses a little ridge at 4.04 miles and begins to lose elevation, slowly at first, then more steeply as it gets into the drainage above Nave Spring.

At 4.52 miles the trail crosses the stream

bed and there are some trail signs. Nave Spring is a few yards downstream, west, from the trail junction. Some pipes have been put into the spring in the past, but the best flow is coming out of the ground now. The flow won't be great, but there should always be at least a trickle of clear, cool water. There is not a good campsite in this canyon anywhere near the spring, so plan to get water here and then continue to Myers Cabin. You should have some extra jugs for carrying water for your stay at Myers Cabin. Also, you should have carried enough water from the car to keep you out of trouble in case the spring is not flowing.

A side trail runs northwest down Nave Canyon. Signs here say, "Shipman Tr. No. 50 (west, the way to Myers Cabin), Forest Road No. 377 5 (west)" and "Shipman Tr. No. 50 (north, where you just came from), Apache Kid Tr. No. 43 2¼ (north), San Mateo Lookout 4 (north)" and "Nave Spring, Nave Tr. No. 86 (northwest), Milo Canyon 1½, San Mateo Canyon 4 (northwest)."

Continue on T-50 as it turns left to climb west, up out of Nave Canyon. You continue to climb for the next three-quarters mile, but the grade eases after a half-mile.

On arrival at Myers Cabin you will have hiked 6.1 fairly hard miles and will likely be ready to make camp for the night. The Forest Map shows that T-50 continues down Shipman Canyon to F.R. 377 (Burma Road). It is about 3.5 miles to F.R. 377 from Myers Cabin. Unless you have a ride available when you arrive at F.R. 377, it is not recommended that you plan to end your hike there. It is a long way (possibly 20 miles) by road back to Springtime Campground.

There is plenty of level ground around Myers Cabin, but no water. A well provided water for the cabin years ago, but not at present. This is a very nice place for an extended camp, with interesting side hikes.

It is a two to four-hour hike southeast to the summit of Vicks Peak and back, plus time that you will spend on the summit. About the same amount of time is required to make the round-trip to San Mateo Mountain, to the southwest. Views from both peaks are spectacular. From San Mateo Mountain you look out over the Black Range of the Gila Mountains, 20 miles to the west (see Hikes #42 and #43).

The map shows Myers Spring to be about three-quarters mile down Shipman Canyon but I haven't been there to see if it is flowing; maybe the Forest Service could tell you about this. You can check out Nave Spring as you pass it, and it is not a long walk down to Myers Spring to check it out to see which would be the best place to get your camp water. It is really fine camping in this area, so plan to spend a few days if you have the time. There is no water on the hikes to the peaks, so be sure and carry enough from camp when you make these day-hikes.

The route you take in getting to Springtime Campground may depend on where you are coming from. The shortest and less steep, all-weather gravel, route is from U.S. 85, 28 miles north of Truth or Consequences and 46 miles south of Socorro. Turn northwest on F.R. 225 and follow it 14 miles to the junction with F.R. 225A, which will take you to the campground. It is suggested that instead of going out this same route, you go out to Monticello. Take F.R. 225 south from the campground to F.R. 139, which is also good all-weather gravel. Some of the views from this route, down through Luna Park, are excellent, particularly when you get in places where you can see the Gila Mountains. Or, if you are coming from the south, you may want to go to Springtime Campground through Monticello. Five miles north of Truth or Consequences on U.S.85/ I-25 turn west on N.M. 52. Go four miles west on N.M. 52 and take the fork to the right on N.M. 142. It is 12 miles from the fork to Monticello. On the west edge of this small cluster of houses and store, turn north across the cattleguard onto F.R. 139. F.R. 377 branches to the left about three miles north of Monticello, but keep to the right on F.R. 139 unless you plan to leave a vehicle at the end of T-50 at Shipman Canyon. Go left on F.R. 225 a mile past the F.R. 377 junction. Luna Park Campground is 10 miles from Monticello and the turnoff to Springtime Campground is seven miles past Luna Park.

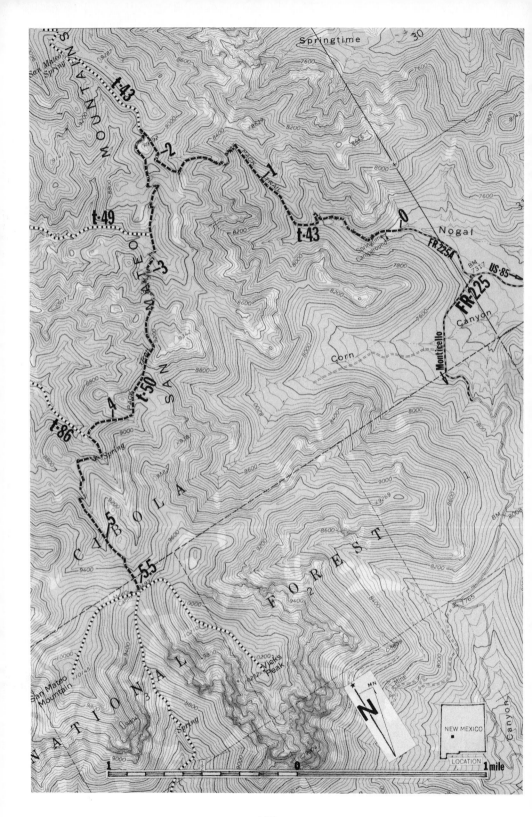

192

The excellent, wide trail for Hike #40 starts at Springtime Campground.

41 COFFEE POT TRAIL
CIBOLA NATIONAL FOREST, MAGDELENA DISTRICT

Distance: 7.2 miles one-way to the top of Blue Mountain
Time: 4 to 6 hours up, with day-pack and longer with backpack; 3 to 4 hours down
Elevation Range: 7,270 to 10,309 feet
Rating: Moderate. Good trail, easy to follow
Water: Good spring at 4.25 miles, emergency water on top of Blue Mountain
Seasons: April through November, but depends on snow
Topographic Map: Blue Mountain
Special Map: Cibola National Forest, Magdelena Ranger District Grid F7

This is an excellent hike and may well become one of your favorites. It is far enough from popular tourist places to limit visitors to this area, though the trail is well maintained and apparently well used. The trail, except for the first 200 feet, is easy hiking, and is very easy to follow with well-marked blazes and signs. Bears seem to find the signs tasty, as they have damaged most of them. Trees all along the way are blazed, and some may not survive the enthusiastic markings. Portions of the path were rerouted or rebuilt in 1979 and all fallen trees were cleared away at that time.

Hike #41 is one of the few routes that has a reliable spring near the top end so you don't have to haul all of your water from the beginning. There are many scenic view points and numerous excellent campsites. Don't camp near the spring, as this is the only water in the vicinity available for wildlife, and they won't drink if you are anywhere close. The dense forest along much of the route offers welcome shade on warm days, which is another plus for this hike. There are good campsites near the summit of Blue Mountain and excellent vistas from the top. Emergency water is available from the cistern of the Forest Service Cabin on the summit. There are a number of optional or additional routes available.

If you are in a hurry, this can be a beautiful all-day hike. If you have a vehicle with adequate clearance you can drive 1.9 miles up Coffee Pot Canyon to the trailhead to reduce distance and time. Times and distances are given from Forest Road 478.

The way to best enjoy this hike is to pack in and stay a while. There are good campsites one-half mile below Cub Spring and one-half mile above it, and also at the summit. From camp, day hikes can be made on the loop of Trails #81 and #87 past Cold Spring and Apache Kid Grave Site. Trails #45, #49 and #43 make a loop with a side trip up San Mateo Peak, or there are other possible hikes which you may prefer. Car shuttles to such places as Burnt Peaks area on F.R. #140; F.R. #76 and Trail No. 45 junction, F.R. #377 and Trail No. 50 junction, or Springtime Campground on F.R. #225 offer a number of interesting alternate routes.

The hike starts from F.R. 478 at the sign that says, "Coffee Pot Trail No. 69, Post Trail No. 90 — 5." The forest road runs along a beautiful flat-bottomed valley with scattered pine trees. The trail goes southeast along a jeep road on the floor of Coffee Pot Canyon for 1.9 miles. At 0.4 mile beyond the end of the jeep road, the trail abruptly goes steeply up the west side of the sloping side of the canyon. After 200 feet the gradient eases and in another 100 feet or so the path is nearly on the crest of a ridge. From here on, the route is easy hiking and well marked, with blazes on trees. In places where the little-used route is indistinct, follow the blazes. Along the ridge at about 2.7 miles (1.9 miles from end of jeep road) there are good vistas to both sides and back to the north. The path generally follows on, or near, the ridge crest to about 3.6 miles where it starts to climb for a short distance and traverses along the west side of a wooded hill, which is a high point on the ridge.

There is a T-59 sign at 4.1 miles on the southwest side of the hill. The trail may lose you briefly at a switchback on a short-steep section which takes you up on the ridge southeast of the wooded peak (4.3 miles). The route continues generally southeast along the ridge, with good views of Mount Withington to the north. There are good campsites along the ridge.

The junction with Post Trail No. 90, which goes to the west, is encountered on the ridge at 5.5 miles. The trail signs have been damaged by bears. From this junction it is 2.75 miles to F.R. 130 on Trail 90, and 1.75 miles along Trail 59 to the summit of Blue Mountain.

The trail in this area is quite wide and easy walking through a mixed forest of aspen, pine, and fir, with many good campsites. The route climbs fairly persistently to Cub Spring, at 6.2 miles. The spring area is fenced to keep animals out and water flows from a pipe into a metal stock water tank. This is a very nice place, and the water is cool, clear, refreshing, and safe to drink. A sign tells you that this is Cub Spring.

There is a trail junction 300 feet along the way, above the spring. Maverick Trail No. 68 goes south nine miles to F.R. 76. Another junction with another fork of Trail No. 68 is found at an additional half-mile farther along (at 6.8 miles).

At 6.9 miles there is another junction that is marked with three signs. Apache Kid Trail No. 43 goes northeast to Tee Pee Peak Trail No. 81 (¼ mile) and to West Red Canyon (6 miles). Your route continues southeast along T-59 and T-43 combined, one-quarter mile to the summit.

There is a Forest Service Cabin and a clearing at the summit of Blue Mountain, which is 7.2 miles from the start, at F.R. 478. There is also an outhouse and a heliport near the cabin. Against the south side of the cabin is a concrete cistern with water in it, accessible by removing a metal cover. Use this water only in case of emergency. Don't contaminate it with dirty hands or cup, and treat it before drinking. And, be sure and replace the cover. Usually there is no one living in the cabin, but do not bother it.

The Apache Kid Trail skirts around the south side of the summit, and a sign 150 feet or so to the southeast of the cabin marks the route. It is 1.5 miles to Cyclone Saddle and seven miles to San Mateo Lookout. (See Hike No. 40 which tells how to get to San Mateo Mountain from the south.)

To get to Coffee Pot Trail, go 12 miles west of Magdalena on U.S. 60 and turn south on N.M. 52. This intersection is near the eastern-most radio telescope antennas that are strung out along Hwy. 60. From Hwy. 60 it is about 46 miles south on N.M. 52 to F.R. 478. A mile or so south of U.S. 90 the pavement ends, but it is very good gravel all the way to F.R. 478. F.R. 478 can be reached from the south also. From I-25, at about five miles north of Truth or Consequences, turn west on N.M. 52. Hwy. 52 is paved to its junction with N.M. 59. Continue seven miles or so north of the end of the pavement to F.R. 478.

F.R. 478 is a good all-weather road, with a few creek crossings that could flood during heavy rains. It is 13.8 miles from N.M. 52 to the Coffee Pot Trail No. 69 sign.

This Forest Service cabin occupies part of a small clearing atop Blue Mountain, the turnaround point for Hike #41. It is possible to continue on the Apache

Kid Trail past Apache Kid Gravesite to join the route covered in Hike #40.

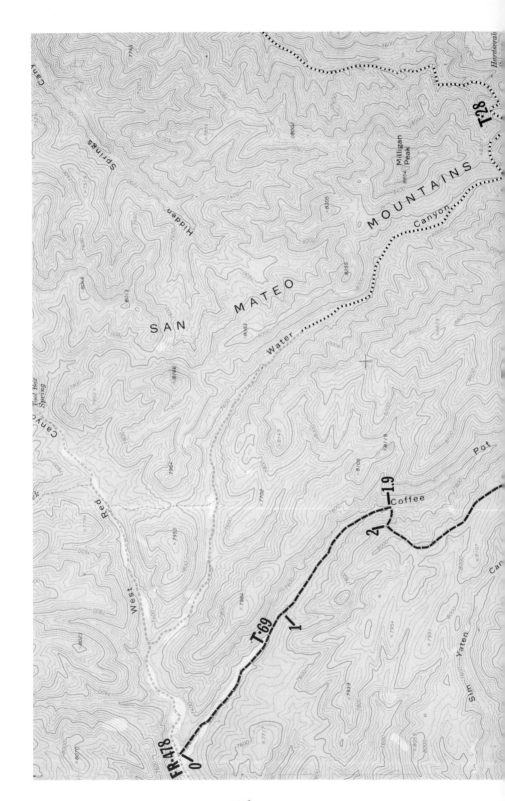

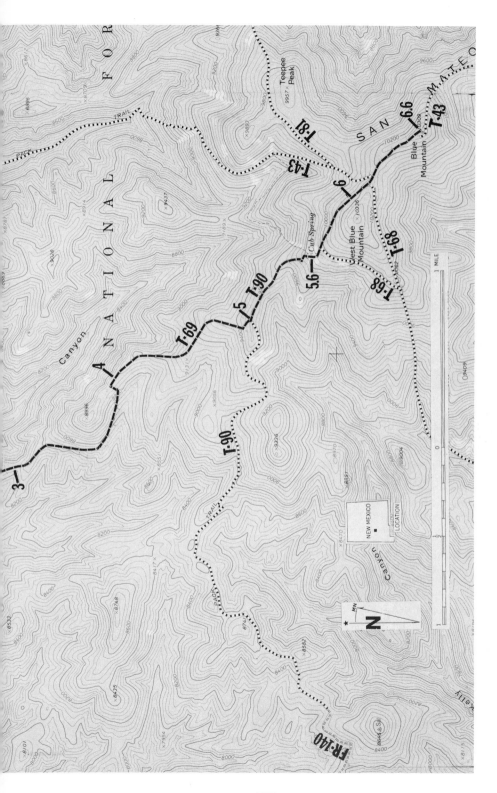

197

42 BLACK RANGE CREST TRAIL
GILA NATIONAL FOREST

Distance: 10.9 miles
Time: 5½ to 10 hours, but plan to take two days
Elevation Range: 8,230 to 10,011 to 7,020 feet
Rating: Moderate
Water: In streams as noted, but you should plan to carry all you will need
Seasons: Depends on snow. April or May to October or November
Topographic Map: San Lorenzo, 15-minute
Special Map: Gila National Forest, Grid L-10
Permit: Not required for this hike, but necessary if you go any farther north, into the Wilderness Area

Gila Crest Trail runs for about 26 miles north, from N.M. 90, along the crest of the Black Range, to join Continental Divide Trail No. 74 at Reed's Peak. Hike #42 follows T-79 for only 6.75 miles, but is a good introduction to the route and to this splendid area. A fast hiker can cover this route in 5½ hours, but if you take your time to eat and leisurely enjoy the scenery along the way and atop Hillsboro Peak, it will take a full day. Get an early start, or better yet, plan to camp in one of the ample good camping places along the trail. Further explorations are made possible this way. There are plenty of optional routes, including continuing farther on T-79. A wilderness permit will be required if you take any of the trails north of the route described here.

This hike, as delineated, will require a car shuttle (two cars) or someone to pick you up at the end. A factor in the selection of this route was that the finish is 1,200 feet lower than the beginning, providing considerably more downhill than uphill hiking. Hillsboro Peak is 1,800 feet higher than the starting point, so the first half of this hike has some uphill hiking. It is 3,000 scenic feet downhill from the peak to the end, in Gallinas Canyon.

I suggest that you carry all of the water you will need. There is no water along the ridge crest. When snow is melting, or while the ground is moist, there is water in a stream at 5.4 miles, but don't count on finding any here later in the summer. There will be water flowing in Railroad Canyon and more in Gallinas Canyon, but this will need to be treated adequately before you can use it.

The hike starts from N.M. Hwy. 90 in Emory Pass. Prior to starting you must shuttle a car west 4.5 miles to T-129 near Railroad Campground in Gallinas Canyon.

A sign at the trailhead says, "Black Range Crest Trail No. 79, Hillsboro Peak 5 (north), Road No. 152 13¼ (north)." At the beginning, the route follows a jeep road that is now closed to vehicles, though the Forest Service may use it occasionally for the first quarter mile to the helicopter pad and corral. The route is easy walking, though a little steep up to the heliport, where it levels off briefly. There is also a small yellow building and an outhouse here. Your route forks at the corral fence. The path to the right follows an abandoned and overgrown road up onto the ridge crest. The path to the left is a foot path with a better gradient and good views to the west and joins the other route at 1.1 miles on the ridge crest. Occasional views to either side of the ridge overlook the beautiful surroundings. To the east it is particularly grand.

There is a nice campsite in a saddle with a good view to the east at 3.1 miles. A side trail goes back down to the east side of the ridge at 3.7 miles and a sign here read, "Ladrone Gulch Trail #127, Kingston 5½ (northeast), Hillsboro Peak 1½ (north, where you are headed), Emory Pass 3½ (south, where you just came from)." Another sign here says, "Hillsboro Bypass Trail No. 412 (and points to a trail that goes down to the west), East Railroad Canyon Trail No. 130 (west)." Face west when you read this second sign so you can better correlate the arrows with the trails. The Crest Trail goes straight, almost north-northwest, from the junction, but it curves around to the west as it approaches the summit of Hillsboro Peak. Bypass Trail No. 412 is convenient to use when the peak is blocked with deep snow, and enables you to hike this route a month or so before the route over the peak is passable.

There is a nice campsite as you cross a

shoulder of the mountain at 3.9 miles. A fence and gate and another sign are at 4.3 miles. The sign points east-southeast to Mineral Creek Trail No. 125 and north to N. (something) "A" road 6.

The summit of Hillsboro Peak is attained at 5.6 miles. This is really a "neat" place. There is a lookout tower here and by climbing the stairs you can see over the trees in all directions. As you would expect, the view is outstanding. There is plenty of level space for camping here on this high point. Trail No. 117 goes north from here, into the wilderness area.

From Hillsboro Peak the remainder of the hike is downhill all the way to Railroad Campground in Gallinas Canyon. There may be a few brief uphill pitches, but none of significance. Bypass Trail No. 412 joins the Crest Trail from the left (southeast) at 5.0 miles. If you don't want to climb the peak, the hike is 0.3 mile shorter via the Bypass route, which is a very good trail. On the Bypass Trail, 0.3 mile west of T-79, there is a junction with T-130, East Railroad Canyon Trail. A sign here says, "Gallinas Canyon Trail No. 129 3½ (to the left, southeast), Hillsboro Bypass Trail No. 412 (both directions, east and west), Ladrone Gulch Trail 127 1¼ (east), Black Range Crest No. ? 1¼ (east)." A quarter of a mile past this junction the trail goes around a high, open corner which affords a fine view over Railroad and Gallinas Canyons and the mountains beyond. Along here the forest is mixed, predominantly conifers, with a few aspen and some oaks.

Near where the Bypass Trail rejoins the Crest Trail you go through a gate. From the gate the route goes downhill to a saddle north of the fence line. There is good water in the drainage at 5.25 miles, when the snow is melting, but it may be dried up later in the summer. A very good place to camp is under the lofty pines near the stream. The route joins a larger drainage, which has water sometimes, and crosses it at 5.9 miles.

At 6.0 miles the trail is in a saddle with good views to the north and south. There is a fence just to the south of the saddle. The path rounds another exposed corner with a good view, turns north, and begins to drop into Railroad Canyon. To the right of the trail (east) at 6.3 miles there appears to be a rock shelter up the steep hillside. I haven't checked to see if it has been occupied. Along here the trail gets into a burn area which has become overgrown with thorn bushes. You really need some tough,

long pants from here to the next junction and for a while as you go down Railroad Canyon.

At 6.75 miles the Crest Trail meets Railroad Canyon Trail. Signs here don't tell you where you are, to my satisfaction. Though it is not identified, T-114 goes north from here. A sign, as you look north, says, "Entering Black Range Primitive Area, Wilderness Permit is Required for Entry." Other signs here tell you, "Road No. 152 5½ (northwest on T-79)" and "Hillsboro Peak 2¾ (east where you just came from), Emory Pass 6½ (east)" and "Hwy. 90 4¼ (south, the way you want to go), ?? Place 6¾ (north, on T-114)."

The trail you want to take is in the drainage on the west side of the stream bed, and goes south down the drainage. T-79 goes up the west bank of the drainage and continues northwest. T-128 remains in the drainage all the way to Railroad Campground at N.M. 90, and crosses the stream 40 times before you get to the car. If there is much water in the stream (check when you shuttle cars) plan to get your feet wet. The farther downstream you go the wider the water gets. It is really not much of a stream above where Railroad Canyon joins Gallinas Canyon, and crossing it is no problem, but the 21 crossings in the last mile give you plenty of opportunity to wet your feet.

West Railroad Canyon, a large side drainage, joins from the west at 8.5 miles. Railroad Canyon widens, with plenty of level area for camping in the forest on the east side above and below the junction with T-130, at mile 8.9. A sign here tells you "East Railroad Canyon Trail No. 130 (east), Hillsboro Peak 4¾ (east), Holden Prong Saddle 1½ (north), Black Range Crest 2½ (north, where you came from), Railroad Spr. 2 (south, where you are going)." T-130 departed from the Crest Trail at 3.70 miles and cuts 2.3 miles off the hike, if you are looking for a shortcut.

There is a fence and gate at 9.2 miles, with good camping areas nearby. The path continues to cross the stream frequently.

Railroad Canyon Trail No. 128, which you have been on, joins Gallinas Canyon Trail No. 129, which comes in from the right at 9.7 miles. A sign here tells you, "Railroad Canyon Trail No. 128 (north), Hillsboro Peak 5¼ (north on T-128), Black Range Crest 4 (north-northwest, on T-129), Highway 90 1½ (south on T-129)." It is a bit difficult to interpret the arrows on this sign without the forest map or topographic map. There is a good campsite near this junction.

The trail continues to cross the stream (which has become wider) frequently in Gallinas Canyon. The path passes a corral at 12.5 miles and it is apparent that the end is near when you come to the picnic table and campsite at 10.8 miles. The parking area and end of hike is at 10.9 miles.

This has been a good introduction to the Black Range. Now you should be ready to hike into the Wilderness Area and spend a few days.

To get to this hike, get on N.M. 90 in Silver City and go east for about 44 miles to Emory Pass, or get on N.M. 90 from I-25 at Caballo and go west about 31 miles to Emory Pass. The car shuttle is to Gallinas Canyon, 4.5 miles west of Emory Pass.

A fairly well marked trail with good Forest Service signs.

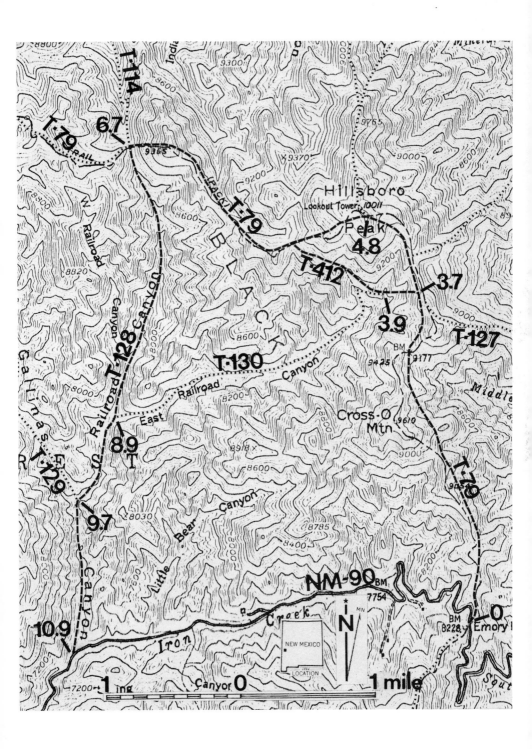

T-114

T-79 RAIL

6.7

T-79

T-412

Hillsboro

Lookout Tower, 10011

Peak

4.8

3.7

3.9

T-127

BM 9177

9425

Cross-O Mtn.

9610

T-79

T-130

Railroad

Railroad Canyon

T-128 Canyon

E

T-129

8.9 T

9.7

8030

Little Bear Canyon

Canyon

8785

NM-90

BM 7754

Creek

BM 8228

Emory

0

10.9

Iron

Canyon O

NEW MEXICO

LOCATION

N MN

1 ing

201

43 WILLOW CREEK TO MOGOLLON BALDY
GILA NATIONAL FOREST

Distance: 40.1 miles round-trip (loop)
Time: 2½ days minimum (allow more time)
Elevation Range: 6,920 to 10,770 feet; start and end at 7,920 feet
Rating: Strenuous. Good trails, but long distance and considerable elevation changes
Water: Reliable in west fork, White Creek, and springs, ordinarily; check with Forest Service about water in springs at 24.1 miles, 28.0 miles (West Fork Saddle), 28.34 miles (Little Hobo), and Hummingbird Saddle
Seasons: Depends on snow, but usually March through November for the route to West Fork of Gila and May or June through October for the high country
Topographic Maps: Negrito Mountain, Mogollon Baldy Peak, Lilley Mountain, Grouse Mountain
Special Map: Gila National Forest, Grids 7F, 8G, 8F, 8E
Permit: Required for all hikes. You can self-permit at box alongside driveway in front of Willow Creek Ranger Station

This is a long, somewhat strenuous, but excellent hike through extremely beautiful country, with a variety of terrain and scenery. The trails are very good, though there are some brief rocky stretches in the first half of the trip. The route is well marked except that the signs do not give trail numbers, and in a couple of places they don't give you enough information to be certain of which way to go without consulting a map. (You must have the forest map or topographic maps, or both, to aid in route-finding, and to help keep you oriented and abreast of your progress.) Maps also show alternate routes and answer questions about where the side trails go. This is such a nice hike, don't try to rush through it in the minimum possible time of 2½ days, if you have more time available. When you look at the map you'll see that there are many other trails which connect with this route, offering numerous alternatives. Since you can't hike them all in one trip, you'll probably find this area luring you back to explore again — and again — and again.

If possible, check with the Forest Service about water availability from the springs on this trip. I have found them to be reliable, but there may be times when one or more stops flowing temporarily. If the springs are questionable you should fill up at White Creek for the remainder of the trip; a gallon or more per day for each person. Emergency water may be available at the cabin atop Mogollon Baldy, but don't plan to get any here, as this is the supply for the rangers on lookout duty and is possibly inadequate for their needs.

This hike begins at Willow Creek Campground and you should try to start walking no later than 8 a.m. if at all possible, if you intend to go to White Creek Cabin area for the first night. This is an eight to 12 hour trip for most hikers, and you need to get to the area, select a site, make camp and cook supper before dark. If you get a late start, or are progressing slowly, you should plan to spend the first night near West Fork Corral. It would be highly desirable to spend at least two nights near White Creek Cabin so you can relax, swim, explore, and just enjoy this wonderful place.

From the West Fork to Mogollon Baldy it is uphill all the way. It takes about eight hours to grind your way up to the spring at 24.1 miles, which is a good place to camp, or 9½ hours to the summit. An average hiker should be able to make it from the summit to Willow Creek in nine hours. It would be better to break the trip down into two five-hour days with an overnight camp in Hummingbird Saddle. There are many possible schedule variations and numerous optional routes, dependent on the whims of the hikers.

In Willow Creek Campground the trailhead parking is on the south side of the creek. A small gravel road crosses through the creek to get to the trailhead, but hikers must look for stepping stones or logs to facilitate getting across with dry feet. From the trailhead follow T-151 uphill to Iron Creek Lake, 1.3 miles distant. Immediately before you get to the lake you pass the junction, on your right, with White Water Baldy Trail (T-172), your return route. A sign at this junction says, "Iron Creek

Lake, Whitewater Baldy 7½ (south), Turkeyfeather Pass 4¾ (east, the way you want to go), Middle Fork 6½ (east), Willow Creek 1¼ (west)." McKinze Trail #151 crosses the small dam of Iron Creek Lake and follows a drainage downhill to Iron Creek, at 2.5 miles. There is another trail junction at 1.52 miles where T-171 continues east and T-151 turns south. Signs here tell you, "Middle Fork 6¼ (east), T.F. Pass 4½ (south)" and "Iron Creek Lake ¼ (west), Willow Creek 1½ (west)."

When you arrive at Iron Creek turn left (east) and follow it downstream. This creek bottom is a beautiful area with many excellent stream-side campsites beneath the lofty pines. The path crosses to the right, (south) side of Iron Creek at 4.10 miles, where the valley narrows. At 4.18 miles T-151, your route, turns to the right and goes south up a side canyon toward Turkeyfeather Pass, two miles distant, while T-157 continues east. Signs at the junction says, "T F Pass 2, West Fork 4½ (south)" and "Willow Creek 4 (west), Clayton Mesa 3½ (east), Middle Fork 5 (east)."

There is a small spring flowing under the trail through two two-inch pipes at 4.68 miles.

The trail is on the hillside with a small stream below and to the left. The trail has crossed this stream a couple of times before you get to the spring, and crosses the drainage five more times before you arrive in Turkeyfeather Pass.

The route levels out in T F Pass at 6.09 miles. The pass is an extensive level area in an open forest of large pine trees. There is not much underbrush and the ground is carpeted with pine needles — great for camping. A little farther along is a grassy clearing to the left of the trail. In T F Pass at 6.14 miles there is a trail junction, with T-102 going to the right, south, to "Crest of Mogollon Mountains 7.75." T-102 goes over Turkeyfeather Mountain to join T-182 near Hobo Spring. The sign here also tells you, "West Fork 2¾ (southeast, the way you are headed), Iron Creek Lake 4¾ (northwest)."

There is another trail junction at 6.3 miles with T-64, which goes east, and T-151 continues southeast. Signs here tell you, "Crest of Jerky Mts. 1¼ (east), Middle Fork 5 (east)" and "Turkeyfeather Pass ¼ (northwest), Iron Creek Lake 5 (northwest), West Fork 2½ (southeast), White Creek 10 (southeast)." Continue on T-151 down T F Creek.

A group of hikers taking a rest stop on their way to camp near Turkeyfeather Pass.

T-165 goes to the left at 8.75 miles. The sign here says, "Lilly Park 5½ (east), T F Pass 2½ (north), White Creek 5½ (south)." Proceed south about 100 yards and turn left when you get to the West Fork of the Gila River, at 8.80 miles. West Fork Corral is nearby and there are plenty of good places to camp near here, if this is where you want to stop. It is really a pretty area, not quite on a par with the area near White Creek Cabin, but superior to most. The trail is very good, though it seems that it is going either up or downhill all the way. Most hikers will be ready to call it a day and make camp when they get here.

The route continues downstream alongside the West Fork. At 9.11 miles the path crosses a portion of the stream to an island, then crosses the main channel (on a fallen tree) to the right (southwest) bank. A sign at 9.92 miles says, "T.F. Pass 3¾ (northwest), White Creek 6¼ (southeast)." Continue downstream for about 0.1 mile to a trail that goes up to the right and crosses Cub Creek. This is T-151 which goes up through Jackass Park, over Cub Mesa and back down to the West Fork near where you may want to spend the next night or two. I don't recommend that you take this route, as it is a steep climb up and down, and is the long way to get to where you are going. Distances shown on my map are for T-151 even though I described a shorter route around the canyon.

The trail you should take is not marked. It follows the route of an old wagon road that roughly parallels the West Fork, nearby, to the northeast. To get on the wagon road, follow the trail alongside the West Fork. After T-151 branches off and starts up Cub Creek, the riverside path quickly starts dropping down to the river. This path appears to go into the canyon with the river, and indeed a path does, but don't go into the canyon if you are looking for the wagon road. Cross the river just upstream of the beginning of the canyon and you should find the trail and wagon road going east up the hillside. As it gets up near the trees, the trail turns southeast into the forest and generally follows along, above the canyon.

The forest map and topographic map both show a trail going immediately alongside the river all the way through the canyon. A trail may have done this prior to the 1978 flood, but now only occasional, brief pieces of it remain. The hike through the canyon is very rocky and you must continually cross from side to side in an effort to walk on the bank, or wade in the very rocky stream bed. It is possible to follow

the river all the way through the canyon, to rejoin T-151 where it comes to the river again from Cub Mesa, but progress in the stream is very wet, tiring, and slow. The wagon road is much easier and faster. The wagon road drops into the canyon where it begins to widen. Level banks on one side or the other of the river get much wider along here. The trail must at times cross the very rocky river bed to make its way on a level, forested bank.

I had some distance measuring problems along the rocky river portion of this hike, so I used the distance via T-151, from where it leaves the river at Cub Creek, to where it comes back down to the river near White Creek. I estimated that T-151 rejoins the river-side trail at 15.64 trail miles from Willow Creek.

The trail junction at 15.64 miles is in the beautiful, wide river valley. The broad, flat banks between river and the low mountains which confine it are covered with grassy, flower bedecked meadows interspersed with open forests of large conifers and deciduous trees. One crisp spring morning I surprised a sizable herd of elk grazing along here. This area is extremely pretty and it gets even better near White Creek Cabin.

The hike distances don't include the 0.6 mile downstream to White Creek Cabin area, but I suggest that that is where you should plan to make camp for a night or two, or more. White Creek joins the West Fork near a couple of Forest Service cabins. One is fairly large and appears to be living quarters for Forest Service personnel who are lucky enough to be working in this area. The smaller building near the corral may be a workshop or storage shed. Downstream from the cabins the West Fork starts dropping more steeply and there are large, clear pools for swimming — a super place to be on a warm summer afternoon! Everyone I know who has been here has told me this area is one of their favorite places to camp. Gila Cliff Dwellings are about 17.5 miles downstream from here.

When you are ready to continue to Mogollon Baldy, return to T-151. Signs here say, "West Fork, to White Creek ¾" and "Snow Park 8½, T.F. Pass 9½, Mogollon Baldy 10¼ (arrows to the places on this last sign all point west, up T-151)." If you did not camp along the West Fork, there are some good places along this next portion of the trip, too. The climb up T-151 from the river, for the first 0.6 mile, is steep and the trail rougher and rockier than any other portion of this hike, aside from the washed out places along the West Fork. After 16.23 miles the grade slackens and progress is quite easy all the way to the summit ridge, except for a short, steep section above the next trail junction.

Trail 151 goes to the right (northwest) at 17.00 miles and T-152, which you want to take, goes west. A sign here tells you, "Raw Meat Creek 5 (west), Mogollon Baldy 9 (west), White Creek 1¾ (southeast), T F Pass 3¼ (northwest)." Take the path west toward Mogollon Baldy. The trail gets steep and rocky briefly, but the gradient eases at 17.38 miles. There is a good view of Mogollon Baldy from the trail at 17.74 miles. The trail crosses White Creek at 17.77 miles and there is plenty of water and some good campsites here. I suggest that you get at least a day's supply of water here, if there is a chance the springs higher up may be dry.

From White Creek the trail gains elevation slowly and continuously for the next 8.0 miles to the summit of Mogollon Baldy. There is a trail junction with T-302 (to the south) at 18.1 miles, but bears have chewed the sign so badly that the distance to Mogollon Baldy has been obliterated. The signs say, "White Creek at West Fork 3 (east)" and "Mogollon Baldy — (west), Raw Meat Creek (south)."

One April when there was quite a bit of snow higher up I encountered a herd of elk near the trail about a half mile above the T-302 junction. What magnificent animals! The trail continues to be excellent on this route.

The route from 18.09 miles to 25.8 miles follows generally along the crest of a ridge, through an open forest of predominantly large pine trees. From 23.8 miles to the summit the route is through aspen groves and open, grassy "balds" along the summit ridge. Exciting views of the varied terrain below (and above) are almost continuous along the summit ridge.

There is a trail junction with T-169 at 23.7 miles, as you join the summit ridge. Signs here tell you, "White Creek 8¾ (east, where you just came from), Raw Meat Creek 6 (south along the ridge), Trail Canyon 6½ (south)" and "Snow Park ¼ (north, towards summit), Mogollon Baldy 2¼ (north), Mogollon Creek 6½." There is another trail junction 175 feet farther along with T-221 at 23.80 miles. The sign here says, "Mogollon Creek 6¼ (south, in the valley below), Raw Meat Creek 6¾ (east),

Looking into a sunset from the summit of Mogollon Baldy.

White Creek 8¼ (east), Mogollon Baldy 2 (west)." A small sign points to the right (northeast) of the trail to "Spring ¼" at 24.11 miles. Along here would be a good place to camp, and to get enough water to last you until you get to the next spring, near West Fork Saddle. Camping here, near the spring, is better than on the summit, but you may want to spend more time on the summit, with its lookout tower and other structures, and its spectacular views in all directions.

Lookout Canyon Trail No. 99 joins from the south at 25 miles. The sign here says, "West Fork Mogollon Creek 4¾, Mogollon Creek 10½ (both south on T-99), Snow Park 1¼ (south, where you just came from), Mogollon Baldy 1 (north, ahead)." Switchbacks ease the grade near the summit. The ridge crest isn't steep, but at this altitude breathing is difficult and even the switchbacks seem steep.

The summit is attained at 25.80 miles, and it is a very accommodating place. There is a cabin with full-length front porch. The lookout tower is behind the cabin and an outhouse is off to the side. Of course, the view is spectacular. From near the cabin you can look over most of your route from the West Fork, though it is all under the canopy of green that appears to be continuous all the way to the eastern horizon.

The cabin on the summit is divided into two rooms: one is for a workshop and the other has a bed and wood stove for the forest ranger when one is up here for lookout duty. In winter the cabin is sometimes left unlocked for use by the rare hiker who ventures this way. It is a spiritual experience to spend a moonlit winter night up here, warmed by a fire in the wood stove and with the world around you sparkling white.

Rainwater and snow melt are collected in gutters on the cabin and piped to a cistern. This supply may be barely adequate for the needs of Forest Service personnel, though they may have an alternate source, so don't plan to use any of it.

The trail, T-182, going down the north side of the mountain is well defined from use, but it is best to locate it prior to starting out with your pack on. Look for blazes on trees anytime you have any doubt about being on the trail. All of the trails on this hike are so well blazed that they can be followed when the ground is blanketed with a few feet of snow — except maybe where there are few trees near the

path, just before mile 34, and a few other brief places.

Black Tail Spring is about 200 yards to the right of the trail at 26.1 miles. Unless you are desperate for water, it would be better to wait and get it from the spring in West Fork Saddle, which is at 28 miles. Trail No. 224 comes up from the south to join T-182 in the saddle about 0.1 mile past the spring. A sign here tells you, "West Fork Saddle, Mogollon Creek 10½ (south), Mogollon Baldy 1½ (east), Sandy Point 10½ (west)." Continue west on T-182 toward Sandy Point and at 28.34 miles there is a spring by the trail. According to the map this is too soon for it to be Little Hobo Spring, but it possibly is.

The junction with T-102, which goes back to Willow Creek via Turkeyfeather Mountain is at about 29.2 miles. It doubles back to the right and I missed it when I was measuring distances. I wouldn't recommend your taking this route back if you are tired or are running behind schedule because it has lots of ups and downs. The route I'm describing is downhill all the way, with a few exceptions.

Continue in the direction of Sandy Point on T-182, but you don't want to go all the way to it, so watch for the T-172 junction. Signs along this part of the route could give more information than just saying Sandy Point is in this direction. At 30.36 miles is the junction with T-181. Signs here point to, "Mogollon Baldy 4½ (east), Spruce Cr. Saddle 3½ (southwest), Sandy Point 7½ (northwest), Mogollon Baldy 4½," and "Spruce Cr. Saddle 3½, Sandy Point 7¼." Take the right fork, towards Sandy Point. At 31.2 miles there is a badly chewed sign pointing west, but this is just a small trail that circles to the west side of a knob you just crossed over.

An important trail junction is at 32.09 miles where T-172 branches off to the right (east). A sign here reads, "Iron Creek Lake 6¾ (northeast), Sandy Point 6¼ (north), Mogollon Baldy 6 (southwest, where you just came from)." If you need water or want to camp soon, you might consider Humming Bird Saddle. There is a good spring and plenty of space for camping there. It is about 0.8 mile on T-182 toward Sandy Point. This is a nice side trip and you might consider a quick visit to it before continuing to Willow Creek, if you don't want to camp there.

From the trail junction proceed northeast on T-172. It is a good trail, downhill just about all the way to Willow Creek. There are many good, but waterless, camping places along the way. I have seen wild turkey and grouse on the trail in this area. There are occasional viewpoints from the ridge the trail follows, and you can see Turkeyfeather Mountain across the valley to the right. The trail continues to lose elevation until you are within a mile of Iron Creek Lake, where it becomes almost level.

Beside Iron Creek Lake, mile 38.8, turn left (west) on T-151. This is the route you started on and should be familiar to you. Soon after the junction you begin descending to Willow Creek, which you reach at 40.1 miles.

This is an excellent, strenuous hike. The trail surface is very good most of the way and is well maintained and routed to keep the gradients as gentle as possible without resorting to too many switchbacks. You don't have to be a very experienced trail finder to follow this route, but you do have to know how to plan your trip: food, water, clothing and equipment, campsites, etc. You should also know how to use your maps and compass.

To get to this hike from the south or west,

get on U.S. 180 and three miles north of Glenwood, or one mile south of Alma, turn east on N.M. 78. It is nine miles east to the old, partially revived, ghost town of Mogollon. Willow Creek Campground is about 17 miles east of Mogollon on N.M. 78. From the north or northeast, get on N.M. 12. There are two routes from N.M. 12 to Willow Creek. The easiest to find, but slowest due to a very winding road, starts from the community of Reserve. Take F.R. 435 south out of Reserve. F.R. 435 soon becomes F.R. 141, which you follow for approximately 35 miles to its junction with N.M. 78. Turn right, southwest, on N.M. 78 and follow it to Willow Creek Campground. I prefer taking F.R. 94 south from Apache Creek on N.M. 12, and going 26 miles to N.M. 78. Again, turn right onto N.M. 78 and follow it to Willow Creek Campground. In the fall or late spring when N.M. 78 is closed between Mogollon and Willow Creek, it may be possible to get to this hike from N.M. 12, particularly via F.R. 94 out of Apache.

There is excellent camping (dry) in the forest and in the meadows near Turkeyfeather Pass.

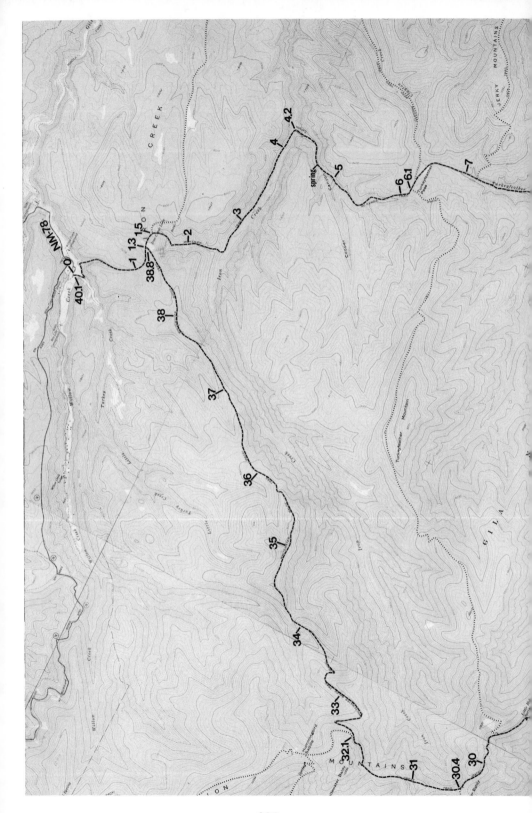

208

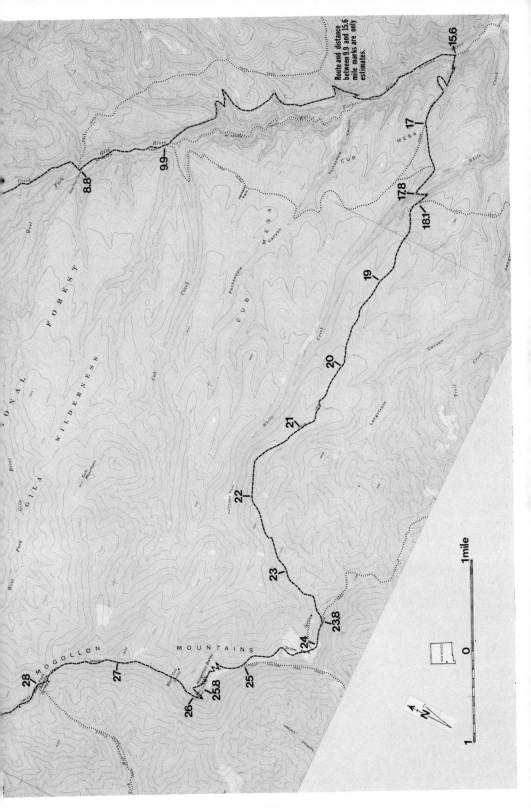

Route and distance between 9.9 and 15.6 mile marks are only estimates.

44 SAND FLAT TRAIL & JEWETT ARAGON TRAIL
APACHE NATIONAL FOREST

Distance: 13.7 miles round-trip
Time: 6 to 10 hours
Elevation Range: 7,360 to 8,080 feet
Rating: Easy hiking, moderate distance and route finding
Water: Unreliable, plan on carrying all you will need
Seasons: Usually March through December, but depends on snow
Topographic Maps: Queens Head, Aragon
Special Map: Gila National Forest, Grids 3E, 3F

The real challenge of this hike may be in finding the trailhead. Sand Flat Trail No. 3 can be considered to start at the east (left) fork of the two-track road which branches near the forest boundary. Trail No. 3 follows the well-worn tracks and enters the forest beside a big pine which has a large blaze chopped in its bark. The path is quite distinct through the forest and is well-marked with blazes on trees along the way. It was rebuilt a few years ago, but is not well-maintained now, and is infrequently used by hikers.

Trail No. 4, which runs from Jewett Work Center to the town of Aragon, (hence the name Jewett Aragon Trail) is not nearly as well defined as Trail No. 3 near the beginning of this hike. The south (right) fork of the two-track road is the beginning of Trail No. 4, but the tracks soon disappear and there are only occasional blazes marking the route through the forest.

This hike needs more use, to take advantage of the effort that went into its construction. I have not hiked the complete loop yet myself. The portion between miles three and 11 is described from information I obtained from maps.

There are two ways to get to the trailhead, which I considered to be at the forest boundary where the two-track road forks. This is at 1.2 miles from the work center, as shown on the accompanying map. When the gate on Forest Road 10, just east of the turnoff into the work center, is open, you can drive to the trailhead. This route is across private land, so stay on the road, close the gates, and don't bother anything.

From the gate on F.R. 10 drive, or walk, east along the road. In a half-mile or so the road forks. The widest, most used branch curves left toward the northeast and goes to a house. Don't go this way. The road that continues straight ahead soon dwindles to two tracks in the grass, paralleling a fence which is on the right (south) side. The two-track soon turns to the right (south), crosses a (sometimes muddy) shallow ditch, and goes through a gate in the fence that has been alongside. After going south through this gate, the tracks parallel a north-south fence which is on the right (west) side. Go south for about 200 yards and there is another gate in an east-west fence. Immediately after this gate the two-track turns left, to the east-southeast. Soon after the left turn, in the open, grassy valley, there is a trail sign on the left between the road and a stream bed. From the sign post it is three-quarter mile back to the Jewett Work Center instead of one-quarter mile as the sign says. Go southeast on the two-track to where it forks, at the forest boundary.

If the gate on F.R. 10 is locked (it was the last time I was there) you must leave your car beside the road at the work center gate (which is always locked), crawl through the fence beside the gate and walk to the work center building. Go through the corral near the building and follow a path south for a half-mile to the east-west fence. Cross through the fence and follow it to the east. There is a fence corner in a clump of trees on a little hill to the east. Cross the north-south fence on the knob and continue east, keeping south of the boundary marker posts which you find at intervals along the way. About three-quarter mile east of the work center the boundary turns north. Follow it north to the two-track road, which forks near where you join it. This is where T-3 goes east and T-4 goes southeast, and is what I call the trailhead.

From the "trailhead" it is a short distance east along the two-track, Trail No. 3, to the big pine with the blaze on it marking where the trail enters the forest.

Whiskey Creek runs west out of the forest just north of where the trail enters. There is often some water in the creek upstream and there is a spring in its drainage in a clump of willows near where the trail enters the forest.

The route goes abruptly from open, grassy meadow into the small, forested valley, with low forested hills on each side. There is plenty of excellent camping space in the forest, under big pine and oak trees, with the flat valley floor carpeted with pine needles and patches of grass. But, you'd better get here soon to enjoy this grove of big trees because many of them have already been marked for cutting by loggers.

Trail No. 3 goes up the valley floor with an easy gradient, but has a rocky surface in places. A fence, with gate, crosses the path at 1.8 miles from the work center. There continue to be good campsites in the valley. At 2.0 miles the gradient steepens as the trail starts its climb up the south side. The route becomes almost level again at 2.4 miles, where it cuts across the gently sloping hillside. From the trail up here you can see the green ridges which surround the valley. Malpais Spring, shown on the map, must be down in the drainage below. The trail, which is quite distinct and easy to follow, though somewhat rocky, continues to

gain elevation gradually until it crosses the broad, forested ridge at 3.5 miles. On the east side of this ridge it drops gradually to 4.1 miles, where the gradient becomes rather steep for the next 0.3 mile. The map shows Trail No. 3 to join F.R. 359 at Castillo Tank, at 5.8 miles, and appears to follow the road as it turns south. I haven't been on the route along here, but the hike should follow F.R. 359 around to where it seems to end at 9.0 miles.

Trail No. 4, coming northeast from Aragon, joins the hike at 8.7 miles and the remainder of the trip will be along it, back to the trailhead.

To get to this hike go north out of Reserve on N.M. 12. At Apache Creek turn north on N.M. 32 and continue north for 10.6 miles to F.R. 356. The sign marking this turn is on the west (left) side of N.M. 32, and points east to Jewett Work Center. Go 2.4 miles northeast on F.R. 356 to the junction with F.R. 10. Turn right onto F.R. 10 and go 0.3 mile to Jewett Work Center.

This is a nice, pleasant hike, primarily over forested hills and in forested valleys, with no particularly dramatic vistas or outstanding features. It is beautiful in its own way and gets you away from people. Perhaps if enough hikers use this trail the Forest Service will provide better access and more signs.

This big pine, with the blaze, marks the trail's entry into the forest. Many of these fine, big trees were marked for logging.

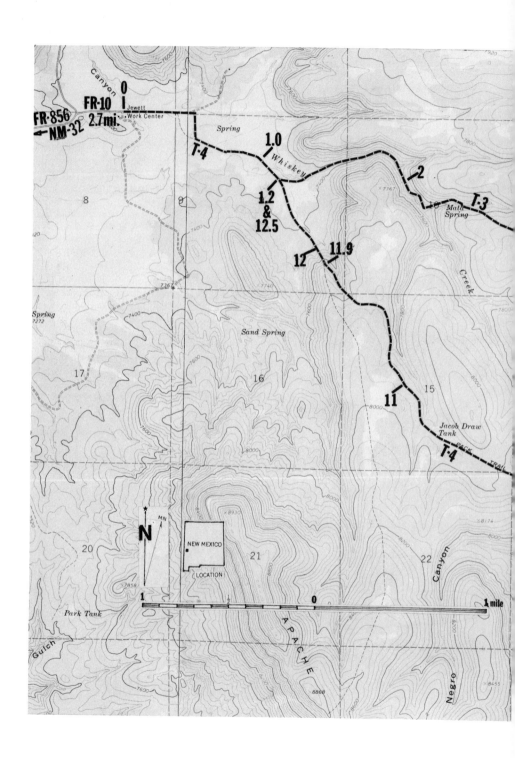

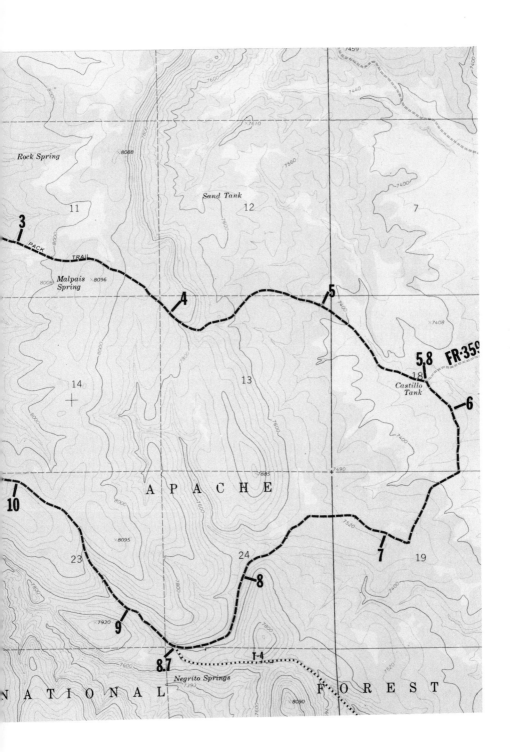

45 MOUNT TAYLOR, SAN MATEO MOUNTAINS
CIBOLA NATIONAL FOREST, MOUNT TAYLOR RANGER DISTRICT

Distance: 5.5 miles round-trip
Time: 2½ to 5 hours round-trip day hiking, longer with a pack
Elevation Range: 9,490 to 11,301 feet
Rating: Easy to moderate
Water: None after Gooseberry Spring
Seasons: Usually May through October, but depends on snow. Can be excellent cross-country skiing in winter. Check with U.S. Forest Service in Grant
Topographic Maps: San Mateo, Cerro Pelon, Lobo Springs, Mount Taylor
Special Map: Cibola National Forest, Mount Taylor Ranger District, Grid I4

When you find the San Mateo Mountains on your map, situated in the middle of the desert, near Grants, between Albuquerque and Gallup, you'll probably assume that they are hot, dry desert mountains. Wrong! Mount Taylor is higher than Sandia Crest which are Albuquerque's ski slopes. Mount Taylor and vicinity is cool and pleasant in summer and snow covered in late fall, winter, and early spring. The forest roads which are not plowed in winter reportedly provide excellent and extensive cross-country skiing.

The forest along the roads leading to this hike appears to be rather open, with large pine and fir trees, and the drive on these roads is a pleasant experience, even if you don't hike.

From I-40 Mount Taylor appears to tower above the surrounding area, and its unforested slopes give it the appearance of being so lofty that timberline must be at its feet. This isn't true, of course, as you will find when you make the climb. This hike takes you to the summit of 11,301 foot Mount Taylor. It is a very scenic trip, with distant vistas much of the way.

To get to this hike, get on U.S. 66 in Grants and turn north on First Street, which is N.M. 547. Go northeast on N.M. 547 for 13 miles to the turnoff onto Forest Road 193. You will pass the other end of F.R. 193 about nine miles from Grants, but don't turn onto it there where the signs say, "Lobo Canyon Campground." After you turn onto the second F.R. 193, it is about five miles to the junction with F.R. 501. Some forest roads are being improved and rerouted, so distances may change some. Turn left, east, on F.R. 501 and watch for the trail sign on the left in about a half-mile.

Park your vehicle near the Trail No. 77 sign and start walking. The trail starts out as a good two-track road, going through a level, open forest of large pines. At 420 feet from F.R. 501 there is a post with two signs on it on the left

side of the road. One sign says, "Rd. No. 501 jct. ⅛." The other says, "Gooseberry Spring ½, Mt. Taylor 2½." Do not interpret the sign as pointing the route along the road, which does go to Gooseberry Spring. Instead, look immediately across the road, to the right, and you will see the path going through the grass into the trees. The trail climbs with an easy gradient up the hillside, while the road goes into a valley. If you miss this turn, the road goes into the small valley but is soon blocked by a barricade, with nearby signs announcing that vehicles are prohibited beyond this point. A short distance beyond the barricade is a metal stock watering tank, with water, apparently from Gooseberry Spring, trickling into it from a pipe. Near the water tank the two-track road turns to the right and climbs steeply out of the valley to join the trail. For the next mile the trail follows this old abandoned route most of the time. It goes up a grassy ridge, which has occasional clumps of coniferous trees, and affords unobstructed views to the west and south.

There is an open aspen, pine, and fir forest along the trail briefly at 0.82 mile and many big, dead trees are on the ground along here. At 0.92 mile the path is out in the open on a grassy slope, with occasional scattered pine trees. The trail rejoins the old two-track at 0.98 mile.

The route crosses a ridge crest at 1.40 miles. The previous 0.3 mile has been fairly steep uphill. The trail is all right, but hasn't been up to the standards of most Cibola National Forest trails. Trail usage appears to be light, and more cows than hikers use it. This is a hike that gets you away from people.

On the side of a ridge the trail leaves the old road, and the gradient eases at 1.7 miles, where the route runs along the ridge top. It soon steepens again and switch backs, climbing toward the summit. A fence, with gate, crosses the path at 2.4 miles, on the grassy mountain side, and the summit is attained at 2.6 miles.

The view from the summit is superb. On a clear day, distant and not so distant mountains can be seen in all directions. Less than a mile to the northeast La Mosca Lookout Tower and microwave towers stand atop a peak only slightly lower than Mount Taylor. There is a well-worn path running from near the summit north to F.R. 453 and La Mosca. This would be an interesting side hike, permitting a traverse

route with a car, or, it could be an alternate route to the summit if you decide to drive to La Mosca.

There is a clump of pine and fir trees northwest of the summit which afford good camping in a few relatively level places. The east slope of the summit is densely forested in places, but is quite steep.

In a pit on the summit is a metal box containing a visitor register. Be sure and sign in. When a cold wind is blowing, this pit offers a welcome shelter while registering.

This is a beautiful area and a nice hike. Try it!

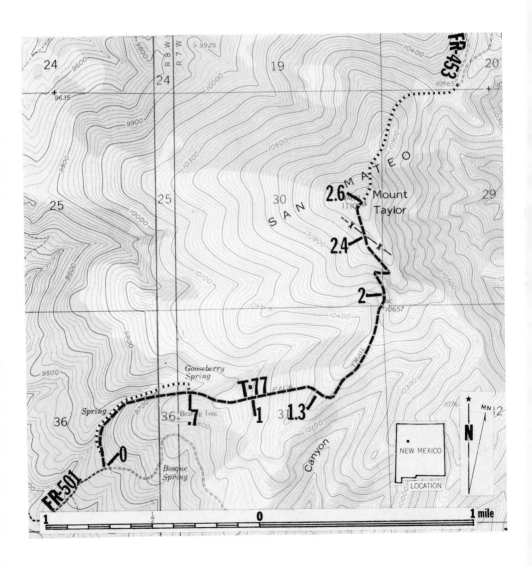

46 EL MORRO INSCRIPTION TRAIL
EL MORRO NATIONAL MONUMENT — INSCRIPTION ROCK

Distance: 2.3 miles
Time: 2 to 3 hours
Elevation Range: 7,218 to 7,440 feet
Rating: Very easy. Could be done by a person in a wheelchair, part way
Water: Available at Visitor Center
Seasons: All year
Topographic Map: El Morro
Special Map: El Morro brochures with map and El Morro Trail guide booklet available at Visitor Center
Permit: Required, day hiking only. Obtain at Visitor Center

This is a truly different hike. It is a very interesting historical experience, suitable for the average tourist's abilities. The following is taken from the El Morro brochure and the El Morro Trails Booklet.

"Rising some 200 feet above the valley floor, El Morro is a massive mesa point of sandstone, forming a striking landmark. It was named by the Spanish Conquistadors who used the place, with its large natural basin of rain and snow melt, as a camping spot in the 17th century. . ."

Many of the travelers left a record of their passage by cutting inscriptions into the soft sandstone, giving the landmark its other name of "Inscription Rock." Two years before the founding of Jamestown and 15 years before the Pilgrims landed at Plymouth Rock, the first

Spanish inscription was made by Don Juan de Onate in April 1605.

But, the Spaniards were not the first to record their presence. On the very top of El Morro lie ruins, still largely unexcavated, of Zuni Indian Pueblos abandoned long before the coming of the Spaniards. And, carved on the rock itself are hundreds of petroglyphs left by these ancient people.

This is such an interesting place that I feel it merits inclusion in "50 Hikes" instead of another overnight backpacking trail. There is an excellent camping area on El Morro Monument a mile or so from the Visitor Center. I suspect that once you get here you won't be in any hurry to leave.

The trail begins directly behind the Visitor Center Headquarters and climbs gradually

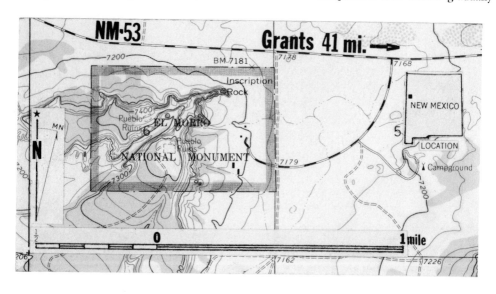

216

toward the rock. Just follow the arrows. . . The hike past the inscriptions and back to the office normally takes 40 to 60 minutes. The distance is about one mile.

After viewing the inscriptions, you may, if you wish, continue up over the top of the rock and visit two large prehistoric Indian ruins. This extra hike will take you another one and a half to two hours. This hike is about 2.3 miles round-trip.

El Morro National Monument is 58 miles southeast of Gallup via N.M. 32 and 53, and it is 43 miles west of Grants on N.M. 53.

Visitors observe the oldest Spanish inscription.

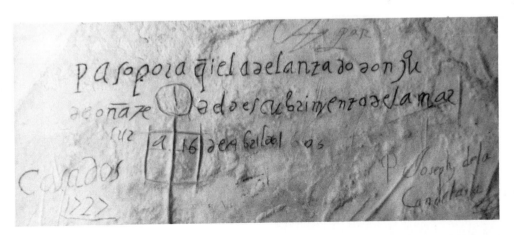

The oldest Spanish inscription is: "Paso por aqui el adelantado Don Juan de Onate del descumbri-miento de la mar del sur a 16 de Abril de 1605." Translated this says: "Passed by here the Governor Don Juan de Onate from the discovery of the Sea of the South on the 16th of April, 1605." He was the first Spaniard to see the Gulf of California.

217

47 OSO RIDGE JEEP TRAIL
CIBOLA NATIONAL FOREST, ZUNI MOUNTAINS

Distance: Varies, 2 to 5 miles one-way, depending on route taken
Time: 2 to 8 hours round-trip
Elevation Range: 8,120 to 8,558 feet
Rating: Easy to moderate walking. Moderate to difficult route finding
Water: None
Seasons: All
Topographic Maps: Page, Ramah
Special Map: Cibola National Forest, Mount Taylor District, Grids C-3, C-4

The Zuni Mountains have no designated hiking trails, but the jeep trails appear to be so infrequently used that they provide very good hiking routes. The hike described here is but one of many such routes available in this area.

The Zuni Mountains were heavily logged in the early 1900s, but now there are abundant trees, both deciduous and coniferous. This forest is very pretty and has a "different" look, possibly because so many of the trees are about the same size.

To get to this hike, turn south off I-40 (U.S. 66) 12 miles east of Gallup on N.M. 400. The sign at I-40 says "McGaffey." On N.M. 400 go about 11 miles south to Forest Road 50. Follow F.R. 50 for 12 miles to its intersection with F.R. 459. F.R. 459 goes west at the junction and F.R. 50 turns east. The trailhead (a jeep road) is about 100 feet east of the intersection and goes almost directly south. On the forest map and the topographic map this is near the Boon Place at the northwest corner of land section 14.

Follow the most heavily used track, as there are a few side tracks. At 0.6 mile there is a small road to the left that goes a short distance in a cool, shady spot with a fireplace and picnic table (not built by the Forest Service). You could drive to this place and camp.

A good half-day hike (round-trip) on this jeep trail is possible. It takes you to a large, relatively level, forested area with plenty of room for camping or picnicking. There is a clearing at 1.25 miles, with a jeep road junction. Take the left fork, to the east, and follow it down into the forest. The area for camping or picnicking is about 1.75 or 2.0 miles from F.R. 50 and you will have to carry all of the water you will need. If you prefer, you might try to drive to this area. Proceed with caution and don't get stuck in the sometimes boggy place or drag on a rock.

If you want a longer hike on an old jeep road that is impassable to vehicles, at 0.8 mile from F.R. 50 a route takes off to the right (south) up a little ridge, as the jeep road curves left. The entry to this route (a long abandoned logging road) has been bulldozed to block it. Go south on this old road a short distance and you will come to a "T" intersection with a wider, but heavily washed road. Go left (east) up the steep, rocky hill and you are on your own for the next four miles or so, if you can follow it that far. All of thes roads fade out in places and join or cross others, making it difficult to follow them. You must use your map and compass in order to know which way to turn. And, remember the route along which you have come so you don't get lost going back. On this route you should come to a trail junction on the crest of Oso Ridge. Take the right route, to the southwest. Use your map and compass from here to get to Dan Valley.

Good luck! You'll need it.

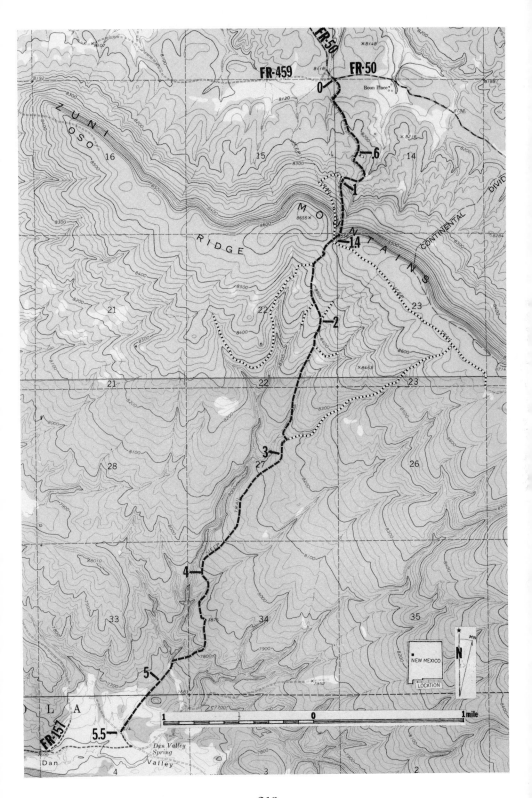

FR-459 FR-50

ZUNI OSO

16

15

0

.6 14

1

RIDGE

M O

14

21

22

2

23

CONTINENTAL DIVIDE

28

27

3

26

22

23

33

34

4

35

5

L A

5.5

Dan Valley Spring

Dan Valley

NEW MEXICO
LOCATION

N MN

1   0   1 mile

48 STRAWBERRY TRAIL TO McGAFFEY LOOKOUT
CIBOLA NATIONAL FOREST, ZUNI MOUNTAINS

Distance: 1.25 miles one-way, 2.5 miles round-trip
Time: ¾ to 1½ hour one-way, 1¼ to 2½ hour round-trip
Rating: Very easy
Water: None
Seasons: All
Topographic Map: Upper Nutria
Special Map: Cibola National Forest, Mount Taylor Ranger District

This is a very easy day hike from McGaffey Campground to McGaffey Lookout Tower. You can drive to both the campground and the lookout, so it is possible to hike this trail in only one direction. The trail is well-routed, constructed, and maintained. The gradient is gentle, culverts take runoff water under the path, and good maintenance keeps the surface almost sidewalk-smooth. I believe that a handicapped person could negotiate this route all the way to the lookout tower in a wheelchair.

The path starts out through a mixed pine and oak forest, with an increase in the percentage of pine, as you gain altitude. About 1910 intensive logging removed most of the trees in this area, so there are few really large trees, but the forest is well-established again, and is very scenic. Occasional openings in the trees provide vistas to the west.

This is an extremely nice little hike and I'd recommend it for the novice and the experienced hiker alike.

To get to this hike, exit from I-40 (Hwy. 66) 12 miles east of Gallup on N.M. 400. Go south on N.M. 400 about 10.7 miles to the turnoff to the right (south) to McGaffey Campground. Follow the road in the campground to the southernmost picnic area. The hike starts from this area. A trail runs from the camping areas nearer N.M. 400 roughly parallel to the road which connects the picnic areas, and joins the Strawberry Trail near its starting point. The trailhead is at a small bridge and a zig-zag through a log fence at the east side of a large, open picnic ground.

Strawberry Trail ends at McGaffey Lookout.

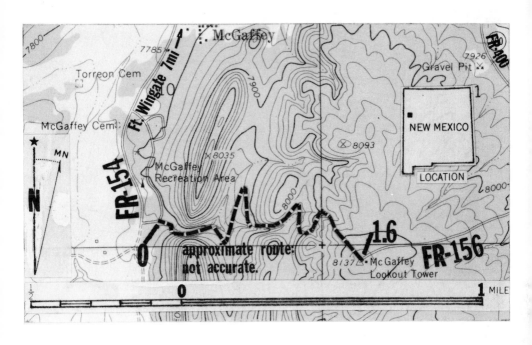

Strawberry Trail is well prepared and maintained, with gentle gradients.

49 PENASCO BLANCO HIKE
CHACO CANYON NATIONAL MONUMENT

Distance: 4.2 miles round-trip
Time: 2 to 4 hours
Elevation Range: 6,110 to 6,260 feet
Rating: Easy
Water: Carry all you will need. There may be muddy water near the ruins, but you would drink it only in a survival situation
Seasons: All — the monument is open all year; summer highs near 100° F, winter lows well below freezing
Topographic Maps: Pueblo Bonito, Kin Klizhin
Special Map: Brochure with map available at Visitor Center
Permit: Required for day-hiking. No overnight hikes permitted. Camp in the campground maintained by the Park Service

This is a day hike in an extremely interesting historical area. It is only recently that the Park Service has started issuing permits to hike to ruins away from the road. This gives you the opportunity to do some desert backcountry hiking and experience some extensive ruins in the solitude of this remote country. Usually you can expect to be alone when you contemplate these impressive structures.

The trip to Penasco Blanco was selected for this book because it is a longer walk than the others, yet it is easier to find and is an extensive and interesting ruin. There are other day-hikes available in Chaco Canyon.

To make this hike, park at Chiquita Ruins. The map available from the Visitor Center will aid you in finding these ruins. From Chiquita walk northwest on an abandoned two-track road which runs alongside Chaco Wash, in the broad valley floor. To the north of the path (right) the first half-mile of the low cliff is decorated extensively with prehistoric rock art.

At about 1.6 miles the road forks. Go left. From here you can see the ruins on the low mesa across the stream bed to the southwest. Cross the stream bed, which may have some muddy water in it, and follow the trail.

Immediately after this crossing, a trail departs to the right from the old road and goes directly to the ruins. The trail is marked with rock cairns, so should be easy to follow. This route takes you to some steps in a small, sloping rock cliff, that were carved in prehistoric times.

The large ruins of Penasco Blanco are some of the earliest of the classic style. Photograph and enjoy them, but please don't disturb them

or pick up any artifacts. The walls are fragile, so please don't climb on them or deface them.

Chaco Canyon and its expertly built, ancient structures is an impressive place, well worth visiting. It is remote and seldom crowded, which adds to its appeal to the venturesome spirited.

No lodging, gasoline, repair services, or food are available at the monument, which is 60 miles from the nearest town. There is a Park Service Campground about a mile from the Visitor Center. There is water at the Campground, but not for drinking. The only drinking water is available at the Visitor Center. Fireplaces are provided in the campground but you will have to bring your own firewood because none is available in the monument.

Though the monument is open year-round, the weather is an important factor to consider. Summer temperatures are extreme and the air dry. Heat exhaustion can happen, so drink plenty of water and protect yourself from the sun near midday. Winter climate is also severe. Sub-zero temperatures are common, so bring warm clothes and adequate camping gear. After a rain or wet snow, the clay surface of dirt roads makes them very slippery. Thunderstorms and flashfloods can make the roads impassable. You'll drive over miles and miles of dirt roads getting to and from Chaco Canyon, so watch the weather. Don't let this warning about weather keep you away from the monument, just let it heighten your spirit of adventure on the trip, and alert you.

To get to Chaco Canyon from the north, turn west off N.M. 44 at Blanco Trading Post, 28 miles south of Bloomfield and follow N.M.

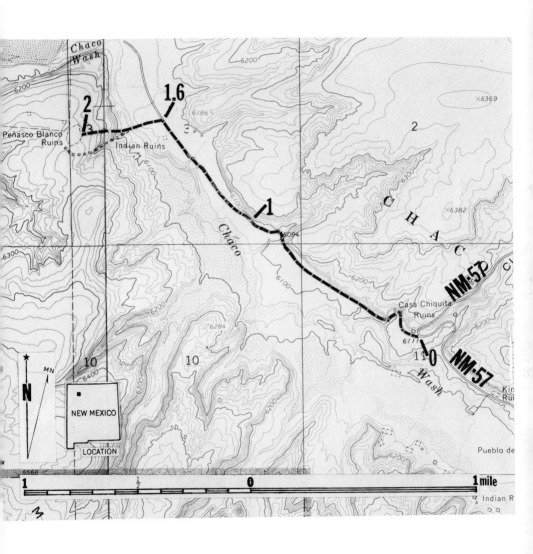

57 for 23 miles to the north entrance of the monument. The Visitor Center is seven miles from this entrance. The trailhead is about two miles from this entrance. From the south turn north on N.M. 57 from U.S. 66 at Thoreau and go 64 miles to the south entrance of the monument. The Visitor Center is less than two miles from this entrance.

Penasco Blanco ruins are silhouetted on the distant horizon.

This is the largest piece of Penasco Blanco wall that remains standing. The rubble covers a large area and at the time of occupation this must have been an impressive structure, situated as it was on the low bluff above Chaco River and Chaco Wash.

50 ANGEL PEAK CAMPGROUND TO VALLEY FLOOR
ANGEL PEAK RECREATION AREA

Distance: 2.25 miles round-trip
Time: 1 to 2½ hours, day hike
Elevation Range: 6,900 to 6,240 feet
Seasons: All year. Hot (100°F) in summer, cold (0°F) in winter possible
Rating: Moderate
Water: None, carry a full canteen
Topographic Map: Bloomfield
Special Map: Recreation Area Brochure with map is available

This is a not a wilderness-type hike. You are in sight of the picnic shelters and an oil well most of the time. It offers an interesting trip through very rough badlands alongside Angel Peak. There are vistas in the horizon, over eroded country with multi-colored bands of sedimentary deposits all about.

The first 1.1 miles follows a hog-back ridge that has occasional rock-capped humps along it. The ridge has a gradual slope down from the picnic area on the mesa to the valley floor nearly 700 feet below.

The trail starts at the northeast corner of the Recreation Area Campground and goes north for 500 feet or so to the beginning of the ridge, which goes downward to the west. About one-quarter mile out on the ridge, Angel Peak is immediately to the north.

This hike is for those who are nimble of foot because there are a couple of places where you have to scramble short distances down rock ledges on the ridge — no real problems. It would be best not to let small children make this hike unattended, as the ridge drops away steeply on each side in many places. The ridge runs out in the valley next to an oil field road.

The return route is optional. If you choose to make a loop instead of climbing back up the ridge, follow the floor of the drainage upstream (east) to the tip of a fairly steep ridge that runs up toward the picnic shelter nearest the starting point. Start up this ridge on its right (west) side until you scramble through the notch in the sandstone ledge. Then, the best path is right up the crest of the ridge, even though there are other paths visible to either side. Near the top, work to the right to scramble over the sandstone ledge that blocks the ridge. This puts you at about the top and 100 yards or so from the starting point.

To get to this hike go 35 miles southeast of Farmington or 71 miles northwest of Cuba on N.M. 44. Turn east at the Angel Peak Recreation Site sign. It is 6.2 miles from Hwy. 44 to Angel Peak Campground and the trailhead.

Joyce Kilmer's poem honors twisted and deformed juniper tree growing on the brink of the canyon.

Atop Wheeler Peak is a plaque and a sturdy container for the register which climbers sign. Here, the author poses with close friends Trevor, Jackie, and Dick, who have been among his companions on numerous hiking, canoeing, and diving outings.

SUGGESTED READING

BIRDS

Peterson, Roger Tory. *A Field Guide to Western Birds (2nd Ed.)*. Houghton Mifflin Co., Boston, MA, 1972.

Robbins, Chandler S., Bertel Bruun and Herbert S. Zim. *Birds of North America: A Guide to Field Identification*. Western Pub., Wisconsin, 1983.

Smith, Gusse Thomas. *Birds of the Southwestern Desert*. Doubleshoe Publisher (Gem Guides Distributor), Scottsdale, AZ, 1955.

Udvardy, Miklow D.F. *The Audubon Society Guide to North American Birds, Western Region*. Alfred A. Knopf, New York, NY, 1977.

BUTTERFLIES

Pyle, Robert Michael. *The Audubon Society Field Guide to North American Butterflies*. Alfred A. Knopf, New York, NY, 1981.

FIRST AID AND MEDICATION

Darvill, Fred T., Jr., M.D. *Mountaineering Medicine, A Wilderness Medical Guide*. Darvil Outdoor, 1980.

Fear, Gene, ed., *Fatigue*. National Park Service (available at most National Park and National Monument Headquarters).

Hackett, Peter H. *Mountain Sickness: Prevention, Recognition, and Treatment*. American Alpine Club, 113 E. 90th St., New York, NY, 1980.

Mitchell, Dick. *Mountaineering First Aid*. The Mountaineers, Seattle, WA, 1975.

SAFECO Insurance Co. *Four Lines of Defense Against Hypothermia*. SAFECO Ins. Co., P.O. Box 5687, Denver, CO 80217, (n.d.).

SAFECO Insurance Co. *Heatcraft*. SAFECO Ins. Co., P.O. Box 5687, Denver, CO 80217, (n.d.).

U.S. Dept. of Agriculture Forest Service. *Winter Recreation Safety Guide, Program Aid No. 1140*. Superintendent of Documents, U.S. Govt. Printing Office, Washington, D.C. 20402, 1976.

Wilkerson, James A., M.D. *Medicine for Mountaineering*. The Mountaineers, 719 Pike St., Seattle, WA, 1977.

FITNESS

Cooper, Kenneth H., M.D. Rev. *The New Aerobics*. Bantam Books, New York, NY, 1975.

Cooper, Mildred. *Aerobics for Women*. Bantam Books, New York, NY, 1973.

FLORA AND FAUNA
Flowers

Craighead, John J. and Frank C. Craighead and Ray J. Davis. *Field Guide to Rocky Mountain Wild Flowers*. Houghton Mifflin Co., Boston, MA, 1974.

Little, Elbert L. *The Audubon Society Field Guide to North American Trees, Western Region*. Alfred A. Knopf, New York, NY, 1980.

Spellenberg, Richard. *The Audubon Society Field Guide to North American Wild Flowers, Western Region*. Alfred A. Knopf, New York, NY, 1979.

Dodge, Natt M. *100 Desert Wildflowers in Natural Color*. SW Parks and Monuments, AZ, 1963.

Ivey, Robert, *Flowering Plants of New Mexico*, Albuquerque, NM, 1983.

Tierney, Gail & Hughes, Phyllis, *Roadside Plants of Northern New Mexico*, Lightning Tree, Santa Fe, NM, 1983.

Fox, Eugene and Sublette, Mary, *Roadside Wildflowers of New Mexico*, Eastern N.M. Univ., Portales, NM, 1978.

Trees

Brockman, C. Frank, *Trees of North America*, Western Pub., Wisconsin, 1968.

Nelson, Dick and Sharon Nelson. *Easy Field Guide to Common Trees of New Mexico*. Gem Guides Book Co., CA, 1977.

Watts, Tom. *Rocky Mountain Tree Finder*. Nature Study Guild, Berkeley, CA, 1972.

FOOD AND COOKING

Barker, Harriett. *The One Burner Gourmet*. Contemporary Books, Chicago, IL, 1981.

Barker, Harriett. *Supermarket Backpacker*. Contemporary Books, Chicago, IL, 1977.

Fleming, June. *The Well Fed Backpacker*. Vintage Books Division of Random House, New York, NY, 1981.

Kinmount, Vikki and Claudia Axcell. *Simple Foods for the Pack*. Sierra Club Books, San Francisco, CA, 1976.

Mendenhall, Ruth Dyar. *Backpack Cookery (revised)*. La Siesta Press, Glendale, CA, 1974.

Prater, Yvonne and Ruth Dyar Mendenhall. *Gorp Glop and Glue Stew*. The Mountaineers, Seattle, WA, 1982.

Thomas, Dian. *Roughing It Easy*. Warner Books, New York, NY, 1974.

Williamson, Darcy. *How to Prepare Common Wild Foods*. Darcy Williamson Publisher, McCall, ID, 1978.

Williamson, Darcy. *Sack It and Pack It*. Maverick Pub., Oregon, 1980.

HIKING, BACKPACKING, AND CAMPING EQUIPMENT AND TECHNIQUES

Hart, John. *Walking Softly in the Wilderness:*

The Sierra Club Guide to Backpacking. Sierra Club Books, San Francisco, CA, 1977.

Manning, Harvey. *Backpacking One Step At A Time.* Vintage Books Division of Random House, New York, NY, 1980.

Peters, Ed, E. *Mountaineering, the Freedom of the Hills.* The Mountaineers, Seattle, WA, 1974.

Mueller, Betty. *Packrat Papers, Volume 2.* Signpost Publications, 16812-P 36th Ave., West Lynnwood, WA, 1977.

Roberts, Harry. *Movin' Out: Equipment and Techniques for Hikers.* Stonewall Press, 5 Byron St., Boston, MA, 1979 (rev.).

Satterfield, Archie and Eddie Bauer. *The Eddie Bauer Guide to Family Camping.* Addison Weseley, 1982.

Satterfield, Archie and Eddie Bauer. *The Eddie Bauer Guide to Backpacking.* Addison Weseley, 1983.

Van Lear, Denise. *The Best About Backpacking.* Sierra Club Books, San Francisco, CA, 1974.

Wheelock, Walt. *Ropes, Knots, and Slings for Climbers.* La Siesta Press, Glendale, CA, 1967.

MAMMALS

Nelson, Dick and Sharon Nelson. *Easy Field Guide to Common Mammals of New Mexico.* Gem Guides, CA, 1977.

Zim, Herbert S. and Donald F. Hoffmeister. *Mammals, a Guide to Familiar American Species.* Western Pub., Wisconsin, 1955.

MAP & COMPASS-ORIENTEERING

Bengtsson, Hans and George Atkinson. *Orienteering for Sport and Pleasure.* Stephen Greene Press, Brattleboro, VT, 1977.

Disley, John. *Orienteering.* Stackpole Books, Harrisburg, PA, 1979.

Kjellstrom, Bjorn. *Be Expert With Map and Compass: The Orienteering Handbook.* Charles Scribner's Sons, New York, NY, 1976 (rev.).

Ratliff, Donald E. *Map, Compass, and Campfire.* Binfords & Mort, Portland, OR, 1970.

NATURE

Larson, Peggy. *A Sierra Club Naturalists Guide: The Deserts of the Southwest.* Sierra Club Books, San Francisco, CA, 1977.

NEW MEXICO INFORMATION

Jackson, Earl. *Your National Park System in the Southwest.* Southwest Parks and Monuments Association, Globe, AZ, 1978.

Jenkins, Myrna Ellen and Albert H. Schroeder. *A Brief History of New Mexico.* The University of New Mexico Press, Albuquerque, NM, 1974.

Kelley, Vincent C. *Albuquerque: Its Mountains, Valley, Water, and Volcanoes.* University of New Mexico Bureau of Mines and Mineral Resources, Socorro, NM, 1974.

Pearce, T.M. Ed. *New Mexico Place Names: A Geographical Dictionary.* University of New Mexico Press, Albuquerque, NM, 1980.

Ungnade, Herbert E. *Guide to the New Mexico Mountains.* University of New Mexico Press, Albuquerque, NM, 1977.

Weigle, Marta. *Brothers of Light, Brothers of Blood.* University of New Mexico Press, Albuquerque, NM, 1976.

Weigle, Marta. *The Penitentes of the Southwest.* Ancient City Press, P.O. Box 5401, Santa Fe, NM, 1980.

PHOTOGRAPHY

Pfeiffer, C. Boyd. *Field Guide to Outdoor Photography.* Stackpole Books, Harrisburg, PA, 1977.

REPTILES

Smith & Brodie. *Reptiles of North America.* Western Pub., Wisconsin, 1982.

SURVIVAL

Fear, Gene. *Surviving the Unexpected Wilderness Emergency.* Survival Education Association, 9035 Golden Given Rd., Tacoma, WA, 1979.

Graves, Richard. *Bushcraft; A Serious Guide to Survival and Camping.* Warner Books, New York, NY, 1978.

Nelson, Dick and Sharon Nelson. *Desert Survival.* Tecolote Press, Glenwood, NM, 1977.

Patterson, Craig E. *Mountain Wilderness Survival.* And/Or Press Inc., P.O. Box 2246, Berkeley, CA, 1979.

WEATHER

Reifsnyder, William F. *Weathering the Wilderness; The Sierra Club Book to Practical Meterology.* Sierra Club Books, San Francisco, CA, 1980.

AGENCIES AND ORGANIZATIONS